250 Essential Diabetes Recipes

250 Essential Diabetes Recipes

Edited by
Sharon Zeiler, BSc, MBA, RD

Robert
ROSE

250 Essential Diabetes Recipes
Text copyright © 2011 Canadian Diabetes Association
Photographs copyright © 2011 Robert Rose Inc.
Cover and text design copyright © 2011 Robert Rose Inc.

Some of the recipes in this book were previously published in *Choice Cooking*, published in 1982 by NC Press Limited, but have been revised to meet today's tastes and health requirements. New recipes were developed by Jennifer MacKenzie.

For complete cataloguing information, see page 327.

Disclaimer
The recipes in this book have been carefully tested by our kitchen and our tasters. To the best of our knowledge, they are safe and nutritious for ordinary use and users. For those people with food or other allergies, or who have special food requirements or health issues, please read the suggested contents of each recipe carefully and determine whether or not they may create a problem for you. All recipes are used at the risk of the consumer.

We cannot be responsible for any hazards, loss or damage that may occur as a result of any recipe use.

For those with special needs, allergies, requirements or health problems, in the event of any doubt, please contact your medical adviser prior to the use of any recipe.

Design and Production: Daniella Zanchetta/PageWave Graphics Inc.
Editor: Sue Sumeraj
Recipe editor: Jennifer MacKenzie
Nutrient analysis: Barbara Selley and Cathie Martin of Food Intelligence
Proofreader: Sheila Wawanash
Indexer: Gillian Watts
Photographer: Colin Erricson
Associate Photographer: Matt Johannsson
Food Stylist: Kathryn Robertson
Prop Stylist: Charlene Erricson

Cover image: Chicken and Snow Pea Stir-Fry (page 204)

We acknowledge the financial support of the Government of Canada through the Book Publishing Industry Development Program (BPIDP) for our publishing activities.

Published by Robert Rose Inc.
120 Eglinton Avenue East, Suite 800, Toronto, Ontario, Canada M4P 1E2
Tel: (416) 322-6552 Fax: (416) 322-6936
www.robertrose.ca

Printed and bound in Canada

1 2 3 4 5 6 7 8 9 TCP 19 18 17 16 15 14 13 12 11

Mixed Sources
Product group from well-managed
forests and other controlled sources
www.fsc.org Cert no. SW-COC-000952
© 1996 Forest Stewardship Council
FSC

Contents

Introduction

WE KNOW — you never read book introductions. But just for once, we hope you'll make an exception. Perhaps you have diabetes, a family member or friend has diabetes or, like many of us, you're always on the lookout for healthy recipes the whole family can enjoy. There's something here for everyone. In this opening section, you will learn:

- important facts about diabetes: what it is, why you should manage it, how you can manage it better and who can help you work out a meal plan;
- tips on choosing and preparing healthy foods and on planning meals;
- ways you can make your meals and snacks "diabetes-friendly," including the plate method of portioning and the American Diabetes Association Exchanges or Canadian Diabetes Association Choices;
- how to use the Nutrition Facts table on packaged foods;
- how to use the nutrition information that appears with the recipes in this book;
- where you can learn more.

We hope you enjoy the easy-to-make recipes in this book. To help you incorporate them into your meal plan, each recipe includes nutrient values per serving, as well as America's Exchanges and Canada's Choices.

Five Things Everyone Should Know About Diabetes

1. Diabetes is a serious chronic disease that affects about one person in 10 in North America — about 35 million people of all ages, and the number is increasing.

2. There are several forms of diabetes:

   - About 10% of those affected have **type 1 diabetes**. It usually appears in childhood but can also develop in adults. The pancreas stops producing insulin, so people with type 1 diabetes need to inject insulin on a regular basis.

   - About 90% have **type 2 diabetes**. Although it typically occurs in adults, it can also affect children and adolescents. Some people with type 2 diabetes are able to bring their blood glucose levels into the healthy range with weight loss and healthy eating habits. Others will also need to take oral hypoglycemic agents (pills), and some will need to inject insulin as well.

   - **Gestational diabetes (GDM)**, a temporary but serious condition, affects 3% to 4% of pregnant women. These mothers and their babies face increased risk for complications in pregnancy and delivery, as well as a risk for type 2 diabetes later in life.

   - **Prediabetes** refers to above-normal blood glucose levels that are not high enough to be diagnosed as diabetes. Untreated, however, prediabetes often progresses to type 2 diabetes.

What Is Insulin?

Insulin, produced by a gland called the pancreas, is a hormone that allows glucose (sugar) to enter body cells, where it is converted to energy. Diabetes occurs when the pancreas doesn't produce enough insulin or when the body's cells don't respond to it. When this happens, blood glucose levels rise above normal and glucose may be found in the urine.

3. All forms of diabetes should be treated to prevent or delay serious complications, including eye problems, heart disease, kidney disease, nerve damage and erectile dysfunction.

4. Healthy eating is an important strategy for preventing type 2 diabetes and for controlling blood glucose levels in all types of diabetes.

5. Even with proper management and good eating habits, diabetes is a progressive disease, so you may find that your blood glucose is not as well controlled as it once was. Your health-care provider may recommend a change in your medication.

The Basics

There's no single "diet" for people with diabetes. You should consult with a registered dietitian, who will help you develop a personalized eating plan that is tailored to your lifestyle, food preferences and customs, the diabetes medications you've been prescribed and your overall health.

How to Find a Registered Dietitian

Your health-care provider or diabetes education center can refer you to a registered dietitian (the exact title varies depending on where you live). Registered dietitians have a university degree in nutrition, have completed an internship and have written a qualifying exam. They are best qualified to help you with meal planning. They may be in private practice or may work in hospitals or diabetes education centers. Contact the American Dietetic Association (www.eatright.org) or Dietitians of Canada (www.dietitians.ca) to learn how you can find a registered dietitian in your state or province.

If you can't see a dietitian immediately, here are some tips to get you started.

1. Eat three meals each day, at regular times, and space meals no more than six hours apart. You may benefit from a healthy snack. Eating at regular times helps your body maintain healthy blood glucose levels.

2. People with diabetes should limit sugars and sweets, such as sugar, regular pop, desserts, candies, jam and honey. The more sugar you eat, the higher your blood glucose will be. Artificial sweeteners can be useful.

3. Limit the amount of high-fat foods you eat, such as fried foods, chips and pastries. They can cause you to gain weight and increase your risk of heart disease. As people with diabetes already have an increased risk of heart disease, cutting back on high-fat foods is a very important step. A healthy weight also helps with blood glucose control.

4. Eat more high-fiber foods, such as whole-grain breads and cereals, lentils, beans and peas, brown rice, vegetables and fruits. Foods high in fiber may help you feel more satisfied and reduce the rise in blood glucose after meals. Over time, a higher fiber intake may also lead to lower cholesterol levels.

5. If you are thirsty, drink water. Avoid regular pop and fruit juice, which will raise your blood glucose.

6. Build more physical activity into your life. Formal exercise programs are very helpful, but there are many ways to boost your activity every day. For example, bypass elevators and escalators, or walk several stops before catching the bus. Increased activity will help you control your weight and improve your blood glucose control. For more tips on increasing your activity level, see "Physical Activity Guidelines for Americans" at www.health.gov or "Tips to Get Active" at www.publichealth.gc.ca.

Source: Adapted from "Just the Basics," Canadian Diabetes Association, March 2010. Available at www.diabetes.ca/files/JTB17x_11_CPGO3_1103.pdf. Used with permission.

Top 10 Tips for Tasty and Healthy Eating

1. **Take a few minutes each week to plan your menus.** This will allow you to schedule a quick and easy meal on Wednesday, when your son plays hockey, and a late dinner after the parent-teacher interview on Thursday.

2. **Cruise the grocery store with a list.** A grocery list will ensure that you bring home everything you need to prepare the meals you've planned — and will help you avoid impulse purchases. Speaking of impulse buying, try not to shop when you're hungry.

3. **In the produce department, favor bright-colored fruits and vegetables.**
   - In general, the darker the color, the higher the nutrients (think bright red peppers or dark green broccoli)
   - When they're available, buy fruits and vegetables in season to enjoy peak flavor.
   - Canned and frozen fruits and vegetables are also high in nutrients. Choose fruits packed in juice. If you purchase vegetables or beans canned with salt, rinse them briefly and drain before use.

4. **Be a smart label reader.**
   - Read the ingredient list on packaged foods.

- Check the Nutrition Facts table, especially for carbohydrate, fat and sodium. See "Take 5 to Read the Facts" on page 13 for tips on how to use the information provided in the Nutrition Facts table.

5. **Equip your kitchen for low-fat food preparation.**
   - Use a steamer for vegetables, cook them in the microwave or boil them covered with a small amount of water.
   - Use a nonstick pan to sauté with very little or no added fat or oil.
   - Place meat on a rack when baking, roasting or broiling, to allow fat to drip away.

6. **Reduce or eliminate high-fat ingredients.**
   - In casseroles and other dishes containing ground meat, replace part of the meat with tofu, bulgur or brown rice.
   - Replace mild cheeses with smaller amounts of stronger varieties.
   - Trim meat well before adding it to soups and stews. When you can, prepare soups and stews the day before, refrigerate in an airtight container and, before reheating, remove any fat that has risen to the top.

7. **Eat small amounts of healthy fats.**
   - Keep saturated fat low by drinking low-fat or skim milk, using reduced-fat cheese, trimming fat from meat and removing skin from chicken.
   - Use soft non-hydrogenated margarine and monounsaturated oils, such as canola and olive oil. Spray oil with a pump spray to minimize the amount used.
   - Eat cold-water fish, such as salmon or tuna, at least twice per week.

8. **Replace salt with spices and herbs to kick up the flavor.**
   - Increase quantities of familiar spices and herbs and experiment with new ones.
   - Always taste food before adding salt.

9. **Let the "space on your plate" guide your portions.** Check out "What to Eat" on page 10.

10. **Fight "portion distortion."**
    - Use a slightly smaller plate than you're used to; that way, the smaller servings will seem more satisfying.
    - Researchers have found that people will help themselves to more snacks from a large container than from a small one. You can make this work for you. When you do splurge — and everyone does now and then — go for a miniature chocolate bar rather than part of a larger one (so you won't be tempted to have "just a little more"). Pick up the $1\frac{1}{2}$-ounce (43 g) package of potato chips, not a 7-ounce (200 g) bag that will greet you every time you open the kitchen cupboard.

Expanding Serving Sizes Can Sneak Up on You

We live in "supersized" times. Packaged foods and restaurant meals are no exception. In 2002, typical hamburgers and bagels were about twice the size of their 1982 "ancestors" and pasta servings were about four times as big as those in 1982. The only thing that hasn't been supersized is the amount of food we actually need. The result is many more people with supersized waistlines.

For an entertaining and thought-provoking look at the "portion distortion" phenomenon and lots of helpful tips for fighting its influence, check out *Mindless Eating: Why We Eat More Than We Think* by Brian Wansink. Another fun eye-opener is the Portion Distortion Interactive Quiz at http://hp2010.nhlbihin.net/portion/portion.cgi?action=question&number=1.

What to Eat

When serving your meal, mentally divide the plate into three sections.

- Fill one-half of the plate with at least two kinds of vegetables.
- Fill one-quarter with grains and starches, such as rice, pasta, couscous or potato.
- Fill one-quarter with lean meat, poultry, fish or alternatives such as beans or lentils.

To complete your meal, add a glass of low-fat or skim milk, or fortified low-fat soy beverage, and choose a piece of fresh fruit for dessert.

Source: Image from "Just the Basics," Canadian Diabetes Association, March 2010. Available at: http://www.diabetes.ca/files/JTB17x_11_CPGO3_1103.pdf. Used with permission.

What Are America's Exchanges and Canada's Choices?

America's Exchanges and Canada's Choices list the foods in each food group, in quantities that contain approximately the same amounts of carbohydrate, fat and protein. Because each food in the list has a similar nutrient profile, you can replace one Exchange or Choice with another from the same list. For example,

- A 1-ounce (30 g) slice of bread and ⅓ cup (150 mL) of cooked rice each contains 15 grams of carbohydrate. Each counts as 1 Starch Exchange or 1 Carbohydrate Choice.
- One ounce (30 g) of cooked meat, 1 ounce (30 g) of hard cheese and one large egg each contains about 7 grams of protein. Each counts as 1 Meat and Meat Substitutes Exchange or 1 Meat and Alternatives Choice.
- One teaspoon (5 mL) of canola or olive oil and 1 teaspoon (5 mL) of soft non-hydrogenated margarine each contains 5 grams of fat. Each counts as 1 Fat Exchange or 1 Fat Choice.

For more examples of the foods in each of the groups, see Appendix 2: Exchange Lists for Diabetes (page 306) and Appendix 3: Canadian Diabetes Association Choice Lists (page 318).

How Many America's Exchanges or Canada's Choices Do You Need?

Your overall calorie requirements determine the amount of food you need each day; your daily routine (including meal times) determines how it should be divided into meals and snacks. The meal plans on page 12 are examples of a division of America's Exchanges and Canada's Choices into meals and snacks for a person needing about 1800 calories per day. Depending on your sex, size, age and activity level, you may need fewer or more calories or a different distribution of Exchanges or Choices. A registered dietitian (see page 7) can help you work out a meal plan that's right for you.

For daily menus based on America's Exchanges and Canada's Choices, using the recipes in this book, see Appendix 1 (page 302).

1800-Calorie Meal Plan Based on America's Exchanges

Exchanges	Breakfast	Lunch	Snack	Dinner	Snack	Total
Carbohydrate Group*						
Starch	2	3	1	3	1	10
Nonstarchy Vegetables	–	2	–	2	–	4
Fruits	1	1	–	1	–	3
Milk, Low-Fat (1%)	½	–	1	–	½	2
Meat and Meat Substitutes (Lean)	1	2	–	3	–	6
Fat	2	2	–	2	–	6

* A Sweets, Desserts and Other Carbohydrates Exchange can on occasion replace a Starch or Fruits Exchange.

1800-Calorie Meal Plan Based on Canada's Choices*

Choices	Breakfast	Lunch	Snack	Dinner	Snack	Total
Carbohydrate (total)**	3½	4	2	4	1½	15
Grains and Starches	2	3	1	3	1	10
Fruits	1	1		1	–	3
Milk and Alternatives (choose skim milk)	½	–	1	–	½	2
Meat and Alternatives	1	2		3	–	6
Fats	2	2		2	–	6

* In addition, over the course of the day, eat 4 servings of "free" vegetables (those not marked with an asterisk in the examples in Appendix 3 on page 323).

** An Other Choice, such as cookies or ice cream, can on occasion replace a choice from the Carbohydrate group.

Take 5 to Read the Facts

Got five minutes? Follow these five easy steps to read the Nutrition Facts table.

Nutrition Facts	
Per 1 cup (55 g)	
Amount	**% Daily Value**
Calories 220	
Fat 2 g	3%
Saturated 0 g + Trans 0 g	0%
Cholesterol 0 mg	11%
Carbohydrate 44 g	15%
Fiber 8 g	32%
Sugars 16 g	
Protein 6 g	
Vitamin A 0% Vitamin C 0%	
Calcium 4% Iron 40%	

(1) (2) (3) (4) (5)

1. **Serving size.** If you eat the serving size shown on the Nutrition Facts table, you will get the amount of calories and nutrients that are listed. Always compare the serving size on the package to the amount that you eat.

2. **Calories.** Calories tell you how much energy you get from one serving of a packaged food.

3. **Percent Daily Value (% Daily Value).** Percent Daily Value puts nutrients on a scale from 0% to 100%. This scale tells you if there is a *little* or a *lot* of a nutrient in one serving of a packaged food.

4. **Get less of these nutrients:**
   - Fat, saturated fat and trans fat
   - Cholesterol
   - Sodium

   Choose packaged foods with a *low* % Daily Value of fat and sodium, especially if you are at risk for heart disease or diabetes.

5. **Get more of these nutrients:**
   - Carbohydrate
   - Fiber
   - Vitamin A and vitamin C
   - Calcium
   - Iron

   Choose packaged foods with a high % Daily Value of these nutrients. If you have diabetes, watch how much carbohydrate you eat, as this will affect your blood glucose levels.

Source: Adapted from Healthy Eating is in Store for You, Fact Sheet #3. © 2011 Canadian Diabetes Association and Dietitians of Canada. Used with permission.

All About Carbohydrate

For people with diabetes, carbohydrate is one of the most important nutrients on the Nutrition Facts table.

How does carbohydrate affect your body?

The carbohydrate you eat changes to glucose (sugar) in your body to provide you with energy. If you are affected by diabetes, you need to watch how much carbohydrate you eat in order to control the amount of glucose in your blood.

What foods supply you with carbohydrate?

Carbohydrate comes from cereals, breads, rice, pasta, other grain products, legumes, some vegetables, fruit, some dairy products and refined sugars.

What are the different types of carbohydrate?

- Starches (bread, pasta, potatoes)
- Sugars (naturally occurring in fruit, vegetables and milk, as well as refined sugars such as granulated sugar, brown sugar, honey or molasses)
- Fiber (whole-grain foods, vegetables and fruit)

Does the type of carbohydrate you eat affect your blood glucose levels?

Yes! For people with diabetes, the type of carbohydrate is one factor in controlling blood glucose. Except for fiber, the different types of carbohydrate you eat turn into glucose in the blood. Eating high-fiber foods may lower your blood glucose and will help you feel full.

Also important in controlling blood glucose is the total amount of carbohydrate eaten at one sitting. Talk with a registered dietitian about the amount of carbohydrate that is right for you.

Is it important to spread the carbohydrate you eat evenly throughout the day?

Dividing your carbohydrate evenly into meals and snacks throughout the day will help your body have better control over your blood glucose levels. Your blood glucose level will also rise more slowly when you eat carbohydrate as part of a complete meal.

Source: Adapted from Healthy Eating is in Store for You, Fact Sheet #6. © 2007 Canadian Diabetes Association and Dietitians of Canada. Used with permission.

What Is Carbohydrate Counting?

Carbohydrate, found in grains and starches, fruits, some vegetables, milk and sugar-containing foods, is the nutrient that has the biggest effect on blood glucose. A dietitian can help you learn to "count carbohydrates" when planning and keeping track of what you eat. This method focuses on carbohydrate, but it's still important to control the amounts of protein and fat you eat in order to avoid excess calories. To learn more about carbohydrate counting, visit www.diabetes.org or www.diabetes.ca.

What Is the Glycemic Index?

The glycemic index (GI) is a measure of how much and how quickly a particular food raises blood glucose. During digestion, low-GI foods release glucose more slowly, over a longer period of time, and raise blood glucose less than high-GI foods.

Foods high in fiber generally have a low GI — think dried beans, peas and lentils, whole-grain breads and crackers, high-fiber cereals and whole grains such as large-flake rolled oats, brown rice and barley. With a few exceptions, vegetables and fruits also have a low GI. Meat, fish, poultry, fats and oils contain no carbohydrate, so they have a GI of zero. They do, however, contain calories and can also have an effect on your blood glucose.

Eating more foods with a low GI may help you control your blood sugar, but remember that the total amount of carbohydrate you eat is still important. Whether the food has a low GI or a high GI, each gram of carbohydrate is equivalent to 4 calories.

To learn more about the glycemic index, visit www.diabetes.org or www.diabetes.ca.

Where Do Calories Come From? Where Do They Go?

Carbohydrate, protein, fat and alcohol in our food and beverages all yield calories (energy). Gram for gram, carbohydrates and protein have less than half the calories of fat.

	Calories per gram
Carbohydrate	4
Protein	4
Fat	9
Alcohol	7

Calories provide the energy for all of our activities. When you eat more calories than you need, your body converts them to fat. If you consistently eat more than you need, your weight will go up — just 100 extra calories a day can add up to 10 pounds (4.5 kg) in a year!

What's the Story on Sodium and Salt?

Sodium is an essential nutrient, but too much can lead to high blood pressure, a major risk factor for stroke and heart disease. You should aim for a total sodium intake of less than 2,300 mg a day, the amount in about 1 tsp (5 mL) of salt.

Most of us get more sodium than we need, much of it from processed and convenience foods. Here are five things you can do to reduce your sodium intake:

1. Look at the Nutrition Facts table when choosing packaged foods. Five percent of the Daily Value (5% DV) for sodium is a little; 15% is a lot.

2. Ask for nutrition information in restaurants and use it to make lower-sodium selections.

3. Choose canned products with reduced sodium or no added salt.

4. Rinse and drain vegetables and legumes that are canned with salt, to reduce sodium by about 40%.

5. Use less salt when you cook, and always taste food before adding any salt.

About the Nutrient Information in this Book

The nutrient information with the recipes in this book will help you fit them into your meal plan. Recipes were evaluated as follows:

- Nutrient calculations were based on common household weights and measures (cup, tsp, lb, etc.) unless a metric package would typically be purchased and a specified portion of it used in the recipe.

- Optional ingredients and unspecified amounts of garnishes and other ingredients were not included in the calculations.

- Where there is a choice of ingredients, the first one listed was used in the calculation.

- When a recipe specifies a maximum amount of salt (e.g., $\frac{1}{8}$ tsp/0.5 mL or less), the maximum amount was used in the calculation.

Food Intelligence (Toronto, Ontario) performed computer-assisted nutrient calculations for the recipes and menus, using Genesis® R&D SQL (ESHA Research). The primary database was the Canadian Nutrient File (version 2007b), supplemented with information from the USDA National Nutrient Database for Standard Reference (Release 21) and other sources. Food Intelligence also assigned America's Exchanges and Canada's Choices to the recipe servings.

America's Exchanges

America's Exchanges calculations were based on the American Diabetes Association food exchange values in the table at right. Carbohydrate exchanges are based on total carbohydrate, including fiber.

Group/Lists	Carbohydrate (g)	Protein (g)	Fat (g)
Carbohydrate Group			
Starches	15	3	–
Fruit	15	–	–
Milk, Low-Fat (1%)	12	8	2
Other Carbohydrates	15	variable	variable
Vegetables	5	2	–
Meat and Meat Substitutes Group			
Lean Meat	–	7	3
Plant-Based Proteins	variable	7	variable
Fat Group	–	–	5

Source: Adapted from *Choose Your Foods — Exchange Lists for Diabetes.* © American Diabetes Association and American Dietetic Association, 2008. Used with permission.

Canada's Choices

Canada's Choices calculations were based on the Canadian Diabetes Association food choice values in the table at right. Carbohydrate choices are based on available carbohydrate (total carbohydrate minus fiber).

Canada's Choice	Carbohydrate (g)	Protein (g)	Fat (g)
Carbohydrate			
Grains & Starches	15	3	0
Fruits	15	0	0
Milk & Alternatives (choose skim milk)	15	8	0
Other Choices	15	variable	variable
Meat & Alternatives	0	7	3
Fats	0	0	5
Extras	< 5	0	0

Source: Adapted from *Beyond the Basics: Meal Planning for Healthy Eating, Diabetes Prevention and Management.* © Canadian Diabetes Association, 2005. Used with permission.

Appetizers

Stuffed Mushrooms

**Makes
12 mushrooms**
Serving size:
2 mushrooms

Select firm white
or creamy beige
mushrooms for these
hot hors d'oeuvres. Do
not substitute other
cheeses — Gruyère works
best and provides good
flavor.

Kitchen Tip

Assemble the stuffed
mushrooms through
step 2, cover and store in
the refrigerator for up to
24 hours before baking.

- **Preheat oven to 400°F (200°C)**
- **Baking sheet, lightly greased**

12	medium mushrooms	12
1/2 cup	shredded Gruyère cheese	125 mL
1/4 cup	Seasoned Bread Crumbs (see recipe, page 72)	60 mL

1. Remove stems from mushrooms and place mushroom caps on prepared baking sheet. Chop stems and measure $\frac{1}{3}$ cup (75 mL).

2. Using a fork, cream cheese until soft. Stir in bread crumbs, mushroom stems and 1 tsp (5 mL) water until blended. Form into 12 balls. Place one ball in each mushroom cap.

3. Bake in preheated oven for 10 minutes. Serve hot.

Nutrients per serving

Calories	67
Carbohydrate	4 g
Fiber	1 g
Protein	4 g
Total fat	4 g
Saturated fat	2 g
Cholesterol	13 mg
Sodium	67 mg

America's Exchanges	
1	Fat
1	Free Food

Canada's Choices	
1/2	Meat & Alternatives
1/2	Fat

Party Mix

This crunchy combination is a real hit with the younger crowd.

Nutrition Tip

Nuts contain protein and fat. While the fat is the healthy unsaturated type, it still contributes calories, so nuts should generally be eaten in small quantities. If you are a vegetarian, a dietitian can advise you about using nuts as a Meat and Meat Substitutes Exchange or a Meat and Alternatives Choice.

- **Preheat oven to 275°F (140°C)**
- **Large, shallow cake pan or roaster**

4 cups	wheat squares cereal, such as Shreddies or Chex	1 L
2 cups	puffed wheat cereal	500 mL
2 cups	toasted oat Os cereal	500 mL
2 cups	small, thin pretzels	500 mL
1 cup	unsalted peanuts or mixed nuts	250 mL
$\frac{1}{3}$ cup	vegetable oil	75 mL
1 tbsp	Worcestershire sauce	15 mL
1 tsp	garlic salt	5 mL

1. In a large bowl, combine wheat squares, puffed wheat, oat cereal, pretzels and peanuts.

2. In a small bowl, combine oil, Worcestershire sauce and garlic salt. Sprinkle over cereal mixture and toss to coat. Spread out in pan.

3. Toast in preheated oven, stirring every 15 minutes, for 1 hour.

Nutrients per Serving	
Calories	92
Carbohydrate	11 g
Fiber	1 g
Protein	2 g
Total fat	5 g
Saturated fat	1 g
Cholesterol	0 mg
Sodium	145 mg

America's Exchanges	
$\frac{1}{2}$	Starch
1	Fat

Canada's Choices	
$\frac{1}{2}$	Carbohydrate
1	Fat

Cheese Puffs

||||||||||||||||||||||||||||||||||||||||||||||||||||||||||||||||||||||||||||||||||||||||||||||||||||||||||||||||||

These tasty special occasion appetizers are surprisingly easy to make. Light as a feather and crisp, they are best served piping hot.

- Preheat oven to 400°F (200°C)
- Baking sheets, lightly greased

¼ cup	margarine or butter	60 mL
½ tsp	salt	2 mL
Pinch	freshly ground black pepper	Pinch
1 cup	all-purpose flour	250 mL
4	eggs, at room temperature	4
1 cup	shredded Swiss cheese	250 mL
½ tsp	dry mustard	2 mL
1 tsp	Dijon mustard	5 mL
2 tbsp	mayonnaise	30 mL
3 tbsp	freshly grated Parmesan cheese	45 mL
Pinch	paprika	Pinch

1. In a saucepan, combine 1 cup (250 mL) water, margarine, salt and pepper. Bring to a rapid boil over high heat. Add flour all at once, beating vigorously with a wooden spoon until mixture forms a ball and comes away from sides of pan. Remove from heat and let cool for 5 minutes.

2. Add eggs, one at a time, beating vigorously for 10 seconds after each addition. Continue beating for 1 to 2 minutes or until smooth and glossy. Stir in Swiss cheese, dry mustard and Dijon mustard. Using two small spoons, drop batter onto prepared baking sheets, making 36 mounds.

Nutrients per Serving

Calories	103
Carbohydrate	6 g
Fiber	0 g
Protein	4 g
Total fat	7 g
Saturated fat	2 g
Cholesterol	48 mg
Sodium	144 mg

America's Exchanges

½	Starch
1	Fat

Canada's Choices

½	Carbohydrate
½	Meat & Alternatives
1	Fat

Kitchen Tips

You can use a food processor in step 2, if you prefer. Process the mixture for 10 seconds after adding each egg, and for 20 seconds after the last egg.

The puffs can be prepared through step 3, cooled and stored in an airtight container at room temperature for up to 3 days. Just before serving, brush with mayonnaise and sprinkle with Parmesan and paprika. Reheat in a 400°F (200°C) oven for 5 minutes.

3. Bake in preheated oven for 20 minutes or until puffed and lightly browned.

4. Brush tops of puffs with mayonnaise and sprinkle with Parmesan and paprika. Serve hot.

Gouda Wafers

||||||||||||||||||||||||||||||||||||||||||||||||||||||||||||||||||||||||||||||||||||||||||||||||||||||||||||||||||||||||||||||||||||||||||||

These homemade crackers are snappy on their own as nibblers or provide the perfect contrast for creamy soups or chunky chowders.

Nutrition Tip

When choosing a margarine, look for a non-hydrogenated soft margarine. These are low in saturated fat and do not contain trans fat. Avoid hard margarines, which contain high amounts of saturated and trans fat.

- **Preheat oven to 400°F (200°C)**
- **Baking sheet, lightly greased**

½ cup	whole wheat flour	125 mL
¼ cup	white rice flour	60 mL
½ tsp	baking powder	2 mL
¼ tsp	celery salt or salt	1 mL
½ cup	shredded medium or aged Gouda cheese	125 mL
1 tbsp	margarine	15 mL
2 tbsp	sesame seeds	30 mL
3 to 4 tbsp	ice water	45 to 60 mL

1. In a bowl, combine whole wheat flour, rice flour, baking powder and celery. Using a pastry blender or two knives, cut in cheese and margarine until mixture resembles fine crumbs. Stir in sesame seeds. Gradually add water, mixing with a fork to form a stiff dough. Form into a ball.

2. On a lightly floured work surface, roll out dough to a thickness of $\frac{1}{8}$ inch (3 mm). Cut into 2-inch (5 cm) squares. Place on prepared baking sheet.

3. Bake in preheated oven for 8 to 10 minutes or until very lightly browned. Transfer wafers to a wire rack and let cool for 2 hours. Store in an airtight container at room temperature.

Nutrients per Serving

Calories	63
Carbohydrate	7 g
Fiber	1 g
Protein	2 g
Total fat	3 g
Saturated fat	1 g
Cholesterol	5 mg
Sodium	81 mg

America's Exchanges	
½	Starch
½	Fat

Canada's Choices	
½	Carbohydrate
½	Fat

Dilly Dip

Like most dips, this one is very versatile. Try a small dollop on a baked potato or a small bowl of salad greens.

Kitchen Tip

Store dip in an airtight container in the refrigerator for up to 5 days. Stir well before serving.

Nutrition Tip

Cottage cheese has traditionally contained a lot of salt, with about 400 mg (17% DV) in ¹⁄₂ cup (125 mL). Some brands now contain less. Be sure to check the Nutrition Facts table when shopping and choose the one that's lowest in sodium.

• Blender or food processor

2 cups	2% cottage cheese	500 mL
¹⁄₂ cup	light sour cream	125 mL
2 tbsp	chopped dill pickle	30 mL
1 tbsp	chopped fresh dill	15 mL
	(or 1 tsp/5 mL dried dillweed)	
¹⁄₄ tsp	freshly ground black pepper	1 mL

1. In blender, purée cottage cheese, sour cream, pickle, dill and pepper until smooth.

Nutrients per Serving

Calories	36
Carbohydrate	2 g
Fiber	0 g
Protein	4 g
Total fat	1 g
Saturated fat	1 g
Cholesterol	4 mg
Sodium	141 mg

America's Exchanges	
1	Lean Meat

Canada's Choices	
¹⁄₂	Meat & Alternatives

Creamy Vegetable Dip

Serve this easy dip with crisp carrot, celery, cucumber and zucchini sticks, along with button mushrooms and plump red radishes.

Kitchen Tip
Store dip in an airtight container in the refrigerator for up to 3 days. Stir well before serving.

● **Blender or food processor**

1 cup	2% cottage cheese	250 mL
3 tbsp	light sour cream	45 mL
2 tbsp	ketchup	30 mL
8	drops hot pepper sauce	8
2 tbsp	chopped green onion	30 mL

1. In blender, purée cottage cheese, sour cream, ketchup and hot pepper sauce for 2 minutes or until very smooth. Add onion and blend just until mixed in.

2. Transfer to a bowl, cover and refrigerate for 1 to 2 hours to blend the flavors.

Nutrients per Serving

Calories	36
Carbohydrate	3 g
Fiber	0 g
Protein	4 g
Total fat	1 g
Saturated fat	1 g
Cholesterol	3 mg
Sodium	166 mg

America's Exchanges

1	Lean Meat
1	Free Food

Canada's Choices

½	Meat & Alternatives

Caramelized Onion and Spinach Dip

**Makes about
1²/₃ cups (400 mL)**
Serving size: 3 tbsp
(45 mL)

In this amazing dip, caramelized onions, spinach and carrots add flavor and goodness. Serve it with a variety of fresh veggies and/or whole-grain crackers.

Variations

Add 2 mashed cloves of roasted garlic with the spinach and carrots.

Replace the onion with 1 cup (250 mL) chopped shallots.

2 tsp	butter	10 mL
1	onion, chopped	1
2 cups	packed chopped fresh spinach	500 mL
¼ cup	shredded carrot	60 mL
²/₃ cup	plain low-fat yogurt	150 mL
½ cup	light mayonnaise	125 mL

1. In a large nonstick skillet, melt butter over medium heat. Cook onion, stirring often, for about 13 minutes or until softened and a rich golden brown (reduce heat if browning too quickly). Add spinach and carrot; sauté for 2 minutes or until spinach is wilted; remove from heat.

2. In a serving bowl, combine yogurt and mayonnaise. Stir in spinach mixture. Cover and refrigerate for at least 1 hour or for up to 2 days to blend the flavors. Let stand at room temperature for 15 minutes before serving.

Nutrients per Serving

Calories	66
Carbohydrate	4 g
Fiber	0 g
Protein	1 g
Total fat	5 g
Saturated fat	1 g
Cholesterol	8 mg
Sodium	108 mg

America's Exchanges	
1	Fat
1	Free Food

Canada's Choices	
1	Fat
1	Extra

Eggplant Dip

||||||||||||||||||||||||||||||||||||||||||||||||||||||||||||||||||||||||||||||||||||||||||||||||||||||||||||||||||||

Eggplant dip (sometimes called "poor man's caviar") is popular in many Mediterranean countries. It's good with raw vegetables or on crisp Melba toast.

Kitchen Tips
To peel a tomato, blanch it in a pot of boiling water for 30 seconds, then immediately plunge it into a bowl of cold water; let stand until cool. Use a paring knife to cut out the core and peel off the thin skin.

A blender or food processor can be used to chop the roasted eggplant, but avoid overprocessing, as this dip is best when it has some crunch.

Store dip in an airtight container in the refrigerator for up to 3 days. Stir well before serving.

Nutrients per Serving	
Calories	21
Carbohydrate	3 g
Fiber	1 g
Protein	0 g
Total fat	1 g
Saturated fat	0 g
Cholesterol	0 mg
Sodium	75 mg

- **Preheat oven to 400°F (200°C)**
- **Baking pan**

1	eggplant	1
3	green onions, finely chopped	3
1	large tomato, peeled and chopped	1
1	small clove garlic, finely chopped	1
½	stalk celery, finely chopped	½
1 tbsp	freshly squeezed lemon juice or white wine vinegar	15 mL
1 tbsp	vegetable oil	15 mL
½ tsp	salt	2 mL
¼ tsp	freshly ground black pepper	1 mL

1. Prick eggplant in several places with a fork. Place in baking pan and roast in preheated oven for 30 minutes. Let cool, then peel and finely chop.

2. In a bowl, combine chopped eggplant, green onions, tomato, garlic and celery. Add lemon juice, oil, salt and pepper. Cover and refrigerate for at least 4 hours to blend the flavors.

America's Exchanges	
1	Free Food

Canada's Choices	
1	Extra

Salmon Cream Cheese Spread

This smooth spread is wonderful on crackers, Melba toast, cucumber or zucchini slices, in celery sticks or as a sandwich filling.

Kitchen Tip
Store spread in an airtight container in the refrigerator for up to 3 days. Stir well before serving.

Nutrition Tips
If you serve crackers with this spread, remember to count them as Starch Exchanges or Carbohydrate Choices.

Use the Nutrition Facts table to compare different varieties of crackers. Look for ones that are lower in fat and sodium, and avoid those containing trans fat. Crackers made from whole grains are higher in fiber.

Nutrients per Serving	
Calories	58
Carbohydrate	2 g
Fiber	0 g
Protein	4 g
Total fat	4 g
Saturated fat	2 g
Cholesterol	11 mg
Sodium	100 mg

1	can (7½ oz/213 g) salmon, drained	1
½ cup	light cream cheese, softened	125 mL
½ cup	light sour cream	125 mL
¼ cup	chopped green onions or chives	60 mL
2 tbsp	chopped fresh dill (or 2 tsp/10 mL dried dillweed)	30 mL
2 tsp	white wine vinegar	10 mL
Pinch	freshly ground black pepper	Pinch

1. In a small bowl, combine salmon and cream cheese until blended. Stir in sour cream, green onions, dill, vinegar and pepper until well combined.

America's Exchanges	
1	Lean Meat
½	Fat

Canada's Choices	
½	Meat & Alternatives
½	Fat

Crabmeat Spread

||||||||||||||||||||||||||||||||||||||||||||||||||||||||||||||||||||||||||||||||||||||||||||||||||||||||||||||||||

**Makes 1¼ cups
(300 mL)**
Serving size: 2 tbsp
(30 mL)

Crabmeat and cottage cheese combine in this elegant but easy party starter. Serve it with celery, carrot or bell pepper spears or on cucumber and zucchini slices or crisp crackers.

Kitchen Tip
To ensure success with any recipe, read it through carefully before you begin to prepare it.

Nutrition Tip
If you serve crackers with this spread, remember to count them as Starch Exchanges or Carbohydrate Choices.

● **Blender or food processor**

½ cup	2% cottage cheese	125 mL
1 tbsp	freshly squeezed lemon juice	15 mL
1 tbsp	dry sherry	15 mL
1 tbsp	ketchup	15 mL
1	can (4½ oz/120 g drained weight) crabmeat, drained	1
2 tbsp	Tangy Salad Cream (see recipe, page 124)	30 mL
2	green onions, finely chopped Freshly ground black pepper	2

1. Drain or press liquid from cottage cheese. In blender, combine cottage cheese, lemon juice, sherry and ketchup; process for 2 to 3 minutes or until very smooth.

2. Rinse crabmeat and pat dry. Remove any pieces of shell. Add crabmeat and dressing to cheese mixture. Pulse 3 to 4 times, just until well blended.

3. Transfer to a bowl and stir in green onions. Season to taste with pepper. Cover and refrigerate for at least 1 hour, to blend the flavors, or for up to 2 days.

Nutrients per Serving	
Calories	26
Carbohydrate	1 g
Fiber	0 g
Protein	3 g
Total fat	0 g
Saturated fat	0 g
Cholesterol	3 mg
Sodium	153 mg

America's Exchanges	
1	Free Food

Canada's Choices	
½	Meat & Alternatives

Cheese 'n' Chutney Spread

Makes 1¼ cups (300 mL)
Serving size: 2 tbsp (30 mL)

Mix and form this spread a few days ahead. It keeps beautifully, wrapped, in the refrigerator. Warm it to room temperature at serving time to bring out the full flavor of the Edam cheese highlighted by the sweet, spicy chutney. It's great on zucchini or cucumber slices.

Kitchen Tip
To make zucchini boats, cut 2 zucchini in half lengthwise and scoop out seeds. Pack Cheese 'n' Chutney Spread into hollow. Chill and serve sliced.

Nutrition Tip
Cheese contains protein, but may also be high in fat and sodium. Because this spread is higher in sodium, save it for special occasions.

Nutrients per Serving	
Calories	92
Carbohydrate	2 g
Fiber	0 g
Protein	6 g
Total fat	6 g
Saturated fat	4 g
Cholesterol	21 mg
Sodium	259 mg

2 cups	shredded Edam cheese	500 mL
4 tsp	mango chutney	20 mL
½ tsp	curry powder	2 mL
2 to 3 tsp	2% milk	10 to 15 mL
4	small green onions, finely chopped	4

1. In a bowl, combine cheese, chutney and curry powder. Beat in milk, 1 tsp (5 mL) at a time, until mixture holds together in a fairly smooth ball.

2. Roll ball in green onions. Wrap and refrigerate for at least 4 hours, to blend the flavors, or for up to 3 days.

America's Exchanges	
1	Lean Meat
½	Fat

Canada's Choices	
1	Meat & Alternatives
½	Fat

Nippy Cheese Log

Feature this log at a snack party. A piece on a crisp cracker, fresh mushroom cap or zucchini or cucumber slice makes a tasty tidbit.

Kitchen Tips
A food processor works well to blend the ingredients in step 1.

All of the recipes in this book have been developed to yield good results whether you use imperial or metric measures. Just be sure to follow one system of measurement throughout the entire preparation of a recipe.

1 cup	shredded Edam cheese	250 mL
½ cup	1% cottage cheese, well mashed	125 mL
¼ cup	shredded aged Cheddar cheese	60 mL
¼ cup	freshly grated Parmesan cheese	60 mL
⅓ cup	finely chopped fresh parsley, divided	75 mL
¼ tsp	garlic powder	1 mL
¼ tsp	paprika	1 mL
Pinch	chili powder	Pinch
2	drops hot pepper sauce	2

1. In a bowl, combine Edam, cottage cheese, Cheddar, Parmesan, 1 tbsp (15 mL) of the parsley, garlic powder, paprika, chili powder and hot pepper sauce until well blended.

2. Form cheese mixture into a log and roll in the remaining parsley. Wrap and refrigerate for at least 5 hours or for up to 3 days. Remove from refrigerator 20 minutes before serving.

Nutrients per Serving

Calories	71
Carbohydrate	1 g
Fiber	0 g
Protein	6 g
Total fat	5 g
Saturated fat	3 g
Cholesterol	16 mg
Sodium	213 mg

America's Exchanges	
1	Lean Meat
½	Fat

Canada's Choices	
1	Meat & Alternative
½	Fat

Beverages

Cranberry Refresher

|||||||||||||||||||||||||||||||||||||||||||||||||||||||||||||||||||||||||||||||||||||||||||||||||||||||||||||||

This bright red cooler is perfect for both summer picnics and Christmas cocktail parties. If a clearer beverage is desired, pour it through a fine sieve or cheesecloth.

| ¼ cup | Cranberry Concentrate (see recipe, opposite) | 60 mL |
| ¾ cup | water, sugar-free ginger ale or soda water | 175 mL |

1. Dilute concentrate with water. Serve chilled, over ice cubes if desired.

Nutrients per Serving

Calories	15
Carbohydrate	4 g
Fiber	1 g
Protein	0 g
Total fat	0 g
Saturated fat	0 g
Cholesterol	0 mg
Sodium	10 mg

America's Exchanges	
1	Free Food

Canada's Choices	
1	Extra

Cranberry Concentrate

The intense flavor of cranberries in this homemade concentrate shines when mixed up into a refreshing beverage.

Kitchen Tip

Freeze cranberry concentrate in 2-tbsp (30 mL) amounts in ice cube trays, then pack the cubes into freezer bags and store in the freezer for up to 9 months. Use 2 cubes to make Cranberry Refresher (opposite); 1 cube to make Frosty Bog (page 40) or Hot Mulled Toddy (page 56); or 5 cubes to make Tea Punch (page 43).

2 cups	cranberries	500 mL
2	slices lemon	2
	Artificial sweetener equivalent to $1/4$ cup (60 mL) granulated sugar	

1. In a stainless steel or enamel saucepan, combine cranberries, lemon slices and $2\frac{1}{2}$ cups (625 mL) water. Bring to a boil over high heat. Reduce heat and simmer for 30 minutes. Add sweetener and stir until dissolved.

2. Strain, stirring and mashing berries until a fairly dry pulp remains in strainer; discard pulp. Transfer liquid to an airtight container and store in the refrigerator for up to 8 weeks.

Nutrients per Serving

Calories	15
Carbohydrate	4 g
Fiber	1 g
Protein	0 g
Total fat	0 g
Saturated fat	0 g
Cholesterol	0 mg
Sodium	6 mg

America's Exchanges	
1	Free Food

Canada's Choices	
1	Extra

Rhubarb Refresher

This chilled beverage is so pretty, and the natural tartness of rhubarb is a great thirst-quencher.

Kitchen Tip
You can add artificial sweetener if a sweeter-tasting beverage is desired.

½ cup	Rhubarb Concentrate (see recipe, opposite)	125 mL
½ cup	water, sugar-free ginger ale or soda water	125 mL

1. Dilute concentrate with water. Serve chilled, over ice cubes if desired.

Nutrients per Serving

Calories	18
Carbohydrate	4 g
Fiber	1 g
Protein	1 g
Total fat	0 g
Saturated fat	0 g
Cholesterol	0 mg
Sodium	10 mg

America's Exchanges	
1	Free Food

Canada's Choices	
1	Extra

**Makes about 3 cups
(750 mL)**
Serving size: $\frac{1}{2}$ cup
(125 mL)

Make a good supply of
rhubarb concentrate
early in the summer,
when garden rhubarb is
plentiful. It freezes well,
so plan to have some
on hand for refreshing
drinks all year long.

Kitchen Tip
Freeze rhubarb concentrate
in 2-tbsp (30 mL) amounts in
ice cube trays, then pack the
cubes into freezer bags and
store in the freezer for up to
9 months.

Rhubarb Concentrate

1 lb	fresh or frozen rhubarb, cut into pieces	500 g
7	whole cloves	7
	Artificial sweetener equivalent to $\frac{1}{4}$ cup (60 mL) granulated sugar	

1. In a stainless steel or enamel saucepan, combine rhubarb, cloves and 3 cups (750 mL) water. Bring to a boil over high heat. Reduce heat and simmer for 30 minutes. Add sweetener and stir until dissolved.

2. Strain and discard pulp. Transfer liquid to an airtight container and store in the refrigerator for up to 8 weeks.

Nutrients per Serving	
Calories	18
Carbohydrate	4 g
Fiber	1 g
Protein	1 g
Total fat	0 g
Saturated fat	0 g
Cholesterol	0 mg
Sodium	6 mg

America's Exchanges	
1	Free Food

Canada's Choices	
1	Extra

Peach Nectar

Makes 1 serving

Peach nectar is a great option on those days when you feel like a change from the usual breakfast juice.

2 tbsp	Peach Nectar Concentrate (see recipe, opposite)	30 mL
½ cup	water, sugar-free ginger ale or soda water	125 mL

1. Dilute concentrate with water. Serve chilled, over ice cubes if desired.

Nutrients per Serving	
Calories	38
Carbohydrate	9 g
Fiber	2 g
Protein	1 g
Total fat	0 g
Saturated fat	0 g
Cholesterol	0 mg
Sodium	8 mg

America's Exchanges	
½	Fruit

Canada's Choices	
½	Carbohydrate

Peach Nectar Concentrate

Makes 1½ cups (375 mL)
Serving size: 2 tbsp (30 mL)

Prepare peach nectar concentrate when peaches are plentiful and at their peak.

Kitchen Tips

Ascorbic acid color keeper is a powder used to prevent fruit from browning once cut. It is often found in the spice aisle of the supermarket or with home canning products.

Freeze peach nectar concentrate in 2-tbsp (30 mL) amounts in ice cube trays, then pack the cubes into freezer bags and store in the freezer for up to 9 months.

- **Blender or food processor**

12	fully ripe peaches	12
	Ice water	
2 tsp	ascorbic acid color keeper	10 mL

1. In a large pot of boiling water, in batches, blanch peaches for 30 to 60 seconds depending on ripeness. Immediately plunge into ice water and let cool. Peel off skins and remove pits.

2. Cut peaches into chunks and sprinkle with ascorbic acid color keeper. In blender, purée peaches until very smooth and liquefied.

3. Pour purée into a heavy saucepan. Bring to a boil over medium heat; reduce heat and boil gently, stirring occasionally, for about 15 minutes or until mixture is reduced by half. Remove from heat and let cool.

4. Transfer to an airtight container and store in the refrigerator for up to 8 weeks.

Nutrients per Serving	
Calories	38
Carbohydrate	9 g
Fiber	2 g
Protein	1 g
Total fat	0 g
Saturated fat	0 g
Cholesterol	0 mg
Sodium	4 mg

America's Exchanges	
½	Fruit

Canada's Choices	
½	Carbohydrate

Frosty Bog

||||||||||||||||||||||||||||||||||||||||||||||||||||||||||||||||||||||||||||||||||||||||||||||||||||||||||||||||||||||||||||

Makes 1 serving

This thick, frosty and tangy beverage is refreshing and can even be served as a light dessert.

Nutrition Tip

If you choose to use sugar or honey instead of artificial sweetener, you'll need to count the carbohydrate it adds. One teaspoon (5 mL) contains about 5 grams of carbohydrate.

• **Blender**

½ cup	crushed ice	125 mL
¼ cup	plain low-fat yogurt	60 mL
2 tbsp	Cranberry Concentrate (see recipe, page 35)	30 mL
	Artificial sweetener equivalent to 1 tsp (5 mL) granulated sugar	
Pinch	ground cinnamon	Pinch

1. In blender, combine ice, yogurt, cranberry concentrate and sweetener. Blend on high speed for 2 minutes or until frosty and thickened.

2. Pour into a glass and sprinkle with cinnamon.

Nutrients per Serving	
Calories	48
Carbohydrate	7 g
Fiber	1 g
Protein	3 g
Total fat	1 g
Saturated fat	1 g
Cholesterol	4 mg
Sodium	44 mg

America's Exchanges	
½	Milk

Canada's Choices	
½	Carbohydrate

Milky Way Cooler

Makes 1 serving

The milk in this refreshing drink makes it a source of calcium. Serve it in a tall glass with a colorful straw, and perhaps a sprig of mint or a sprinkle of nutmeg as a garnish.

• **Blender**

1 cup	chilled sugar-free carbonated beverage, any flavor	250 mL
1/2 cup	1% or skim milk	125 mL
3	ice cubes	3

1. In blender, combine carbonated beverage and milk. Blend until frothy. Continue blending, adding ice cubes one at a time through the feed tube, until mixture is slightly thickened.

Nutrients per Serving	
Calories	51
Carbohydrate	6 g
Fiber	0 g
Protein	4 g
Total fat	1 g
Saturated fat	1 g
Cholesterol	6 mg
Sodium	93 mg

America's Exchanges	
1/2	Milk

Canada's Choices	
1/2	Carbohydrate

Sparkling Fruit Punch

|||||||||||||||||||||||||||||||||||||||||||||||||||||||||||||||||||||||||||||||||||||||||||||||||||||||||||||

**Makes about 5 cups
(1.25 L)**
Serving size: $^2/_3$ cup
(150 mL)

When you need a festive drink for a shower, afternoon tea or anniversary party, this is sure to please with its fresh flavor and pretty color.

Variation
Replace the ginger ale with dry sparkling wine or Champagne. This will not change the amount of carbohydrate, but the alcohol will add about 40 calories per serving.

1 $^1/_2$ cups	Rhubarb Concentrate (see recipe, page 37)	375 mL
$^1/_2$ cup	unsweetened orange juice	125 mL
$^1/_3$ cup	unsweetened apple juice	75 mL
1 tsp	vanilla extract	5 mL
3	drops red food coloring (optional)	3
2 cups	chilled sugar-free ginger ale	500 mL
1 cup	strawberries, halved	250 mL
	Artificial sweetener	
	Ice cubes	

1. In a pitcher or punch bowl, combine rhubarb concentrate, orange juice, apple juice, vanilla and food coloring (if using). Refrigerate until thoroughly chilled.

2. Stir in ginger ale and strawberries. Sweeten to taste with sweetener. Add ice cubes.

Nutrients per Serving

Calories	26
Carbohydrate	6 g
Fiber	1 g
Protein	0 g
Total fat	0 g
Saturated fat	0 g
Cholesterol	0 mg
Sodium	12 mg

America's Exchanges	
$^1/_2$	Fruit

Canada's Choices	
1	Extra

Tea Punch

||||||||||||||||||||||||||||||||||||||||||||||||||||||||||||||||||||||||||||||||||||||||||||||||||||

**Makes about 4 cups
(1 L)**
Serving size: $2/3$ cup
(150 mL)

This punch is quite concentrated, so don't be afraid to use plenty of ice.

Nutrition Tip

If you choose to use sugar or honey instead of artificial sweetener, you'll need to count the carbohydrate it adds. One teaspoon (5 mL) contains about 5 grams of carbohydrate.

1 cup	boiling water	250 mL
2	2-cup tea bags (or 4 tsp/20 mL tea leaves)	2
1	lemon, thinly sliced	1
2 cups	cold water	500 mL
$2/3$ cup	Cranberry Concentrate (see recipe, page 35)	150 mL
$1/2$ cup	unsweetened white grape juice	125 mL
$1/3$ cup	unsweetened apple juice	75 mL
	Artificial sweetener equivalent to 4 tsp (20 mL) granulated sugar	
	Ice cubes	

1. Pour boiling water over tea; let steep for 5 minutes. Remove tea bags (or strain out leaves).

2. Stir in lemon slices, cold water, cranberry concentrate, grape juice, apple juice and sweetener until well mixed. Serve over ice cubes in tall glasses.

Nutrients per Serving	
Calories	31
Carbohydrate	8 g
Fiber	1 g
Protein	0 g
Total fat	0 g
Saturated fat	0 g
Cholesterol	0 mg
Sodium	5 mg

America's Exchanges	
$1/2$	Fruit

Canada's Choices	
$1/2$	Carbohydrate

Morning Sunshine Smoothie

Makes 3 servings

This frosty smoothie packed with fresh fruit flavors will help get you going in the morning — or any time of day.
For a terrific breakfast on the go, add some reduced-fat cheese or a hard-boiled egg, along with some whole-grain crackers.

Kitchen Tips

Ripe yellow bananas, freckled and fragrant, make all the difference in this smoothie. For faster ripening, place bananas in a paper bag and leave at room temperature.

Peel ripe bananas, then wrap them in plastic wrap and freeze them so you have them on hand when you get a craving for a smoothie.

Variation

To boost your fiber, add 1 to 2 tbsp (15 to 30 mL) ground flax seeds (flaxseed meal).

Nutrients per Serving	
Calories	104
Carbohydrate	22 g
Fiber	1 g
Protein	3 g
Total fat	1 g
Saturated fat	0 g
Cholesterol	2 mg
Sodium	32 mg

● **Blender**

1	frozen very ripe banana, broken into chunks	1
¼ cup	fresh or frozen strawberries	60 mL
¾ cup	unsweetened orange juice	175 mL
½ cup	plain low-fat yogurt	125 mL
¼ cup	unsweetened pomegranate juice	60 mL

1. In blender, combine banana, strawberries, orange juice, yogurt and pomegranate juice; purée until smooth. Pour into glasses and serve immediately.

America's Exchanges	
1½	Fruits

Canada's Choices	
1½	Carbohydrates

Tropical Smoothie

Makes 4 servings

Bursting with tropical flavors, this refreshing smoothie can be enjoyed any time of the year.

Kitchen Tip
The secret to a thick, refreshing smoothie is to use frozen fruit and chilled juice.

Nutrition Tips
When buying canned fruit, choose ones packed in fruit juice or water, not syrup.

Read juice labels carefully to make sure you are buying pure juice. Fruit drinks have added sugar and fewer vitamins than pure juice.

● **Blender**

1	frozen very ripe banana, broken into chunks	1
1 cup	fresh, frozen or canned pineapple chunks	250 mL
¾ cup	fresh or frozen mango chunks	175 mL
1 cup	unsweetened pineapple juice	250 mL

1. In blender, combine banana, pineapple, mango and pineapple juice; purée until smooth. Pour into glasses and serve immediately.

Nutrients per Serving

Calories	100
Carbohydrate	25 g
Fiber	2 g
Protein	1 g
Total fat	0 g
Saturated fat	0 g
Cholesterol	0 mg
Sodium	2 mg

America's Exchanges	
1½	Fruits

Canada's Choices	
1½	Carbohydrates

Just Peachy Smoothie

Creamy and yummy, this peach smoothie is sure to become a favorite. This recipe is for two, but it can easily be doubled or tripled as required.

Kitchen Tips
If using frozen peaches, let them thaw slightly for easier blending.

Depending on the sweetness of your peaches, you may want to add up to 1 tsp (5 mL) of honey or sugar or an equivalent amount of artificial sweetener.

Nutrition Tip
Whole fruits contain more vitamins and fiber than fruit juices. Smoothies are a delicious way to enjoy whole fruits.

● Blender

1 cup	fresh or frozen sliced peaches	250 mL
1/2 cup	1% milk or fortified soy beverage	125 mL
1/4 cup	low-fat peach-flavored yogurt	60 mL
1 tbsp	frozen orange juice concentrate	15 mL

1. In blender, combine peaches, milk, yogurt and orange juice concentrate; purée until smooth. Pour into glasses and serve immediately.

Nutrients per Serving

Calories	106
Carbohydrate	19 g
Fiber	2 g
Protein	4 g
Total fat	2 g
Saturated fat	1 g
Cholesterol	7 mg
Sodium	43 mg

America's Exchanges	
1	Fruit
1/2	Milk

Canada's Choices	
1 1/2	Carbohydrates
1/2	Fat

Berrylicious Smoothie

||||||||||||||||||||||||||||||||||||||||||||||||||||||||||||||||||||||||||||||||||||||||||||||||||||||||||||||||||||||

This nourishing, delicious berry smoothie is a perfect treat for kids of all ages.

Kitchen Tips

Instant skim milk powder is available packaged or in bulk and can be found in the baking section in most supermarkets. Like liquid skim milk, it is fat-free. In a smoothie it provides extra thickness and boosts the calcium content

When berries are in season, freeze them on a baking sheet until hard, then transfer them to an airtight container or freezer bag. If you don't have any frozen berries on hand, frozen mixed berries are available in most supermarkets.

Nutrition Tip

Red and dark-colored berries supply antioxidants. These plant compounds protect body cells from damage by free radicals.

Nutrients per Serving

Calories	101
Carbohydrate	20 g
Fiber	2 g
Protein	5 g
Total fat	1 g
Saturated fat	1 g
Cholesterol	5 mg
Sodium	52 mg

● **Blender**

1	frozen very ripe banana, broken into chunks	1
1 cup	fresh or frozen mixed berries	250 mL
1 cup	1% milk	250 mL
2 tbsp	instant skim milk powder	30 mL

1. In blender, combine banana, berries, milk and milk powder; purée until smooth. Pour into glasses and serve immediately.

America's Exchanges

1	Fruit
½	Milk

Canada's Choices

1	Carbohydrate

Fiber Boost Smoothie

|||||||||||||||||||||||||||||||||||||||||||||||||||||||||||||||||||||||||||||||||||||||||||||||||||||||||||

Makes 3 servings

Here's a novel way to get fiber on the run (no pun intended). If you're heading out the door, pour this smoothie into an insulated mug, and you're good to go.

Kitchen Tips

Flax seeds, well-known for their fiber and omega-3 fat content, can be purchased packaged or in bulk at most supermarkets. Refrigerate or freeze them in an airtight container for up to 3 months.

Buy flax seeds already ground or grind them yourself before adding to recipes. If they are left whole, the tough outer coat will prevent them from being digested and you won't get the benefit of their nutrients.

● Blender

1	frozen very ripe banana, broken into chunks	1
1 cup	fresh or frozen blueberries	250 mL
1 cup	unsweetened orange juice	250 mL
2 tbsp	ground flax seeds (flaxseed meal)	30 mL

1. In blender, combine banana, blueberries, orange juice and flax seeds; purée until smooth. Pour into glasses and serve immediately.

Nutrients per Serving

Calories	128
Carbohydrate	26 g
Fiber	4 g
Protein	2 g
Total fat	3 g
Saturated fat	0 g
Cholesterol	0 mg
Sodium	3 mg

America's Exchanges	
1½	Fruits
½	Fat

Canada's Choices	
1½	Carbohydrates
½	Fat

Gouda Wafers (page 24)

Dilly Dip (page 25)

Tea Punch (page 43)

Tropical Smoothie (page 45)

Hearty Beef Minestrone (page 89)

Clam Chowder (page 94)

Orange and Sprout Salad (page 103)

Cucumber and Fruit Salad (page 104)

Strawberry Instant Breakfast

‖‖

Makes 1 serving

This filling drink containing milk, fruit and cottage cheese is quick, easy and nourishing, ideal for busy mornings when a sit-down breakfast is not in the cards.

Nutrition Tip

Cottage cheese has traditionally contained a lot of salt, with about 400 mg (17% DV) in ½ cup (125 mL). Some brands now contain less. Be sure to check the Nutrition Facts table when shopping and choose the one that's lowest in sodium.

• Blender

1 cup	skim milk	250 mL
½ cup	frozen unsweetened strawberries	125 mL
¼ cup	1% cottage cheese or plain low-fat yogurt	60 mL
1 tsp	vanilla extract	5 mL
	Artificial sweetener (optional)	

1. In blender, combine milk, strawberries, cottage cheese and vanilla. Blend on high speed for 1 minute or until smooth. Sweeten to taste with sweetener, if desired.

Nutrients per Serving

Calories	163
Carbohydrate	21 g
Fiber	2 g
Protein	16 g
Total fat	1 g
Saturated fat	1 g
Cholesterol	7 mg
Sodium	341 mg

America's Exchanges

½	Fruit
1	Milk
1	Lean Meat

Canada's Choices

1	Carbohydrate
1	Meat & Alternatives

Chocolate Banana Instant Breakfast

Makes 1 serving

This quick milkshake makes a wonderful addition to breakfast on the run — and it's delicious at any time of day.

Variation

Pear Instant Breakfast: Replace the banana with ½ very ripe peeled pear, coarsely chopped, and omit the chocolate sauce.

● **Blender**

1	small frozen banana, broken into chunks	1
1 cup	skim milk	250 mL
¼ cup	plain low-fat yogurt	60 mL
2 tsp	Chocolate Sauce (see recipe, page 284)	10 mL
½ tsp	vanilla extract	2 mL

1. In blender, combine banana, milk, yogurt, chocolate sauce and vanilla. Blend on high speed for 1 minute or until smooth and thick.

Nutrients per Serving

Calories	182
Carbohydrate	36 g
Fiber	2 g
Protein	10 g
Total fat	1 g
Saturated fat	0 g
Cholesterol	5 mg
Sodium	105 mg

America's Exchanges

1½	Fruits
1	Milk

Canada's Choices

2	Carbohydrates

Slimmer's Shake

‖‖‖

Makes 1 serving

No bowl or spoon is required for this milk, cereal and fruit combo. For added fiber, make it with bran flakes.

Variation

Replace the strawberries with ¼ banana, ¼ peeled pear, coarsely chopped, or ½ peach, coarsely chopped.

Nutrition Tip

If you choose to use sugar or honey instead of artificial sweetener, you'll need to count the carbohydrate it adds. One teaspoon (5 mL) contains about 5 grams of carbohydrate.

• Blender

½ cup	fresh or frozen unsweetened strawberries	125 mL
⅓ cup	corn flakes or bran flakes cereal	75 mL
½ cup	1% milk	125 mL
	Artificial sweetener equivalent to 1 tsp (5 mL) granulated sugar	

1. In blender, combine strawberries, cereal, milk, ¼ cup (60 mL) water and sweetener. Blend on high speed until thick and frothy.

Nutrients per Serving

Calories	112
Carbohydrate	20 g
Fiber	2 g
Protein	5 g
Total fat	1 g
Saturated fat	1 g
Cholesterol	6 mg
Sodium	114 mg

America's Exchanges	
1	Fruit
½	Milk

Canada's Choices	
1	Carbohydrate

Chocolate Milk

|||||||||||||||||||||||||||||||||||||||||||||||||||||||||||||||||||||||||||||||||||||||||||||||||||||||||||||

Makes 1 serving

Chocolate lovers of all ages will be delighted with the rich flavor that develops when our chocolate sauce is stirred into milk.

| 1 cup | 1% or skim milk | 250 mL |
| 1 tbsp | Chocolate Sauce (see recipe, page 284) | 15 mL |

1. Pour milk into a tall glass and stir in chocolate sauce.

Nutrients per Serving

Calories	107
Carbohydrate	13 g
Fiber	0 g
Protein	8 g
Total fat	3 g
Saturated fat	2 g
Cholesterol	12 mg
Sodium	108 mg

America's Exchanges

1	Milk

Canada's Choices

1	Carbohydrate
½	Fat

Hot Chocolate

||||||||||||||||||||||||||||||||||||||||||||||||||||||||||||||||||||||||||||||||||||||||||||||||||||||||||||||||||||||||||||

Makes 1 serving

A pinch of cinnamon adds pizzazz to hot chocolate.

Nutrition Tip

This hot drink is very high in calcium and vitamin D and is a source of vitamin A.

1 cup	hot 1% or skim milk	250 mL
1 tbsp	Chocolate Sauce (see recipe, page 284)	15 mL
	Ground cinnamon (optional)	

1. Pour milk into a mug and stir in chocolate sauce. Sprinkle lightly with cinnamon, if desired.

Nutrients per Serving

Calories	107
Carbohydrate	13 g
Fiber	0 g
Protein	8 g
Total fat	3 g
Saturated fat	2 g
Cholesterol	12 mg
Sodium	108 mg

America's Exchanges

1	Milk

Canada's Choices

1	Carbohydrate
1/2	Fat

Swiss Mocha

Swiss Mocha is a delicious after-dinner treat when you feel like a change from tea or coffee.

Variation

Café Bavarian: To each mug, add a pinch of ground cinnamon and/or a few drops of peppermint extract.

Nutrition Tip

If you choose to use sugar or honey instead of artificial sweetener, you'll need to count the carbohydrate it adds. One teaspoon (5 mL) contains about 5 grams of carbohydrate.

2 tbsp	Instant Swiss Mocha Mix (see recipe, opposite)	30 mL
1 cup	boiling water	250 mL
	Artificial sweetener	

1. Place mocha mix in a mug and slowly pour in boiling water, stirring until mix dissolves. Stir in sweetener to taste.

Nutrients per Serving	
Calories	39
Carbohydrate	6 g
Fiber	1 g
Protein	4 g
Total fat	0 g
Saturated fat	0 g
Cholesterol	2 mg
Sodium	55 mg

America's Exchanges	
½	Milk

Canada's Choices	
1	Extra

**Makes ¹/₂ cup
(125 mL)**
Serving size: 2 tbsp
(30 mL)

With this homemade mix on hand, it only takes seconds to make a good hot drink. It is also an easy, economical way to include milk in meals.

Instant Swiss Mocha Mix

¹/₂ cup	instant skim milk powder	125 mL
2 tbsp	unsweetened cocoa powder	30 mL
2 tbsp	instant coffee granules	30 mL

1. In a jar, combine skim milk powder, cocoa and instant coffee. Seal and shake until very well mixed. Store at room temperature for up to 3 months.

Nutrients per Serving

Calories	39
Carbohydrate	6 g
Fiber	1 g
Protein	4 g
Total fat	0 g
Saturated fat	0 g
Cholesterol	2 mg
Sodium	48 mg

America's Exchanges	
¹/₂	Milk

Canada's Choices	
1	Extra

Hot Mulled Toddy

A hot toddy is an old-fashioned warmer-upper, perfect for chilly days. Take it along in a Thermos for a special outdoor treat.

⅔ cup	unsweetened apple juice	175 mL
2 tbsp	Cranberry Concentrate (see recipe, page 35)	30 mL
2	whole allspice	2
1	2-inch (5 cm) cinnamon stick	1
1	whole clove	1
2	thin lemon slices	2

1. In a saucepan, combine $1\frac{1}{4}$ cups (300 mL) water, apple juice, cranberry concentrate, allspice, cinnamon stick and clove. Bring to a boil over high heat. Reduce heat to low, cover and simmer for 20 minutes. Discard allspice, cinnamon and clove, if desired.

2. Pour into mugs and garnish with lemon slices.

Nutrients per Serving	
Calories	30
Carbohydrate	8 g
Fiber	0 g
Protein	0 g
Total fat	0 g
Saturated fat	0 g
Cholesterol	0 mg
Sodium	5 mg

America's Exchanges	
½	Fruit

Canada's Choices	
½	Carbohydrate

Sauces
and Basics

Basic White Sauce

You'll find dozens of uses for this sauce and its variations, all of which are trimmed of fat and starch. They keep in the refrigerator for up to a week, so when preparing them, you might want to make extra to have on hand.

Variation

Herb Sauce: Stir in $1/2$ tsp (2 mL) each dried thyme, basil, oregano and parsley with the salt. Serve over cooked vegetables, meat or fish, or use as a base for crêpe fillings.

1 cup	2% milk	250 mL
1 tbsp	all-purpose flour	15 mL
1 tsp	cornstarch	5 mL
$1/4$ tsp	salt	1 mL
1 tsp	vegetable oil	5 mL
Pinch	freshly ground white pepper (optional)	Pinch

1. In a small saucepan, combine milk, flour, cornstarch and salt, whisking until no dry bits of flour or cornstarch remain. Heat over medium-high heat, stirring constantly, for about 2 minutes or until mixture boils and thickens. Stir in oil. Season with white pepper, if desired.

Nutrients per Serving	
Calories	50
Carbohydrate	5 g
Fiber	0 g
Protein	2 g
Total fat	2 g
Saturated fat	1 g
Cholesterol	5 mg
Sodium	171 mg

America's Exchanges	
$1/2$	Fat
1	Free Food

Canada's Choices	
$1/2$	Fat
1	Extra

Béchamel Sauce

**Makes 1 cup
(250 mL)**
Serving size: $1/4$ cup
(60 mL)

This classic sauce adds an elegant touch to cooked vegetables, meats and fish and as a base for crêpe fillings.

Kitchen Tip

Cooled sauce can be stored in an airtight container in the refrigerator for up to 1 week. Reheat in a saucepan over medium-low heat, stirring often, until steaming.

1 tsp	vegetable oil	5 mL
1 tbsp	finely chopped onion	15 mL
1 tbsp	all-purpose flour	15 mL
1 tsp	cornstarch	5 mL
$1/4$ tsp	salt	1 mL
1 cup	2% milk	250 mL
Pinch	freshly ground white pepper (optional)	Pinch

1. In a small saucepan, heat oil over medium heat. Sauté onion for about 3 minutes or until softened (do not let brown).

2. In a bowl, whisk together flour, cornstarch, salt and milk until no dry bits of flour or cornstarch remain. Gradually pour into saucepan, whisking constantly. Increase heat to medium-high and cook, stirring constantly, for about 2 minutes or until mixture boils and thickens. Season with white pepper, if desired.

Nutrients per Serving	
Calories	52
Carbohydrate	5 g
Fiber	0 g
Protein	2 g
Total fat	2 g
Saturated fat	1 g
Cholesterol	5 mg
Sodium	171 mg

America's Exchanges	
$1/2$	Fat
1	Free Food

Canada's Choices	
$1/2$	Fat
1	Extra

Velouté Sauce

Velouté makes an ideal sauce for crêpe fillings and is also delicious served with chicken.

Kitchen Tip
In place of the homemade chicken stock, you can use store-bought reduced-sodium chicken broth. If you do this, omit the salt in the recipe.

1 cup	Chicken Stock (see recipe, page 78)	250 mL
1 tbsp	all-purpose flour	15 mL
1 tsp	cornstarch	5 mL
$1/4$ tsp	salt	1 mL
1 tsp	vegetable oil	5 mL
Pinch	freshly ground white pepper (optional)	Pinch

1. In a small saucepan, combine stock, flour, cornstarch and salt, whisking until no dry bits of flour or cornstarch remain. Heat over medium-high heat, stirring constantly, for about 2 minutes or until mixture boils and thickens. Stir in oil. Season with white pepper, if desired.

Nutrients per Serving	
Calories	41
Carbohydrate	4 g
Fiber	0 g
Protein	2 g
Total fat	2 g
Saturated fat	0 g
Cholesterol	2 mg
Sodium	158 mg

America's Exchanges	
$1/2$	Fat
1	Free Food

Canada's Choices	
$1/2$	Fat
1	Extra

Cheese Sauce

||||||||||||||||||||||||||||||||||||||||||||||||||||||||||||||||||||||||||||||||||||||||||||||||||||||||||||||||

**Makes 18 tbsp
(270 mL)**
Serving size: 3 tbsp
(45 mL)

This is the perfect sauce for cooked cauliflower, broccoli and asparagus. It is also sensational over hard-cooked eggs on toast.

1 cup	2% milk	250 mL
1 tbsp	all-purpose flour	15 mL
1 tsp	cornstarch	5 mL
$\frac{1}{4}$ tsp	salt	1 mL
$\frac{1}{2}$ cup	shredded Cheddar cheese	125 mL
1 tsp	vegetable oil	5 mL
Pinch	freshly ground white pepper (optional)	Pinch

1. In a small saucepan, combine milk, flour, cornstarch and salt, whisking until no dry bits of flour or cornstarch remain. Heat over medium-high heat, stirring constantly, for about 2 minutes or until mixture boils and thickens. Stir in cheese and oil, stirring briskly until cheese melts (do not let sauce boil, or it may curdle). Season with white pepper, if desired.

Nutrients per Serving

Calories	71
Carbohydrate	3 g
Fiber	0 g
Protein	4 g
Total fat	5 g
Saturated fat	3 g
Cholesterol	13 mg
Sodium	173 mg

America's Exchanges	
1	Fat
1	Free Food

Canada's Choices	
$\frac{1}{2}$	Meat & Alternatives
$\frac{1}{2}$	Fat

Speedy Barbecue Sauce

Brush this spicy, easy-to-prepare barbecue sauce sparingly on pork chops, steaks or chicken pieces.

Nutrition Tip

Use this delicious barbecue sauce instead of commercial varieties, which typically contain 120 to 240 mg of sodium per tbsp (15 mL). If you do use a commercial sauce, be sure to choose one that is as low as possible in sodium.

½ cup	undiluted condensed tomato soup	125 mL
3 tbsp	red wine or cider vinegar	45 mL
1 tbsp	light (fancy) molasses	15 mL
1 tsp	celery seeds	5 mL
½ tsp	chili powder	2 mL

1. In a jar, combine tomato soup, wine, molasses, celery seeds and chili powder. Cover tightly and shake until mixed. Store, tightly covered, in the refrigerator for up 2 weeks.

Nutrients per Serving

Calories	15
Carbohydrate	3 g
Fiber	0 g
Protein	0 g
Total fat	0 g
Saturated fat	0 g
Cholesterol	0 mg
Sodium	66 mg

America's Exchanges	
1	Free Food

Canada's Choices	
1	Extra

Celery Sauce

||||||||||||||||||||||||||||||||||||||||||||||||||||||||||||||||||||||||||||||||||||||||||||||||||||||||||||||||

No starchy thickener is required in our celery sauce, which is delicious over hard-cooked eggs, steamed salmon and other fish.

Kitchen Tips

In place of the homemade chicken stock, you can use store-bought reduced-sodium chicken broth. If you do this, omit the salt in the recipe.

The sauce can be cooled and stored in an airtight container in the refrigerator for up to 3 days. Reheat in a saucepan over medium heat, stirring often, until hot and bubbling.

• **Blender, food processor or food mill**

1	potato, peeled and chopped	1
1½ cups	sliced celery (about 4 stalks)	375 mL
¼ tsp	salt	1 mL
¼ tsp	dried oregano	1 mL
Pinch	freshly ground black pepper	Pinch
Pinch	ground nutmeg	Pinch
2 cups	Chicken Stock (see recipe, page 78)	500 mL

1. In a saucepan, combine potato, celery, salt, oregano, pepper, nutmeg and stock. Bring to a boil over high heat. Reduce heat and simmer for 15 minutes.

2. Remove about ¼ cup (60 mL) celery slices. Transfer the remaining potato mixture to blender and purée until smooth. Transfer to a bowl and stir in the reserved celery slices.

Nutrients per Serving	
Calories	38
Carbohydrate	7 g
Fiber	1 g
Protein	2 g
Total fat	0 g
Saturated fat	0 g
Cholesterol	0 mg
Sodium	140 mg

America's Exchanges	
½	Starch
1	Free Food

Canada's Choices	
1	Extra

Mushroom Sauce

||||||||||||||||||||||||||||||||||||||||||||||||||||||||||||||||||||||||||||||||||||||||||||||||||||||||||||||

Fresh mushrooms make the best sauce, but drained canned mushrooms can be used if fresh are unavailable.

Kitchen Tip

In place of store-bought beef broth, you can use homemade Beef Stock (page 76). You may need to add up to ¼ tsp (1 mL) salt to bring out the flavors of the sauce. Taste the finished sauce and add just enough salt to perk up the flavor.

	Vegetable cooking spray	
1½ cups	chopped mushrooms	375 mL
1½ cups	reduced-sodium beef broth	375 mL
⅛ tsp	freshly ground black pepper	0.5 mL
1 tbsp	all-purpose flour	15 mL
1½ tsp	cornstarch	7 mL

1. Lightly coat a skillet with cooking spray and heat over medium-high heat. Sauté mushrooms for about 5 minutes or until they start to brown. Add broth and pepper; bring to a boil. Reduce heat and simmer for 5 minutes.

2. In a small bowl, combine flour, cornstarch and 3 tbsp (45 mL) water to form a smooth paste (or shake together in a small jar). Add to mushroom mixture and cook, stirring, for about 2 minutes or until sauce thickens.

Nutrients per Serving	
Calories	11
Carbohydrate	2 g
Fiber	0 g
Protein	1 g
Total fat	0 g
Saturated fat	0 g
Cholesterol	0 mg
Sodium	98 mg

America's Exchanges	
1	Free Food

Canada's Choices	
1	Extra

Stroganoff Sauce

For a quick stroganoff, heat cooked beef strips or meatballs in this sauce. You'll have a succulent topping for cooked whole wheat noodles.

Nutrition Tip

Cottage cheese has traditionally contained a lot of salt, with about 400 mg (17% DV) in ¹⁄₂ cup (125 mL). Some brands now contain less. Be sure to check the Nutrition Facts table when shopping and choose the one that's lowest in sodium.

• **Blender or food processor**

¹⁄₂ cup	2% cottage cheese	125 mL
¹⁄₄ cup	2% plain yogurt	60 mL
1 cup	Mushroom Sauce (see recipe, page 64)	250 mL

1. In blender, purée cottage cheese and yogurt.

2. Transfer to a saucepan and stir in mushroom sauce. Bring to a simmer over medium-low heat (do not let boil). Serve immediately.

Nutrients per Serving

Calories	34
Carbohydrate	3 g
Fiber	0 g
Protein	4 g
Total fat	1 g
Saturated fat	0 g
Cholesterol	2 mg
Sodium	182 mg

America's Exchanges	
1	Lean Meat

Canada's Choices	
¹⁄₂	Meat & Alternatives

Spaghetti Sauce

||||||||||||||||||||||||||||||||||||||||||||||||||||||||||||||||||||||||||||||||||||||||||||||||

Serve this meatless sauce over whole wheat noodles. For a more substantial meal, add crumbled cooked ground meat or cooked meatballs with the tomatoes.

Kitchen Tips

In place of store-bought vegetable broth, you can use homemade Vegetable Stock (page 79). You may need to add up to $1/4$ tsp (1 mL) more salt to bring out the flavors of the sauce. Taste the finished sauce and add just enough salt to perk up the flavor.

Make a double or triple batch of this sauce and let cool, then measure sauce into single portions and freeze in airtight containers for up to 6 months to have on hand for quick meals.

1 tsp	vegetable oil	5 mL
2	cloves garlic, chopped	2
1	onion, chopped	1
1	can (28 oz/796 mL) no-salt-added tomatoes, mashed or puréed	1
1 cup	reduced-sodium vegetable broth	250 mL
$1/4$ cup	tomato paste	60 mL
1 tbsp	dried parsley	15 mL
$1/2$ tsp	dried oregano	2 mL
$1/2$ tsp	dried thyme	2 mL
$1/2$ tsp	dried basil	2 mL
$1/4$ tsp	ground cloves	1 mL
$1/4$ tsp	salt	1 mL
$1/4$ tsp	freshly ground black pepper	1 mL

1. In a heavy saucepan, heat oil over medium heat. Sauté garlic and onion for 3 minutes or until softened.

2. Stir in tomatoes, broth, tomato paste, parsley, oregano, thyme, basil, cloves, salt and pepper; bring to a boil. Reduce heat and simmer, stirring occasionally, for 1 hour or until sauce is reduced by one-quarter.

Nutrients per Serving	
Calories	53
Carbohydrate	10 g
Fiber	2 g
Protein	2 g
Total fat	1 g
Saturated fat	0 g
Cholesterol	0 mg
Sodium	204 mg

America's Exchanges	
2	Vegetables

Canada's Choices	
1	Extra

Fat-Free Gravy

||||||||||||||||||||||||||||||||||||||||||||||||||||||||||||||||||||||||||||||||||||||||||||||||||||

Makes about 1 cup (250 mL)
Serving size: $1/4$ cup (60 mL)

Call this a waist-watcher gravy: there are only 13 calories in one serving. Serve it over meatloaf or roast meat and mashed potatoes.

Kitchen Tips
If you've made a roast, skim off the fat from the pan juices and add the juices to the broth, keeping the total amount to 1 cup (250 mL).

In place of store-bought beef broth, you can use homemade Beef Stock (page 76). You may need to add up to $1/4$ tsp (1 mL) salt to bring out the flavors of the gravy. Taste the finished gravy and add just enough salt to perk up the flavor.

1 cup	reduced-sodium beef broth	250 mL
2 tsp	all-purpose flour	10 mL
1 tsp	cornstarch	5 mL
1 tsp	ketchup	5 mL
Pinch	dried basil	Pinch
Pinch	freshly ground black pepper	Pinch

1. Combine broth, flour and cornstarch in a screw-top jar, cover and shake until well combined.

2. Pour into saucepan; stir in ketchup, basil and pepper. Cook, stirring, over medium heat for about 2 minutes or until gravy thickens.

Nutrients per Serving

Calories	13
Carbohydrate	2 g
Fiber	0 g
Protein	1 g
Total fat	0 g
Saturated fat	0 g
Cholesterol	0 mg
Sodium	161 mg

America's Exchanges	
1	Free Food

Canada's Choices	
1	Extra

Whole Wheat Flour Tortillas

||||||||||||||||||||||||||||||||||||||||||||||||||||||||||||||||||||||||||||||||||||||||||||||||||||||||||||||||||

Makes twelve 5½-inch (14 cm) tortillas
Serving size: 2 tortillas

½ cup	all-purpose flour	125 mL
½ cup	whole wheat flour	125 mL
¼ tsp	salt	1 mL
6 tbsp	warm water	90 mL
1 tbsp	vegetable oil, divided	15 mL

Tortillas are definitely a staple in the Mexican diet, used to make everything from tacos and enchiladas to nachos. For added nutrition, use these whole wheat tortillas any time a recipe calls for flour tortillas.

Kitchen Tip

Cooled tortillas can be stacked in a sealable storage bag and refrigerated for up to 3 days. To reheat, lightly moisten each tortilla with water and stack on a large piece of foil. Fold foil around tortillas, pinching edges to seal. Heat in a 350°F (180°C) oven for 5 to 10 minutes or until hot.

1. In a bowl, combine all-purpose flour, whole wheat flour and salt.

2. In a small bowl, combine warm water and 2 tsp (10 mL) of the oil. Stir into flour mixture to make a soft dough. Knead in the bowl about 5 times or until dough is smooth. Divide dough into 12 even pieces and form each into a small ball.

3. Coat your palms with the remaining oil and roll each ball in your hands. Place in a bowl and cover with a damp towel or plastic wrap. Let stand for 15 minutes.

4. Working with one ball at a time, use your fingers to flatten ball into a 2-inch (5 cm) round patty. On a lightly floured work surface, roll out to a 6-inch (15 cm) circle, pausing frequently to let dough relax and to dust surface and rolling pin with flour to prevent sticking. Stack rolled tortillas and cover with a slightly damp towel while rolling remaining tortillas.

Nutrients per Serving

Calories	92
Carbohydrate	15 g
Fiber	2 g
Protein	2 g
Total fat	3 g
Saturated fat	0 g
Cholesterol	0 mg
Sodium	99 mg

America's Exchanges	
1	Starch
½	Fat

Canada's Choices	
1	Carbohydrate
½	Fat

Nutrition Tip

Tortillas are handy wraps for sandwiches, but commercial varieties contain a surprising amount of sodium. These homemade ones contain less than half the sodium.

Variation

Soft Taco Shells: To make soft taco shells, cook as directed in step 5, gently folding each tortilla in half as soon as you remove it from the pan. Place tortillas in a single layer on a tray, cover with a dry towel and let cool.

5. Heat a dry skillet over medium-low heat. Cook one tortilla at a time, for about 30 seconds or until bubbles form on top and underside is flecked with brown. Flip tortilla over and use a scrunched-up dry towel to press any bubbles down as they form. Cook for about 10 seconds or until underside is flecked with brown but not too crisp and still flexible. Transfer to a plate, stacking cooked tortillas and keeping them covered with a dry towel. Repeat with remaining tortillas, adjusting heat as necessary to prevent them from getting too crisp or burning.

6. Once all tortillas are cooked, transfer stack to a sealable storage bag to keep soft and pliable. Serve warm or let cool completely.

Crêpes

‖‖

Freeze or refrigerate crêpes to have on hand for a variety of special main dishes and elegant desserts. If crêpes are cooked in a well-seasoned pan or one with a nonstick finish, very little oil is required to prevent sticking.

Kitchen Tip

Store cooked crêpes between layers of waxed paper in an airtight container or freezer bag in the refrigerator for up to 2 days or in the freezer for up to 3 months. To reheat, lightly moisten each crêpe with water and stack on a large piece of foil. Fold foil around crêpes, pinching edges to seal. Heat in a 350°F (180°C) oven for 5 to 10 minutes or until hot.

- 6- to 7-inch (15 to 18 cm) crêpe pan or nonstick skillet

2	eggs	2
$^2\!/_3$ cup	1% milk	150 mL
1$^1\!/_2$ tsp	vegetable oil, divided	7 mL
$^1\!/_2$ cup	all-purpose flour	125 mL

1. In a bowl, using an electric mixer, beat eggs, milk and 1 tsp (5 mL) of the oil until well blended. Beat in flour until combined. Let stand for 1 hour.

2. Brush crêpe pan with a little of the remaining oil. Heat over medium heat until water dropped on the surface dances. Pour $^1\!/_4$ cup (60 mL) batter into pan, lifting pan off heat and turning so batter coats all surfaces evenly. Return to heat, continuing to rotate pan for 30 to 40 seconds or until top is dry and bottom is light brown. Loosen edges and flip crêpe over; cook other side for 15 seconds. Slide crêpe out of pan onto waxed paper. Repeat with the remaining batter.

Nutrients per Serving

Calories	63
Carbohydrate	7 g
Fiber	0 g
Protein	3 g
Total fat	2 g
Saturated fat	1 g
Cholesterol	48 mg
Sodium	24 mg

America's Exchanges	
$^1\!/_2$	Starch
$^1\!/_2$	Fat

Canada's Choices	
$^1\!/_2$	Carbohydrate
$^1\!/_2$	Fat

Fluffy Dumplings

These dumplings are
not doughy at all, but
become light and fluffy
as they steam over
simmering stew or soup.

Nutrition Tip
When choosing a margarine,
look for a non-hydrogenated
soft margarine. These are
low in saturated fat and do
not contain trans fat. Avoid
hard margarines, which
contain high amounts of
saturated and trans fat.

Variation
Add $\frac{1}{2}$ to 1 tsp (2 to 5 mL)
dried dill, caraway seeds
or dried basil to the flour
mixture.

1 cup	all-purpose flour	250 mL
2 tsp	baking powder	10 mL
$\frac{1}{4}$ tsp	salt	1 mL
1 tbsp	margarine or butter	15 mL
$\frac{1}{3}$ cup	1% milk	75 mL

1. In a bowl, combine flour, baking powder and salt.
   Cut in margarine until mixture resembles fine
   crumbs. Stir in milk until just moistened.

2. Divide dough into 6 portions and spoon onto
   simmering stew. Cover tightly and simmer for
   15 minutes without lifting lid.

Nutrients per Serving	
Calories	101
Carbohydrate	17 g
Fiber	1 g
Protein	3 g
Total fat	2 g
Saturated fat	0 g
Cholesterol	1 mg
Sodium	222 mg

America's Exchanges	
1	Starch
$\frac{1}{2}$	Fat

Canada's Choices	
1	Carbohydrate
$\frac{1}{2}$	Fat

Seasoned Bread Crumbs

2 cups	fine dry bread crumbs	500 mL
1	clove garlic, finely chopped	1
1/2 cup	finely chopped onion	125 mL
1/2 cup	finely chopped fresh parsley (or 2 tbsp/30 mL dried parsley)	125 mL
1/3 cup	freshly grated Parmesan cheese	75 mL
1 tsp	dried oregano	5 mL

Makes about 3 cups (750 mL)
Serving size: 3 tbsp (45 mL)

These seasoned crumbs make a tasty topping for casseroles and baked vegetables, and are also handy for breading fish, chicken, pork or veal.

1. In a bowl, combine bread crumbs, garlic, onion, parsley, cheese and oregano. Store in an airtight container in the freezer for up to 6 months.

Nutrients per Serving

Calories	65
Carbohydrate	11 g
Fiber	0 g
Protein	3 g
Total fat	1 g
Saturated fat	1 g
Cholesterol	2 mg
Sodium	132 mg

America's Exchanges	
1	Starch

Canada's Choices	
1/2	Carbohydrate

All-Purpose Dry Rub

Use this rub on chicken, steak, fish or pork. It adds a terrific flavor without any salt or sugar.

Variation

For a smoky flavor, replace 1 tsp (5 mL) of the sweet paprika with smoked paprika.

2 tbsp	dried basil	30 mL
¹/₄ cup	sweet paprika	60 mL
1 tbsp	garlic powder	15 mL
1 tbsp	ground cumin	15 mL
1 tsp	freshly ground black pepper	5 mL

1. Using your fingers, crumble basil into smaller pieces. In a glass jar or airtight container, combine basil, paprika, garlic powder, cumin and pepper. Use immediately or seal jar and store in a cool, dark, dry place for up to 6 months.

2. To use, rub 1 tsp (5 mL) all over each 3-oz (90 g) portion of meat, fish or poultry. Let stand for 5 minutes, then cook as desired.

Nutrients per Serving

Calories	6
Carbohydrate	1 g
Fiber	1 g
Protein	0 g
Total fat	0 g
Saturated fat	0 g
Cholesterol	0 mg
Sodium	1 mg

America's Exchanges	
1	Free Food

Canada's Choices	
1	Extra

Every-Day Salt-Free Herb Seasoning

||||||||||||||||||||||||||||||||||||||||||||||||||||||||||||||||||||||||||||||||||||||||||||||||||||||||||||||||||

Makes about ½ cup (125 mL)

Serving size: 2 tsp (10 mL)

Use this herb seasoning in place of salt to spruce up vegetables, salads, meats, fish and poultry.

Kitchen Tip

For the best flavor, when purchasing dried herbs and spices, be sure to buy them from a store with a high turnover and make sure they are bright-colored and fragrant. They lose their flavor over time, so check your stores regularly and discard any that are faded or have lost their aroma.

¼ cup	dried parsley	60 mL
2 tbsp	dried oregano	30 mL
2 tbsp	dried basil	30 mL
1 tsp	dried thyme	5 mL
½ tsp	dried rosemary	2 mL
Pinch	hot pepper flakes (optional)	Pinch

1. In a bowl, combine parsley, oregano, basil, thyme and rosemary. Using your fingers, rub herbs together to crumble into smaller pieces. Stir in hot pepper flakes (if using). Use immediately or transfer to a jar or airtight container and store in a cool, dark, dry place for up to 6 months.

Nutrients per Serving	
Calories	3
Carbohydrate	1 g
Fiber	0 g
Protein	0 g
Total fat	0 g
Saturated fat	0 g
Cholesterol	0 mg
Sodium	2 mg

America's Exchanges	
1	Free Food

Canada's Choices	
1	Extra

Soups

Beef Stock

2 lbs	beef neck bones with meat	1 kg
16 cups	cold water	4 L
2	carrots, cut into ¾-inch (2 cm) pieces	2
1	onion, stuck with 3 whole cloves	1
1	leek, chopped	1
1	stalk celery, chopped	1
1	clove garlic, chopped	1
6	sprigs fresh parsley (or 1 tbsp/15 mL dried parsley)	6
1	large bay leaf	1
¼ tsp	dried thyme	1 mL
3 cups	hot water	750 mL

Makes about 8 cups (2 L)
Serving size: ½ cup (125 mL)

Beef stock is derived from the gentle simmering of meaty bones, vegetables and herbs. It's easy to make, but you must allow plenty of time for the cooking. The best thing about making your own stock is that you can leave out the salt.

Kitchen Tip
Measure cold stock into portions and pour into airtight containers for freezing. Be sure to leave space at the top of the container for expansion when the stock freezes.

1. Place bones in a stockpot and cover with cold water. Bring to a boil over high heat. Reduce heat and simmer, skimming occasionally, for 1 hour. Do not stir, or the broth will cloud.

2. Add carrots, onion, leek, celery, garlic, parsley, bay leaf, thyme and hot water; increase heat and bring to a boil. Reduce heat and simmer for 4 hours or until stock is flavorful.

3. Strain into a clean container, discarding solids. Chill until fat sets on the top; remove fat and discard. Cover and refrigerate for up to 5 days or freeze for up to 3 months.

Nutrients per Serving

Calories	16
Carbohydrate	1 g
Fiber	0 g
Protein	2 g
Total fat	0 g
Saturated fat	0 g
Cholesterol	0 mg
Sodium	24 mg

America's Exchanges	
1	Free Food

Canada's Choices	
1	Extra

Brown Beef Stock

Browning the bones
and vegetables before
making stock creates
a deeper flavor and
color than you get with
stock made with raw
ingredients. Brown beef
stock is ideal for rich
soups with stronger-
flavored ingredients.

Kitchen Tip

Measure cold stock into
portions and pour into
airtight containers for
freezing. Be sure to leave
space at the top of the
container for expansion
when the stock freezes.

Nutrients per Serving	
Calories	16
Carbohydrate	1 g
Fiber	0 g
Protein	2 g
Total fat	0 g
Saturated fat	0 g
Cholesterol	0 mg
Sodium	24 mg

- **Preheat oven to 350°F (180°C)**
- **Roasting pan**

2 lbs	beef neck bones with meat	1 kg
2	carrots, cut into $3/4$-inch (2 cm) pieces	2
1	onion, stuck with 3 whole cloves	1
1	leek, chopped	1
1	stalk celery, chopped	1
1	clove garlic, chopped	1
$1/2$ cup	cold water	125 mL
6	sprigs fresh parsley (or 1 tbsp/15 mL dried parsley)	6
1	large bay leaf	1
$1/4$ tsp	dried thyme	1 mL

1. Place bones in roasting pan and roast in preheated oven for 20 minutes. Add carrots, onion, leek, celery and garlic; roast for 10 to 20 minutes or until bones are well browned. Transfer bones and vegetables to a stockpot.

2. Add cold water to roasting pan and scrape up any brown bits, then add to stockpot along with parsley, bay leaf and thyme. Add 18 cups (4.5 L) water.

3. Bring to a boil over high heat. Reduce heat and simmer, skimming occasionally, for 4 hours or until stock is flavorful. Do not stir, or the broth will cloud.

4. Strain into a clean container, discarding solids. Chill until fat sets on the top; remove fat and discard. Cover and refrigerate for up to 5 days or freeze for up to 3 months.

America's Exchanges	
1	Free Food

Canada's Choices	
1	Extra

Chicken Stock

2 lbs	chicken backs and necks	1 kg
2	stalks celery, chopped	2
1	onion, sliced	1
1	carrot, sliced	1
1	clove garlic	1
8	whole black peppercorns	8
1	bay leaf	1
1/2 tsp	dried basil	2 mL
1/2 tsp	dried thyme	2 mL

**Makes about
7 cups (1.75 L)**
Serving size: 1/2 cup
(125 mL)

Pale stocks are made
from chicken, veal, lamb
or fish bones. They are
best if the bones are raw
and not browned.

Kitchen Tip
Measure cold stock into
portions and pour into
airtight containers for
freezing. Be sure to leave
space at the top of the
container for expansion
when the stock freezes.

1. Rinse chicken parts under cold water. Place in a
   stockpot and cover with 10 cups (2.5 L) water. Add
   celery, onion, carrot, garlic, peppercorns, bay leaf,
   basil and thyme. Bring to a boil over high heat.
   Reduce heat and simmer, skimming occasionally,
   for 2 to 2 1/2 hours or until stock is flavorful.

2. Strain into a clean container, discarding solids.
   Chill until fat sets on the top; remove fat and
   discard. Cover and refrigerate for up to 5 days or
   freeze for up to 3 months.

Nutrients per Serving	
Calories	16
Carbohydrate	1 g
Fiber	0 g
Protein	2 g
Total fat	0 g
Saturated fat	0 g
Cholesterol	0 mg
Sodium	24 mg

America's Exchanges	
1	Free Food

Canada's Choices	
1	Extra

Vegetable Stock

6	carrots, chopped	6
4	stalks celery, chopped	4
3	onions, cut into quarters	3
3	leeks, halved lengthwise and cut into chunks	3
1 cup	packed parsley sprigs (including stems)	250 mL
4	bay leaves	4
1 tbsp	whole black peppercorns	15 mL

Makes about 8 cups (2 L)
Serving size: $1/2$ cup (125 mL)

This multipurpose stock can be used as a base for a bevy of recipes. Keep it on hand in the freezer so you can create soups, stews and sauces in no time. Be sure not to use any vegetables that are spoiled to make stock — only use quality vegetables you still want to eat.

Kitchen Tips

Some people don't peel vegetables for stock, or they include peels along with the vegetables, and that's fine, but you do get a fresher, cleaner vegetable flavor when you discard the peels. Be sure to clean or scrub vegetables regardless of whether you're peeling them.

1. In a large pot, combine carrots, celery, onions, leeks, parsley, bay leaves, peppercorns and 12 cups (3 L) water. Bring to a boil over medium heat. Reduce heat and simmer gently for about 1 hour or until liquid is flavorful.

2. Set a fine-mesh sieve over another large pot or bowl; ladle in stock, emptying solids from sieve as necessary. Strain again, if necessary, to remove any solids from the stock. Cover and refrigerate for up to 5 days or freeze for up to 6 months (see tip, page 78).

Nutrients per Serving

Calories	15
Carbohydrate	3 g
Fiber	1 g
Protein	1 g
Total fat	0 g
Saturated fat	0 g
Cholesterol	0 mg
Sodium	12 mg

America's Exchanges	
1	Free Food

Canada's Choices	
1	Extra

Borscht

||||||||||||||||||||||||||||||||||||||||||||||||||||||||||||||||||||||||||||||||||||||||||||||||||||||||||||||||||||||||||||||||||||||||||||||||||||||||

**Makes about
10 cups (2.5 L)**
Serving size: 1¼ cups
(300 mL)

This quick and easy
borscht can be prepared
without the cabbage,
but it does add more
body, character and
flavor to the soup.

Kitchen Tip
In place of the homemade
beef stock, you can use
store-bought reduced-
sodium beef broth. If you
do this, omit the salt in the
recipe.

Nutrition Tip
If you add the sour cream
garnish, count it as an Extra
or Free Food.

1	can (19 oz/540 mL) beets, with juice	1
2 cups	finely shredded cabbage	500 mL
1 cup	chopped celery	250 mL
½ cup	chopped onion	125 mL
1	large bay leaf	1
½ tsp	salt	2 mL
¼ tsp	freshly ground black pepper	1 mL
2½ cups	Beef Stock (see recipe, page 76)	625 mL
2 tbsp	freshly squeezed lemon juice	30 mL
½ cup	light sour cream (optional)	125 mL
	Chopped fresh dill or dried dillweed	

1. Drain beets, reserving juice. Cut beet slices into julienne strips. Add enough water to beet juice to make 4 cups (1 L).

2. In a large saucepan, combine beets, cabbage, celery, onion, bay leaf, salt, pepper, beet juice mixture and stock. Bring to a boil over high heat. Reduce heat and simmer for 30 minutes or until vegetables are soft and soup is flavorful. Discard bay leaf. Stir in lemon juice.

3. Ladle into warmed bowls and top each with 1 tbsp (15 mL) sour cream, if desired. Sprinkle with dill.

Nutrients per Serving	
Calories	42
Carbohydrate	8 g
Fiber	2 g
Protein	2 g
Total fat	0 g
Saturated fat	0 g
Cholesterol	0 mg
Sodium	279 mg

America's Exchanges	
1	Vegetable

Canada's Choices	
1	Extra

Cream of Cauliflower Soup

|||||||||||||||||||||||||||||||||||||||||||||||||||||||||||||||||||||||||||||||||||||||||||||||||||||||||||||

Homemade cauliflower soup is really very easy to make, and the result is wonderful.

Kitchen Tips

In place of store-bought chicken broth, you can use homemade Chicken Stock (page 78). You may need to add up to ¹⁄₄ tsp (1 mL) salt to bring out the flavors of the soup. Taste the finished soup and add just enough salt to perk up the flavor.

Heat milk-based soups just to a simmer. If they are allowed to boil, they may curdle.

Variation

Cream of Broccoli Soup:
Replace the cauliflower with broccoli.

• **Blender, food processor or immersion blender**

2 cups	cauliflower florets	500 mL
¹⁄₂ cup	chopped celery	125 mL
1¹⁄₂ cups	reduced-sodium chicken broth	375 mL
1 cup	evaporated 2% milk	250 mL
Pinch	freshly ground white pepper	Pinch
1	green onion, thinly sliced	1

1. In a saucepan, combine cauliflower, celery and broth. Bring to a boil over high heat. Reduce heat and simmer for 10 minutes or until vegetables are tender.

2. Working in batches, transfer soup to blender (or use immersion blender in saucepan) and purée until smooth. Return soup to saucepan (if necessary) and stir in milk and white pepper. Heat over medium heat, stirring occasionally, until hot (do not let boil).

3. Ladle into warmed bowls and garnish with green onion.

Nutrients per Serving	
Calories	79
Carbohydrate	10 g
Fiber	1 g
Protein	7 g
Total fat	2 g
Saturated fat	1 g
Cholesterol	5 mg
Sodium	298 mg

America's Exchanges	
1	Vegetable
¹⁄₂	Milk

Canada's Choices	
¹⁄₂	Carbohydrate
¹⁄₂	Fat

Creamy Celery Soup

‖‖‖

If you make the celery sauce ahead of time and store it in the refrigerator, it takes minutes to transform it into soup.

Kitchen Tip
In place of the homemade chicken stock, you can use store-bought reduced-sodium chicken broth.

2 cups	Celery Sauce (see recipe, page 63)	500 mL
1 cup	2% milk	250 mL
1 cup	Chicken Stock (see recipe, page 78)	250 mL

1. In a saucepan, combine celery sauce, milk and stock, stirring well. Bring to a simmer over medium heat, stirring often (do not let boil).

Nutrients per Serving

Calories	64
Carbohydrate	10 g
Fiber	1 g
Protein	4 g
Total fat	1 g
Saturated fat	1 g
Cholesterol	3 mg
Sodium	262 mg

America's Exchanges

$1/2$	Starch
1	Free Food

Canada's Choices

$1/2$	Carbohydrate

Iced Cucumber Soup

Makes about 4 cups (1 L)
Serving size: 1 cup (250 mL)

This refreshing soup is just the thing to serve on a hot summer day. It makes a nice starter to a meal or a light lunch with a piece of cheese and a crusty whole-grain roll.

Kitchen Tip
In place of store-bought chicken broth, you can use homemade Chicken Stock (page 78). You may need to add up to $1/4$ tsp (1 mL) more salt to bring out the flavors of the soup. Taste the finished soup and add just enough salt to perk up the flavor.

• Blender or food processor

1	cucumber	1
1	green onion	1
$1/2$ tsp	dried mint	2 mL
$1/8$ tsp	salt	0.5 mL
Pinch	garlic powder	Pinch
1 cup	reduced-sodium chicken broth	250 mL
1 tsp	freshly squeezed lemon juice	5 mL
$1/2$ cup	light sour cream	125 mL
$1 1/2$ cups	low-fat plain yogurt	375 mL

1. Cut 4 thin slices from cucumber, wrap in plastic wrap and reserve for garnish. Peel the remaining cucumber, remove seeds and chop.

2. In blender, combine chopped cucumber, green onion, mint, salt, garlic powder, broth and lemon juice. Process until vegetables are finely chopped but not liquefied.

3. In a large bowl, combine sour cream and yogurt. Stir in cucumber mixture. Cover and refrigerate for at least 4 hours, to blend the flavors, or for up to 1 day.

4. Spoon into chilled bowls and garnish with reserved cucumber slices.

Nutrients per Serving	
Calories	103
Carbohydrate	12 g
Fiber	0 g
Protein	7 g
Total fat	3 g
Saturated fat	2 g
Cholesterol	12 mg
Sodium	311 mg

America's Exchanges	
$1/2$	Milk
$1/2$	Other Carbohydrate
$1/2$	Fat

Canada's Choices	
$1/2$	Carbohydrate
$1/2$	Fat

Clear Mushroom Soup

||||||||||||||||||||||||||||||||||||||||||||||||||||||||||||||||||||||||||||||||||||||||||||||||||||||||||

In this easy appetizer soup, mushroom slices simmer in a tantalizing base, creating flavors ideal for whetting the appetite at the start of a meal.

Kitchen Tip
In place of the homemade chicken stock, you can use 1 cup (250 mL) store-bought reduced-sodium chicken broth plus 2 cups (500 mL) water. If you do this, omit the salt in the recipe.

Nutrition Tip
Regular soy sauce typically contains about 900 mg of sodium per tbsp (15 mL) — over 30% of the Daily Value. You can significantly reduce the sodium content of recipes by using sodium-reduced soy sauce, which usually has 30% to 40% less sodium.

Nutrients per Serving	
Calories	41
Carbohydrate	5 g
Fiber	1 g
Protein	5 g
Total fat	0 g
Saturated fat	0 g
Cholesterol	0 mg
Sodium	272 mg

8 oz	mushrooms, sliced	250 g
3 cups	Chicken Stock (see recipe, page 78) or Beef Stock (see recipe, page 76)	750 mL
2 tsp	reduced-sodium soy sauce	10 mL
½ tsp	grated lemon zest	2 mL
¼ tsp	salt	1 mL
Pinch	freshly ground black pepper	Pinch
2 tsp	dry sherry	10 mL

1. In a saucepan, combine mushrooms, stock and soy sauce. Bring to a boil over high heat. Reduce heat and simmer for 20 minutes or until mushrooms are soft and soup is flavorful. Stir in lemon zest, salt and pepper; simmer for 2 minutes. Stir in sherry.

America's Exchanges	
1	Vegetable

Canada's Choices	
1	Extra

French Onion Soup

Makes 4 servings

This classic makes a wonderful main course when served with a crispy green salad dressed with a vinaigrette.

Kitchen Tip

In place of the homemade beef stock, you can use 2 cups (500 mL) store-bought reduced-sodium beef broth plus 3 cups (750 mL) water. If you do this, omit the salt in the recipe.

- Preheat oven to 325°F (160°C)
- 4 ovenproof bowls, heated

1 tbsp	butter	15 mL
1	large sweet onion, such as Spanish, Vidalia or other mild onion, thinly sliced	1
2 tsp	all-purpose flour	10 mL
1/4 cup	dry white wine	60 mL
5 cups	Beef Stock (see recipe, page 76)	1.25 L
1/4 tsp	salt	1 mL
	Freshly ground black pepper	
4	slices French bread (about 1 inch/2.5 cm thick)	4
1 cup	shredded Swiss cheese	250 mL

1. In a heavy skillet, melt butter over low heat. Add onion, cover and cook for about 5 minutes or until onion is tender. Uncover, increase heat to medium-high and cook, stirring, for 5 to 10 minutes or until onion is golden.

2. Reduce heat to low and stir in flour and wine; simmer for 1 minute. Add stock and salt; increase heat and bring to a boil. Reduce heat and simmer for 5 minutes. Season to taste with pepper.

3. Meanwhile, place bread on a baking sheet and bake in preheated oven for 5 minutes to dry.

4. Place ovenproof bowls on a baking sheet. Pour soup into bowls. Place a slice of bread on top of each; let bread soak up soup, then sprinkle with cheese, dividing evenly.

5. Bake for 25 to 30 minutes or until cheese is lightly browned.

Nutrients per Serving	
Calories	224
Carbohydrate	18 g
Fiber	1 g
Protein	15 g
Total fat	10 g
Saturated fat	6 g
Cholesterol	28 mg
Sodium	367 mg

America's Exchanges	
1	Starch
1 1/2	Lean Meats
1	Fat

Canada's Choices	
1	Carbohydrate
1 1/2	Meat & Alternatives
1	Fat

Tomato Basil Soup

||||||||||||||||||||||||||||||||||||||||||||||||||||||||||||||||||||||||||||||||||||||||||||||||||||||

Hot herb-flavored tomato soup is an excellent starter for a meal featuring a substantial entrée, such as a roast or steak. It's superb in late summer, when fresh tomatoes are at their prime.

Kitchen Tips

If you prefer, you can use 6 chopped fresh tomatoes in place of the canned tomatoes.

In place of the homemade chicken stock, you can use 2 cups (500 mL) store-bought reduced-sodium chicken broth plus 2 cups (500 mL) water. If you do this, omit the salt in the recipe.

Nutrients per Serving

Calories	57
Carbohydrate	9 g
Fiber	2 g
Protein	4 g
Total fat	1 g
Saturated fat	0 g
Cholesterol	0 mg
Sodium	252 mg

- **Blender, food processor or immersion blender**

1 tsp	vegetable oil or butter	5 mL
1	large green onion, chopped	1
1	clove garlic, finely chopped	1
½ cup	chopped carrots	125 mL
⅓ cup	chopped leek (white part only)	75 mL
1	can (28 oz/796 mL) no-salt-added tomatoes	1
4 cups	Chicken Stock (see recipe, page 78)	1 L
1	bay leaf	1
1 tsp	dried basil	5 mL
½ tsp	salt	2 mL
Pinch	dried thyme	Pinch
Pinch	freshly ground black pepper	Pinch
	Chopped fresh parsley	

1. In a large, heavy saucepan, heat oil over medium heat. Sauté green onion, garlic, carrots and leek for 2 to 3 minutes or until softened. Add tomatoes, stock, bay leaf, basil, salt, thyme and pepper; reduce heat to low, cover and simmer for 30 minutes or until carrots are soft and soup is flavorful. Discard bay leaf.

2. Working in batches, transfer soup to blender (or use immersion blender in saucepan) and purée until smooth. Strain soup through a sieve, discarding solids. Return to pan (if necessary) and reheat over medium heat, stirring often, until steaming.

3. Ladle into warmed bowls and garnish with parsley.

America's Exchanges

1	Vegetable
1	Free Food

Canada's Choices

1	Extra

Creamy Vegetable Soup

This blend of seven vegetables becomes a thick, creamy soup when you purée the vegetables in the broth.

Kitchen Tip

In place of the homemade chicken stock, you can use 3 cups (750 mL) store-bought reduced-sodium chicken broth plus 2 cups (500 mL) water. If you do this, omit the salt in the recipe.

Variation

This soup also tastes great cold. After step 2, transfer soup to an airtight container and let cool, then refrigerate for at least 8 hours, until chilled, or for up to 3 days. Garnish with cilantro just before serving.

• **Blender, food processor or immersion blender**

3	stalks celery, sliced	3
1	leek (white and light green parts only), sliced	1
1	small carrot, chopped	1
1	small turnip, peeled and chopped	1
1	kohlrabi (or $1/4$ small cabbage), chopped	1
1	potato, peeled and chopped	1
$1/2$ cup	green peas	125 mL
5 cups	Chicken Stock (see recipe, page 78)	1.25 L
$3/4$ tsp	salt	3 mL
1 tbsp	chopped fresh cilantro or parsley (or 1 tsp/5 mL dried parsley)	15 mL

1. In a large saucepan, combine celery, leek, carrot, turnip, kohlrabi, potato, peas and stock. Bring to a boil over high heat. Reduce heat and boil gently for 20 minutes or until vegetables are tender. Stir in salt and boil gently for 1 minute.

2. Working in batches, transfer soup to blender (or use immersion blender in saucepan) and purée until smooth. Return to pan (if necessary) and reheat over medium heat, stirring often, until steaming.

3. Ladle into warmed bowls and garnish with cilantro.

Nutrients per Serving

Calories	59
Carbohydrate	11 g
Fiber	2 g
Protein	4 g
Total fat	0 g
Saturated fat	0 g
Cholesterol	0 mg
Sodium	277 mg

America's Exchanges	
2	Vegetables

Canada's Choices	
$1/2$	Carbohydrate

Lentil Soup

Split lentils require
a surprisingly short
simmering time in this
flavorful all-vegetable
soup.

Nutrition Tip

Lentils, beans and peas
belong to the legume family.
They are available both
dried and canned. Like meat,
they contain protein. As a
bonus, they're high in fiber
and (with the exception of
soybeans) low in fat. Count
2 tbsp (30 mL) dry or $^1/_2$ cup
(125 mL) cooked or canned
legumes as 1 Meat and
Meat Substitutes Exchange
plus 1 Carbohydrate
Exchange, or 1 Meat and
Alternatives Choice plus
1 Carbohydrate Choice.

3	stalks celery, coarsely chopped	3
2	carrots, sliced	2
1	small green bell pepper, chopped	1
1	small onion, chopped	1
1 cup	dried split red lentils, rinsed	250 mL
$^1/_3$ cup	chopped fresh parsley	75 mL
1$^1/_4$ tsp	salt	6 mL
$^1/_4$ tsp	freshly ground black pepper	1 mL

1. In a large saucepan, combine celery, carrots, green
   pepper, onion, lentils, parsley, salt, pepper and
   6 cups (1.5 L) water. Bring to a boil over high heat.
   Reduce heat and simmer for 25 minutes or until
   vegetables are tender.

Nutrients per Serving

Calories	76
Carbohydrate	14 g
Fiber	3 g
Protein	5 g
Total fat	0 g
Saturated fat	0 g
Cholesterol	0 mg
Sodium	316 mg

America's Exchanges	
1	Other Carbohydrate
1	Lean Meat

Canada's Choices	
$^1/_2$	Carbohydrate
1	Meat & Alternatives

Hearty Beef Minestrone

||||||||||||||||||||||||||||||||||||||||||||||||||||||||||||||||||||||||||||||||||||||||||||||||||||||||||||||||||||||||||

Makes about 14 cups (3.5 L)
Serving size: 1 cup (250 mL)

Minestrone is a substantial, tasty, inexpensive Italian country soup. One serving is hearty enough to be the foundation of a meal.

Kitchen Tip
This recipe makes a large amount of soup, so you can freeze some to have meals on hand. Portion soup into airtight containers, leaving room for expansion at the top, let cool and freeze for up to 3 months. Let thaw in the refrigerator overnight or defrost in the microwave before reheating.

Nutrition Tip
Cheese is high in fat and sodium, but used sparingly it can give a lift to soups and other dishes. Two teaspoons (10 mL) of grated Parmesan add about 1 gram of fat and 60 milligrams of sodium.

Nutrients per Serving	
Calories	120
Carbohydrate	14 g
Fiber	3 g
Protein	9 g
Total fat	3 g
Saturated fat	1 g
Cholesterol	17 mg
Sodium	273 mg

1 lb	lean ground beef	500 g
1	can (28 oz/796 mL) no-salt-added diced tomatoes	1
1 cup	chopped onion	250 mL
1 cup	chopped celery	250 mL
1 cup	chopped green bell pepper or zucchini	250 mL
1 cup	shredded cabbage	250 mL
1 cup	diced potatoes	250 mL
1 cup	sliced carrots	250 mL
2	bay leaves	2
1 tsp	salt	5 mL
1/4 tsp	freshly ground black pepper	1 mL
1 tsp	Worcestershire sauce	5 mL
1	can (14 oz/398 mL) red kidney beans, drained and rinsed	1
1/2 cup	elbow macaroni	125 mL
	Freshly grated Parmesan cheese (optional)	

1. In a deep, heavy pot, over medium-high heat, cook beef, breaking it up with the back of a spoon, for about 8 minutes or until no longer pink. Drain off fat.

2. Stir in tomatoes, onion, celery, green pepper, cabbage, potatoes, carrots, bay leaves, salt, pepper, 6 cups (1.5 L) water and Worcestershire sauce; bring to a boil. Reduce heat to low, cover and simmer for 1 hour. Stir in beans and macaroni; cover and simmer for 30 minutes or until vegetables are soft and pasta is tender.

3. Ladle into warmed bowls and sprinkle with Parmesan, if desired.

America's Exchanges	
1/2	Starch
1	Vegetable
1	Lean Meat

Canada's Choices	
1/2	Carbohydrate
1	Meat & Alternatives

Pea Soup

||||||||||||||||||||||||||||||||||||||||||||||||||||||||||||||||||||||||||||||||||||||||||||||||||||||||||||||||||||

Hearty pea soup offers an economical and satisfying way to round out a light meal — or can even act as the meal itself.

Kitchen Tip

If you prefer pea soup with a smooth texture, transfer the finished soup, in batches, to a blender or food processor (or use an immersion blender in the pot) and purée until smooth. Return to pot (if necessary) and reheat over medium heat, stirring often, until steaming.

2 cups	dried split peas	500 mL
2 cups	chopped peeled turnip	500 mL
1 cup	chopped carrot	250 mL
½ cup	chopped potato	125 mL
½ cup	chopped onion	125 mL
⅓ cup	chopped celery leaves	75 mL
1 tsp	salt	5 mL
¼ tsp	freshly ground black pepper	1 mL

1. In a large pot, combine peas and 10 cups (2.5 L) water. Bring to a rapid boil over high heat; boil for 2 minutes. Turn off heat and let stand for 1 hour.

2. Add turnip, carrot, potato, onion, celery leaves, salt and pepper to peas; bring to a boil over high heat. Reduce heat and simmer for 1½ hours or until vegetables are tender.

Nutrients per Serving	
Calories	195
Carbohydrate	36 g
Fiber	5 g
Protein	13 g
Total fat	1 g
Saturated fat	0 g
Cholesterol	0 mg
Sodium	315 mg

America's Exchanges	
2	Other Carbohydrates
2	Lean Meat

Canada's Choices	
2	Carbohydrates
2	Meat & Alternatives

Tortilla Soup

The crunch of the bite-size tortilla chips is a surprise in this Mexican-style soup.

Kitchen Tips

Use 1 cup (250 mL) drained canned no-salt-added diced tomatoes when fresh tomatoes are not in season.

In place of the homemade chicken stock, you can use 2 cups (500 mL) store-bought reduced-sodium chicken broth plus 2 cups (500 mL) water. If you do this, omit the salt in the recipe.

To crisp tortillas, place on a baking sheet and bake in a 350°F (180°C) oven for 5 minutes or until starting to crisp. Flip tortillas over and bake for 5 to 10 minutes, until lightly toasted and crisp.

2 tsp	vegetable oil	10 mL
1	small onion, thinly sliced	1
1	clove garlic, finely chopped	1
2	tomatoes, chopped	2
¼ tsp	freshly ground black pepper	1 mL
4 cups	Chicken Stock (see recipe, page 78)	1 L
½ tsp	salt	1 mL
½ cup	finely chopped celery	125 mL
½ cup	finely chopped carrot	125 mL
4	crisp Whole Wheat Flour Tortillas (see recipe, page 68), broken into bite-size pieces	4
½ cup	crumbled Mexican queso fresco or farmer's cheese	125 mL
¼ cup	crumbled crisp bacon (2 slices) Hot pepper sauce	60 mL

1. In a medium saucepan, heat oil over medium heat. Sauté onion and garlic for 5 minutes or until onion is softened. Stir in tomatoes and pepper; sauté for 10 to 15 minutes or until tomatoes are soft and juicy.

2. Stir in stock and salt; reduce heat and simmer for 15 minutes. Stir in celery and carrot; simmer for 10 minutes or until tender.

3. Divide tortilla pieces among warmed bowls. Ladle soup over tortillas. Sprinkle with cheese, bacon and hot pepper sauce to taste.

Nutrients per Serving	
Calories	113
Carbohydrate	12 g
Fiber	2 g
Protein	7 g
Total fat	4 g
Saturated fat	1 g
Cholesterol	7 mg
Sodium	307 mg

America's Exchanges	
1	Other Carbohydrate
1	Lean Meat

Canada's Choices	
½	Meat & Alternatives
½	Fat
1	Extra

Chicken Soup

Makes about 12 cups (3 L)

Serving size: 1½ cups (375 mL)

The flavors of the chicken, vegetables and herbs blend to make an excellent broth, and the barley makes this soup very satisfying, perfect for a wintery day.

3 lbs	bone-in skin-on chicken pieces	1.5 kg
3	large stalks celery, leaves reserved, stalks chopped	3
1	small onion, chopped	1
½ cup	finely chopped carrot	125 mL
½ cup	chopped fresh parsley	125 mL
½ cup	pearl barley	125 mL
1 tsp	salt	5 mL
½ tsp	freshly ground black pepper	2 mL
¼ tsp	celery seeds	1 mL
2 tbsp	freshly squeezed lemon juice	30 mL
1½ cups	sliced green beans (1-inch/2.5 cm pieces)	375 mL

1. In a large pot, combine chicken, celery leaves, small onion and 9 cups (2.25 L) water. Cover and bring to a boil over high heat. Reduce heat to low and simmer for 1½ hours or until chicken is tender and broth is flavorful.

2. Transfer chicken to a cutting board and let cool slightly. Strain broth into a bowl and refrigerate until fat sets on top; remove and discard fat. Remove skin and bones from chicken; discard skin and bones. Cut chicken into bite-size pieces; set aside.

3. Return broth to pot and stir in celery stalks, chopped onion, carrot, parsley, barley, salt, pepper, celery seeds and lemon juice. Bring to a simmer over high heat. Reduce heat to low, cover and simmer for 20 minutes. Stir in beans and reserved chicken; cover and simmer for 15 minutes or until barley and beans are tender.

Nutrients per Serving

Calories	174
Carbohydrate	14 g
Fiber	2 g
Protein	19 g
Total fat	5 g
Saturated fat	1 g
Cholesterol	53 mg
Sodium	371 mg

America's Exchanges

½	Starch
1	Vegetable
2	Lean Meats

Canada's Choices

½	Carbohydrate
2	Meat & Alternatives

Fish Chowder

**Makes about
8 cups (2 L)**
Serving size: 1 cup
(250 mL)

The word "chowder" comes from the French word *chaudière*, which was the name for the pot French fishermen cooked their seafood stews in.

Kitchen Tips

If good fresh fish is hard to come by in your area, you can use partially thawed frozen fish fillets or even smoked fish fillets.

Heat milk-based soups just to a simmer. If they are allowed to boil, they may curdle.

1 tbsp	butter or margarine	15 mL
1 cup	chopped onion	250 mL
½ cup	chopped celery	125 mL
1½ cups	cubed potatoes	375 mL
½ cup	coarsely chopped carrot	125 mL
½ tsp	dried summer savory or thyme	2 mL
½ tsp	salt	2 mL
¼ tsp	freshly ground black pepper	1 mL
1 lb	skinless fish fillets, cut into bite-size pieces	500 g
2 cups	2% milk	500 mL

1. In a heavy saucepan, melt butter over medium heat. Sauté onion and celery for 5 minutes or until softened.

2. Stir in potatoes, carrot, savory, salt, pepper and 2 cups (500 mL) water; bring to a boil. Reduce heat to low, cover and simmer for 20 minutes or until vegetables are tender.

3. Stir in fish, cover and simmer for 10 minutes or until fish is opaque and flakes easily when tested with a fork. Stir in milk and return to a simmer (do not let boil).

Nutrients per Serving	
Calories	134
Carbohydrate	10 g
Fiber	1 g
Protein	15 g
Total fat	4 g
Saturated fat	2 g
Cholesterol	27 mg
Sodium	227 mg

America's Exchanges	
½	Other Carbohydrate
2	Lean Meats

Canada's Choices	
½	Carbohydrate
1½	Meat & Alternatives

Clam Chowder

1	can (5 oz/142 g) clams, with liquid	1
1 cup	cubed potatoes ($\frac{1}{2}$-inch/1 cm cubes)	250 mL
$\frac{1}{2}$ cup	chopped celery	125 mL
$\frac{1}{4}$ cup	chopped onion	60 mL
2 tbsp	instant skim milk powder	30 mL
$\frac{1}{2}$ tsp	salt	2 mL
$\frac{1}{4}$ tsp	freshly ground white pepper	1 mL
4 cups	2% milk	1 L
1 tbsp	margarine or butter	15 mL

1. In a large, heavy saucepan, combine clams with liquid, potatoes, celery, onion, skim milk powder, salt, pepper, milk and margarine. Bring to a simmer over low heat. Simmer, stirring occasionally, for about 20 minutes or until potatoes are tender (do not let boil).

Makes about 7 cups (1.75 L)
Serving size: 1 cup (250 mL)

Classic chowders are made with whole milk or cream. This lighter clam chowder uses 2% milk and skim milk powder — and it still tastes delightfully rich.

Kitchen Tip
Heat milk-based soups just to a simmer. If they are allowed to boil, they may curdle.

Nutrition Tip
When choosing a margarine, look for a non-hydrogenated soft margarine. These are low in saturated fat and do not contain trans fat. Avoid hard margarines, which contain high amounts of saturated and trans fat.

Nutrients per Serving

Calories	119
Carbohydrate	12 g
Fiber	1 g
Protein	8 g
Total fat	5 g
Saturated fat	2 g
Cholesterol	18 mg
Sodium	280 mg

America's Exchanges	
1	Other Carbohydrate
1	Lean Meat

Canada's Choices	
$\frac{1}{2}$	Carbohydrate
1	Meat & Alternatives

Salads

continued...

Classic Greek Salad

||||||||||||||||||||||||||||||||||||||||||||||||||||||||||||||||||||||||||||||||||||||||||||||||||||||||||||||||||||||

Makes 8 servings

When served with whole wheat baguette slices, this easy, fresh-tasting salad makes a great light lunch. Or serve it as a side salad with your main meal.

Kitchen Tip

Many good-quality kalamata olives have the pits in them. You can slice the olive flesh away from the pits before adding them to the salad or, if you prefer olives with pits in them, just point it out to your guests when serving the salad.

Variations

Add 1 tbsp (15 mL) drained rinsed capers with the tomatoes and sprinkle salad with hot pepper flakes to taste.

Replace the dried oregano with 1 tbsp (15 mL) chopped fresh oregano in the dressing and 1½ tsp (7 mL) on top.

Dressing

1	clove garlic, minced	1
1 tsp	dried oregano	5 mL
¼ tsp	salt	1 mL
1 tbsp	red wine vinegar	15 mL
1 tbsp	freshly squeezed lemon juice	15 mL
3 tbsp	extra virgin olive oil	45 mL
	Freshly ground black pepper	

Salad

2	plum (Roma) tomatoes, cut into chunks	2
1	green bell pepper, chopped	1
3 cups	torn romaine lettuce	750 mL
1 cup	sliced English cucumber	250 mL
¼ cup	slivered red onion	60 mL
⅓ cup	crumbled feta cheese	75 mL
⅓ cup	kalamata olives	75 mL
½ tsp	dried oregano	2 mL

1. *Dressing:* In a small bowl, whisk together garlic, oregano, salt, vinegar and lemon juice. Gradually whisk in oil until blended. Season to taste with pepper.

2. *Salad:* In a large serving bowl, combine tomatoes, green pepper, romaine, cucumber and red onion.

3. Whisk dressing and pour over salad; toss gently to coat. Scatter feta cheese, olives and oregano on top.

Nutrients per Serving

Calories	83
Carbohydrate	4 g
Fiber	1 g
Protein	2 g
Total fat	7 g
Saturated fat	2 g
Cholesterol	6 mg
Sodium	186 mg

America's Exchanges

1½	Fats
1	Free Food

Canada's Choices

1½	Fats

Caesar Salad

||||||||||||||||||||||||||||||||||||||||||||||||||||||||||||||||||||||||||||||||||||||||||||||||||||||||||||||||||

This Caesar is on the mild side, but you can increase the amounts of garlic, mustard and Worcestershire sauce if you like.

Kitchen Tip

If you like anchovies in your Caesar salad, you can substitute them for all or part of the bacon (replace 1 slice bacon with 1 finely chopped anchovy fillet). Add them with the garlic.

1	clove garlic, finely chopped	1
¼ tsp	salt	1 mL
¼ tsp	dry mustard	1 mL
¼ cup	light mayonnaise	60 mL
2 tbsp	freshly squeezed lemon juice	30 mL
1 tsp	Worcestershire sauce	5 mL
4	slices bacon, cooked crisp and crumbled	4
1	large head romaine lettuce, torn into bite-size pieces	1
1 cup	toasted bread cubes	250 mL
1 tbsp	freshly grated Parmesan cheese	15 mL

1. In a large salad bowl, combine garlic, salt, mustard, mayonnaise, lemon juice and Worcestershire sauce.

2. Add bacon, romaine, bread cubes and Parmesan; toss well.

Nutrients per Serving

Calories	101
Carbohydrate	8 g
Fiber	2 g
Protein	4 g
Total fat	6 g
Saturated fat	1 g
Cholesterol	10 mg
Sodium	356 mg

America's Exchanges	
½	Starch
1	Fat

Canada's Choices	
1	Fat
1	Extra

Broccoli Ranch Salad

|||||||||||||||||||||||||||||||||||||||||||||||||||||||||||||||||||||||||||||||||||||||||||||||||||||

Here's a wonderful creamy yet low-fat way to prepare a broccoli salad. The onions add some zip, and the almonds contribute a delightful nuttiness and crunch.

Kitchen Tips
Save time by buying 1 lb (500 g) of precut broccoli, often available in the produce section at the supermarket.

To make the salad ahead, prepare the vegetables and dressing, but don't mix them together. Cover and refrigerate separately for up to 1 day. Just before serving, toss together.

Variation
Stir in 1 chopped apple with the onion.

1	large bunch broccoli	1
1/3 cup	chopped red onion	75 mL
2 tbsp	chopped or sliced almonds, toasted (see tip, page 103)	30 mL

Dressing

1/2 cup	2% plain yogurt	125 mL
1/2 cup	light mayonnaise	125 mL
2 tsp	cider vinegar	10 mL
1 tsp	dried dillweed	5 mL
1/8 tsp	dried thyme	0.5 mL

1. Separate broccoli heads from stalks. Cut heads into small florets. Peel thick outer surface from stalks and chop stalks into bite-size pieces. You should have about 6 cups (1.5 L) florets and stalks.

2. In a medium saucepan of boiling water, boil broccoli for 3 minutes or until bright green and slightly tender. Drain and rinse with cold water until chilled; drain again. Pat with paper towels to remove excess water. Transfer to a serving bowl and add onion. Refrigerate while preparing dressing.

3. *Dressing:* In a small bowl, whisk together yogurt, mayonnaise, vinegar, dill and thyme.

4. Pour dressing over broccoli mixture and toss gently to coat. Sprinkle with almonds. Serve immediately.

Nutrients per Serving

Calories	143
Carbohydrate	12 g
Fiber	3 g
Protein	5 g
Total fat	10 g
Saturated fat	2 g
Cholesterol	9 mg
Sodium	206 mg

America's Exchanges

1	Vegetable
2	Fats
1	Free Food

Canada's Choices

2	Fats
1	Extra

Crunchy Layered Salad

||||||||||||||||||||||||||||||||||||||||||||||||||||||||||||||||||||||||||||||||||||||||||||||||||||||||||||||||||||||||||

Makes 9 servings

A thin coating of dressing spread over this salad keeps the air out, allowing the lettuce and vegetables to remain crisp and fresh during the long chilling time. It's a perfect choice when company is coming.

Kitchen Tips

Choose sturdy lettuce, such as iceberg or romaine, rather than more tender leaf lettuce.

Children prefer raw vegetables to cooked ones. Keep an assortment of washed raw vegetables in a covered container in the refrigerator.

- 9-inch (23 cm) square glass dish or salad bowl

6 cups	coarsely shredded lettuce	1.5 L
1	red onion, chopped	1
1 cup	chopped green or red bell pepper	250 mL
1 cup	chopped celery	250 mL
1 cup	frozen green peas	250 mL
1 cup	Tangy Salad Cream (see recipe, page 124)	250 mL
3	slices bacon, cooked crisp and crumbled	3
1 cup	shredded Cheddar cheese	250 mL

1. Place lettuce in an even layer in glass dish. Add layers of red onion, green pepper, celery and peas. Spoon salad cream over top, spreading to all edges of dish. Sprinkle with bacon and cheese.

2. Cover and refrigerate for at least 6 hours, until well chilled, or for up to 3 days. To serve, cut into squares.

Nutrients per Serving	
Calories	131
Carbohydrate	10 g
Fiber	2 g
Protein	7 g
Total fat	7 g
Saturated fat	3 g
Cholesterol	40 mg
Sodium	226 mg

America's Exchanges	
1/2	Starch
1	Vegetable
1 1/2	Fats

Canada's Choices	
1	Meat & Alternatives
1	Fat
1	Extra

Mushroom Salad

||||||||||||||||||||||||||||||||||||||||||||||||||||||||||||||||||||||||||||||||||||||||||||||||||

Sliced mushrooms add distinction to this tossed salad.

1	head romaine lettuce, torn into bite-size pieces	1
½	English cucumber, chopped	½
1 cup	sliced mushrooms	250 mL
¼ cup	Thousand Island Dressing (see recipe, page 130)	60 mL
¼ cup	unsalted sunflower or pumpkin seeds	60 mL

1. In a salad bowl, combine romaine, cucumber and mushrooms. Add dressing and toss to coat. Sprinkle with sunflower seeds.

Nutrients per Serving

Calories	63
Carbohydrate	6 g
Fiber	2 g
Protein	3 g
Total fat	4 g
Saturated fat	0 g
Cholesterol	0 mg
Sodium	47 mg

America's Exchanges	
1	Fat
1	Vegetable

Canada's Choices	
1	Fat
1	Extra

Spinach Salad

||||||||||||||||||||||||||||||||||||||||||||||||||||||||||||||||||||||||||||||||||||||||||||||||||||||||||||||||||||

Fresh spinach is available throughout the year and makes a nice change from lettuce. Like other dark green leafy vegetables, spinach is a valuable source of folate, iron and potassium.

Nutrition Tip

Vitamin C in oranges and other fruits and vegetables improves the body's absorption of iron from grains and dark green vegetables, such as spinach.

6 cups	lightly packed baby spinach (about 5 oz/150 g)	1.5 L
1	large sweet onion, such as Spanish, Vidalia or other mild onion, cut into rings	1
1	large orange	1
	Unsweetened orange juice	
1	clove garlic, finely chopped	1
¼ tsp	salt	1 mL
¼ tsp	freshly ground black pepper	1 mL
2 tsp	vegetable oil	10 mL

1. In a salad bowl, combine spinach and onion.

2. Peel orange and cut into sections. Cut each section in half and add to the spinach mixture.

3. Squeeze juice from remaining orange membranes into a measuring cup and pour in enough orange juice to make ¼ cup (60 mL). Stir in garlic, salt, pepper and oil.

4. Pour dressing over salad and toss to coat. Cover and refrigerate for 4 to 6 hours to let the flavors mellow.

Nutrients per Serving

Calories	69
Carbohydrate	11 g
Fiber	2 g
Protein	2 g
Total fat	2 g
Saturated fat	0 g
Cholesterol	0 mg
Sodium	169 mg

America's Exchanges

1	Vegetable
½	Fruit
½	Fat

Canada's Choices

½	Fat
1	Extra

Orange and Sprout Salad

Makes 4 servings
Serving size: 1 cup
(250 mL)

Cool, crunchy bean sprouts combine with tangy orange for a scrumptious salad that makes a star appetizer.

Kitchen Tips

Toast almonds in a small dry skillet over medium heat, stirring constantly, for about 3 minutes or until golden and fragrant.

You can also shake the dressing ingredients together in a small jar.

When you're shopping, keep fresh vegetables and fruit separate from raw meat, poultry and seafood, and store them separately in the refrigerator. Wash thoroughly before using.

2	small oranges, peeled and sectioned	2
2	stalks celery, sliced	2
2 cups	torn lettuce	500 mL
1 cup	bean sprouts	250 mL
2 tbsp	slivered almonds, toasted (see tip, at left)	30 mL

Dressing

2 tbsp	unsweetened orange juice	30 mL
1 tbsp	cider vinegar	15 mL
1 tbsp	vegetable oil	15 mL
½ tsp	celery seeds	2 mL
¼ tsp	salt	1 mL
¼ tsp	granulated sugar	1 mL

1. In a salad bowl, combine oranges, celery, lettuce, bean sprouts and almonds.

2. *Dressing:* In a small bowl, whisk together orange juice, vinegar, oil, celery seeds, salt and sugar.

3. Pour dressing over salad and toss to coat.

Nutrients per Serving	
Calories	96
Carbohydrate	11 g
Fiber	2 g
Protein	3 g
Total fat	6 g
Saturated fat	0 g
Cholesterol	0 mg
Sodium	168 mg

America's Exchanges	
1	Vegetable
½	Fruit
1	Fat

Canada's Choices	
½	Carbohydrate
1	Fat

Cucumber and Fruit Salad

||||||||||||||||||||||||||||||||||||||||||||||||||||||||||||||||||||||||||||||||||||||||||||||||||||||||||||||||||||||||||||

Makes 8 servings
Serving size: $\frac{1}{2}$ cup
(125 mL)

Cucumber, apples and cantaloupe team up in a sprightly salad that is refreshing as a starter or as a side salad with the main course.

Nutrition Tip
Most dark green leafy vegetables and yellow fruits and vegetables, including apricots, broccoli, cantaloupe, carrots, nectarines, peaches, spinach and squash, are good sources of vitamin A.

2	red apples, cut into bite-size pieces	2
1	large English cucumber, cut into bite-size pieces	1
1	small cantaloupe or honeydew melon, peeled, seeded and cut into bite-size pieces	1
$\frac{1}{4}$ cup	low-fat plain yogurt	60 mL
2 tbsp	freshly squeezed lime or lemon juice	30 mL
$\frac{1}{2}$ tsp	dried mint (or 1 tsp/5 mL chopped fresh mint)	2 mL
	Lettuce or spinach leaves	
1 tbsp	unsalted sunflower seeds	15 mL

1. In a large bowl, combine apples, cucumber and cantaloupe.

2. In a small bowl, whisk together yogurt, lime juice and mint. Pour over apple mixture and toss to coat.

3. Serve salad on a bed of lettuce, sprinkled with sunflower seeds.

Nutrients per Serving

Calories	48
Carbohydrate	10 g
Fiber	1 g
Protein	1 g
Total fat	1 g
Saturated fat	0 g
Cholesterol	0 mg
Sodium	12 mg

America's Exchanges	
$\frac{1}{2}$	Fruit
1	Free Food

Canada's Choices	
$\frac{1}{2}$	Carbohydrate

Variety Coleslaw

||||||||||||||||||||||||||||||||||||||||||||||||||||||||||||||||||||||||||||||||||||||||||||||||||||||||

Makes 4 servings
Serving size: 1/2 cup
(125 mL)

Shredded cabbage
has been used for
generations to make
economical, crisp salads
with a pleasant, sweet
taste. Chopped apple
transforms basic coleslaw
into a special occasion
salad.

Variation
Replace the apple with
1/3 cup (75 mL) drained
canned unsweetened
pineapple chunks or 2 tbsp
(30 mL) raisins.

1	carrot, finely chopped	1
1/2	red apple, chopped	1/2
2 cups	shredded cabbage	500 mL
2 tbsp	chopped green bell pepper	30 mL
1/4 cup	Tangy Salad Cream (see recipe, page 124)	60 mL
2 tbsp	low-fat plain yogurt	30 mL

1. In a large bowl, combine carrot, apple, cabbage and green pepper.

2. In a small bowl, whisk together salad cream and yogurt. Pour over salad and toss to coat.

Nutrients per Serving

Calories	51
Carbohydrate	9 g
Fiber	1 g
Protein	2 g
Total fat	1 g
Saturated fat	0 g
Cholesterol	14 mg
Sodium	53 mg

America's Exchanges	
1/2	Other Carbohydrate

Canada's Choices	
1	Extra

Marinated Vegetable Medley

In this relish salad, marinating gives the garden vegetables a lightly pickled taste. The longer you refrigerate the salad, the better the flavor will be.

Kitchen Tips

Choose the flavor of vinegar you enjoy most. If you like a mild vinegar, choose white wine vinegar, distilled white vinegar or cider vinegar. For a bolder flavor, use red wine vinegar, balsamic vinegar or malt vinegar. Herb-flavored vinegar would add a nice flavor too.

You can also shake the dressing ingredients together in a small jar.

1	carrot, sliced	1
$1/2$	cucumber, sliced	$1/2$
1 cup	cauliflower florets	250 mL
1 cup	broccoli florets	250 mL
1 cup	sliced celery	250 mL
$1/4$ cup	vinegar (any variety)	60 mL
1 tbsp	vegetable oil	15 mL
$1/2$ tsp	onion salt	2 mL
$1/2$ tsp	freshly ground black pepper	2 mL
1	firm tomato, cut into 8 wedges	1

1. In a large bowl, combine carrot, cucumber, cauliflower, broccoli and celery.

2. In a small bowl, whisk together vinegar, oil, onion salt and pepper. Pour over salad and toss to coat. Cover and refrigerate for at least 3 hours or for up to 3 days to marinate. Add tomato wedges just before serving.

Nutrients per Serving

Calories	45
Carbohydrate	5 g
Fiber	2 g
Protein	1 g
Total fat	2 g
Saturated fat	0 g
Cholesterol	0 mg
Sodium	184 mg

America's Exchanges

1	Vegetable
$1/2$	Fat

Canada's Choices

$1/2$	Fat

Marinated Cucumbers

Makes 4 servings

Few salads are as easy to make as this one. Remember to drain the cucumbers well before serving them with fish, chicken or cold meats.

Kitchen Tip

English cucumbers have a more tender and easily digestible skin than field cucumbers, so you don't have to peel them, making them a terrific choice for this salad.

1	cucumber, cut into thin slices	1
½ cup	Herb Dressing (see recipe, page 125)	125 mL

1. Layer cucumber in a bowl with drizzles of dressing. Refrigerate overnight. Drain to serve.

Nutrients per Serving	
Calories	18
Carbohydrate	4 g
Fiber	1 g
Protein	1 g
Total fat	0 g
Saturated fat	0 g
Cholesterol	1 mg
Sodium	67 mg

America's Exchanges	
1	Free Food

Canada's Choices	
1	Extra

Celery Victor

||||||||||||||||||||||||||||||||||||||||||||||||||||||||||||||||||||||||||||||||||||||||||||||||||||||||||||||||||||||||||||

Makes 6 servings

Celery simmered in a broth fragrant with lemon and herbs makes a distinctive salad after it is chilled. It makes the taste buds tingle when served as either an appetizer or a side salad.

Kitchen Tip

If you don't have celery hearts and are using mature stalks of celery, you may want to peel the outer strings off with a vegetable peeler to make sure the celery is tender.

6	celery hearts (or twenty-four 4-inch/10 cm celery stalks)	6
3 cups	water	750 mL
1/4 tsp	salt	1 mL
1/2 cup	red wine vinegar	125 mL
1 tbsp	freshly squeezed lemon juice	15 mL
1	bay leaf	1
2 tsp	dried parsley	10 mL
1 tsp	dried oregano	5 mL
1/2 tsp	dried thyme	2 mL
1/4 tsp	freshly ground black pepper	1 mL
Pinch	cayenne pepper	Pinch
	Lettuce leaves	
2 tbsp	drained capers	30 mL
2 tbsp	chopped pimentos	30 mL

1. Cut celery hearts in half lengthwise. In a pot, bring water to a boil. Add salt and celery hearts; cook for about 7 minutes or until tender-crisp. Add vinegar, lemon juice, bay leaf, parsley, oregano, thyme, black pepper and cayenne; simmer for 4 minutes. Remove from heat and let cool.

2. Remove celery hearts from liquid, draining well. Place each piece on a lettuce leaf. Sprinkle with capers and pimentos.

Nutrients per Serving

Calories	20
Carbohydrate	4 g
Fiber	1 g
Protein	1 g
Total fat	0 g
Saturated fat	0 g
Cholesterol	0 mg
Sodium	201 mg

America's Exchanges	
1	Free Food

Canada's Choices	
1	Extra

Jellied Beet Mold

Makes 6 servings
Serving size: ½ cup
(125 mL)

Beets are refreshing in this icy-cold molded salad.

Kitchen Tip

Most jellied salads call for the gelatin mixture to be partially set before other ingredients are folded into it. Gelatin in this state is syrupy-thick, similar to the consistency of an unbeaten egg white.

● **4-cup (1 L) jelly mold**

1	can (14 oz/398 mL) diced beets, with juice	1
¾ cup	unsweetened orange juice	175 mL
2 tsp	white vinegar	10 mL
1	envelope (¼ oz/7 g) unflavored gelatin powder	1
1 cup	shredded zucchini	250 mL
½ cup	finely chopped celery	125 mL

1. Drain juice from beets into a small saucepan; reserve beets. Stir orange juice and vinegar into beet juice. Sprinkle gelatin over top and let stand for 5 minutes to soften.

2. Heat gelatin mixture over medium heat, stirring, until all granules dissolve. Pour into a bowl and let cool. Refrigerate for about 30 minutes or until partially set.

3. Spread zucchini and celery on paper towels and blot out excess moisture. Fold reserved beets, zucchini and celery into gelatin mixture.

4. Rinse jelly mold with cold water. Spoon gelatin mixture into mold. Refrigerate for at least 4 hours, until set, or for up to 2 days.

5. To serve, dip mold in warm water and pat dry. Invert a serving plate on top of the mold, then flip over to unmold jelly.

Nutrients per Serving

Calories	43
Carbohydrate	9 g
Fiber	1 g
Protein	2 g
Total fat	0 g
Saturated fat	0 g
Cholesterol	0 mg
Sodium	110 mg

America's Exchanges	
1	Vegetable

Canada's Choices	
½	Carbohydrate

Salad Royale

‖‖

Makes 8 servings
Serving size: $1/3$ cup
(75 mL)

The combination of canned beets and pineapple makes a wonderful winter salad.

Kitchen Tip
If you don't have a jelly mold, you can make this in a pretty, clear glass bowl and skip step 5.

● **4-cup (1 L) jelly mold**

1	can (14 oz/398 mL) diced beets, with juice	1
$3/4$ cup	unsweetened grape juice	175 mL
2 tsp	freshly squeezed lemon juice	10 mL
1	envelope ($1/4$ oz/7 g) unflavored gelatin powder	1
1	can (14 oz/398 mL) unsweetened crushed pineapple, drained	1
1 tsp	prepared horseradish	5 mL
Pinch	ground cinnamon	Pinch

1. Drain juice from beets into a small saucepan; reserve beets. Stir grape juice and lemon juice into beet juice. Sprinkle gelatin over top and let stand for 5 minutes to soften.

2. Heat gelatin mixture over medium heat, stirring, until all granules dissolve. Pour into a bowl and let cool. Refrigerate for about 30 minutes or until partially set.

3. Fold reserved beets, pineapple, horseradish and cinnamon into gelatin mixture.

4. Rinse jelly mold with cold water. Spoon gelatin mixture into mold. Refrigerate for at least 4 hours, until set, or for up to 2 days.

5. To serve, dip mold in warm water and pat dry. Invert a serving plate on top of the mold, then flip over to unmold jelly.

Nutrients per Serving

Calories	54
Carbohydrate	13 g
Fiber	1 g
Protein	1 g
Total fat	0 g
Saturated fat	0 g
Cholesterol	0 mg
Sodium	79 mg

America's Exchanges	
1	Fruit

Canada's Choices	
$1/2$	Carbohydrate

Cucumber Lime Mold

||||||||||||||||||||||||||||||||||||||||||||||||||||||||||||||||||||||||||||||||||||||||||||||||||||||||||||||||||

This creamy molded salad, spiked with the tang of lime, is cool as a cucumber. It's a great accompaniment for hot or cold fish, pork or ham.

Nutrition Tip

Cottage cheese has traditionally contained a lot of salt, with about 400 mg (17% DV) in 1/2 cup (125 mL). Some brands now contain less. Be sure to check the Nutrition Facts table when shopping and choose the one that's lowest in sodium.

Nutrients per Serving	
Calories	47
Carbohydrate	4 g
Fiber	0 g
Protein	7 g
Total fat	1 g
Saturated fat	0 g
Cholesterol	3 mg
Sodium	260 mg

- **Blender or food processor**
- **4-cup (1 L) jelly mold**

1 tbsp	freshly squeezed lime juice	15 mL
1 tbsp	white vinegar	15 mL
1	envelope (1/4 oz/7 g) unflavored gelatin powder	1
1 cup	2% cottage cheese	250 mL
1/4 tsp	salt	1 mL
1/2 tsp	Worcestershire sauce	2 mL
2	drops hot pepper sauce	2
1 1/2 cups	coarsely shredded unpeeled seeded cucumber (1 large)	375 mL
2 tsp	finely grated onion	10 mL

1. In a small saucepan, combine 1 cup (250 mL) water, lime juice and vinegar. Sprinkle gelatin over top and let stand for 5 minutes to soften.

2. Heat gelatin mixture over medium heat, stirring, until all granules dissolve. Pour into a bowl and let cool.

3. In blender, combine cottage cheese, salt, Worcestershire sauce and hot pepper sauce; process until smooth. Stir into gelatin mixture. Refrigerate for about 45 minutes or until partially set.

4. Press cucumber between paper towels to remove excess moisture. Fold cucumber and onion into gelatin mixture.

5. Rinse jelly mold with cold water. Spoon gelatin mixture into mold. Refrigerate for at least 4 hours, until set, or for up to 2 days.

6. To serve, dip mold in warm water and pat dry. Invert a serving plate on top of the mold, then flip over to unmold jelly.

America's Exchanges	
1	Lean Meat

Canada's Choices	
1/2	Meat & Alternatives
1	Extra

Molded Cranberry Salad

‖‖

Makes 6 servings
Serving size: 1 cup
(250 mL)

Ruby red cranberries make this molded salad look like a jewel on the holiday table. It is wonderful not only with roast turkey but also with ham, pork and chicken.

Kitchen Tip
To grate the orange zest, use the fine side of a box cheese grater or a Microplane-style grater. If you use a five-hole zester, chop the zest into smaller pieces with a knife.

- 6-cup (1.5 L) jelly mold

1	envelope ($\frac{1}{4}$ oz/7 g) unflavored gelatin powder	1
2 cups	sugar-free ginger ale, divided	500 mL
2 cups	cranberries, coarsely chopped	500 mL
1 tbsp	freshly squeezed lemon juice	15 mL
2 tsp	grated orange zest	10 mL
	Artificial sweetener equivalent to 5 tsp (25 mL) granulated sugar	
$\frac{1}{2}$	apple, finely chopped	$\frac{1}{2}$
$\frac{1}{2}$ cup	finely chopped celery	125 mL

1. In a small bowl, sprinkle gelatin over $\frac{1}{4}$ cup (60 mL) of the ginger ale and let stand for 5 minutes to soften.

2. In a saucepan, combine the remaining ginger ale, cranberries, lemon juice and orange zest. Bring to a boil over high heat. Remove from heat and stir in gelatin mixture and sweetener until all granules dissolve. Pour into a bowl and let cool. Refrigerate for about 45 minutes or until partially set.

3. Fold apple and celery into gelatin mixture.

4. Rinse jelly mold with cold water. Spoon gelatin mixture into mold. Refrigerate for at least 4 hours, until set, or for up to 2 days.

5. To serve, dip mold in warm water and pat dry. Invert a serving plate on top of the mold, then flip over to unmold jelly.

Nutrients per Serving

Calories	30
Carbohydrate	7 g
Fiber	2 g
Protein	1 g
Total fat	0 g
Saturated fat	0 g
Cholesterol	0 mg
Sodium	23 mg

America's Exchanges	
$\frac{1}{2}$	Fruit

Canada's Choices	
1	Extra

Festival Fruit Salad

Makes 6 servings

Jellied fruit is sure to rate tops with the kids. Serve it as a salad or a dessert. For an elegant-looking dessert treat for adults, spoon it into six parfait glasses to set.

Kitchen Tip

Don't attempt to replace the canned pineapple with fresh. There's an enzyme in fresh pineapple that prevents gelatin from setting properly.

Nutrients per Serving	
Calories	63
Carbohydrate	12 g
Fiber	1 g
Protein	4 g
Total fat	0 g
Saturated fat	0 g
Cholesterol	1 mg
Sodium	35 mg

- 8- by 4-inch (20 by 10 cm) loaf pan

2½ cups	sugar-free carbonated orange beverage, divided	625 mL
2	envelopes (each ¼ oz/7 g) unflavored gelatin powder	2
2 tbsp	freshly squeezed lemon juice	30 mL
½ tsp	almond extract	2 mL
½ cup	low-fat plain yogurt	125 mL
1	small orange, peeled and sectioned	1
½	banana, sliced	½
½ cup	seedless red grapes, halved	125 mL
½ cup	seedless green grapes, halved	125 mL
⅓ cup	drained canned unsweetened pineapple chunks	75 mL

1. In a small bowl, sprinkle gelatin over ¼ cup (60 mL) of the orange beverage and let stand for 5 minutes to soften.

2. In a saucepan, combine the remaining orange beverage and lemon juice. Bring to a boil over high heat. Remove from heat and stir in gelatin mixture and almond extract until all granules dissolve. Pour into a bowl and let cool. Refrigerate for about 45 minutes or until partially set.

3. Stir yogurt into gelatin mixture. Fold in orange, banana, red grapes, green grapes and pineapple.

4. Rinse loaf pan with cold water. Spoon gelatin mixture into pan. Refrigerate at least 4 hours, until set, or for up to 1 day.

5. To serve, dip loaf pan in warm water and pat dry. Invert a serving plate on top of the pan, then flip over to unmold jelly. Cut into 6 slices.

America's Exchanges	
1	Fruit

Canada's Choices	
1	Carbohydrate

Sunburst Salad

Bright, cheery salads add color and texture to meals at any time of the year.

Nutrition Tip

Nuts contain protein and fat. While the fat is the healthy unsaturated type, it still contributes calories, so nuts should generally be used in small quantities, as garnishes. If you are a vegetarian, a dietitian can advise you about using nuts as a Meat and Meat Substitutes Exchange or a Meat and Alternatives Choice.

Variation

Vary the flavor of this colorful mold by replacing $1/4$ cup (60 mL) of the cabbage with chopped green bell pepper or chopped green onion.

Nutrients per Serving

Calories	93
Carbohydrate	11 g
Fiber	2 g
Protein	3 g
Total fat	5 g
Saturated fat	0 g
Cholesterol	0 mg
Sodium	27 mg

- 4-cup (1 L) jelly mold

1	envelope ($1/4$ oz/7 g) unflavored gelatin powder	1
$1/4$ cup	cold water	60 mL
$1/2$ cup	boiling water	125 mL
1 cup	sugar-free ginger ale	250 mL
$1/4$ cup	unsweetened orange juice	60 mL
$1/4$ tsp	ground ginger	1 mL
2	small oranges, peeled and sectioned	2
1 cup	finely shredded cabbage	250 mL
$1/2$ cup	grated carrot	125 mL
$1/4$ cup	chopped pecans or walnuts	60 mL

1. In a large bowl, sprinkle gelatin over cold water and let stand for 5 minutes to soften.

2. Add boiling water to gelatin mixture and stir until all granules dissolve. Stir in ginger ale, orange juice and ginger. Let cool. Refrigerate for about 45 minutes or until partially set.

3. Fold oranges, cabbage, carrot and pecans into gelatin mixture.

4. Rinse jelly mold with cold water. Spoon gelatin mixture into mold. Refrigerate for at least 4 hours, until set, or for up to 2 days.

5. To serve, dip mold in warm water and pat dry. Invert a serving plate on top of the mold, then flip over to unmold jelly.

America's Exchanges	
1	Fruit
1	Fat

Canada's Choices	
$1/2$	Carbohydrate
1	Fat

Wholesome Pasta and Veggie Salad

Makes 6 servings
Serving size: 1½ cups
(375 mL)

Pasta salads are always popular. This one uses whole wheat pasta and is packed with a rainbow of veggies — it's sure to become a favorite.

Kitchen Tip

A garlic press is a great kitchen tool that works well when you're mincing garlic for salad dressing. As an added bonus, you don't have to peel the garlic before placing it in the press.

Variations

Omit the dried dillweed and add 2 tbsp (30 mL) chopped fresh dill with the parsley.

Stir in ½ cup (125 mL) mini bocconcini cheese with the tomatoes.

Dressing

1	clove garlic, minced	1
½ tsp	dried dillweed	2 mL
½ tsp	salt	2 mL
¼ tsp	freshly ground black pepper	1 mL
2½ tbsp	vegetable oil	37 mL
4 tsp	red wine vinegar	20 mL
¼ tsp	Dijon mustard	1 mL

Salad

6 oz	whole wheat rotini, fusilli or penne pasta (about 2 cups/500 mL)	175 g
1½ cups	sliced green beans (1-inch/2.5 cm pieces)	375 mL
2	green onions, sliced	2
1	red bell pepper, chopped	1
1	stalk celery, chopped	1
1 cup	grape or cherry tomatoes, cut in half	250 mL
2 tbsp	chopped fresh parsley	30 mL

1. *Dressing:* In a small bowl, whisk together garlic, dill, salt, pepper, oil, vinegar and mustard until blended. Set aside.

2. *Salad:* In a large pot of boiling water, cook pasta according to package directions until just tender, adding green beans for the last 5 minutes of cooking time. Drain and rinse under cold water until cool. Drain well and transfer to a serving bowl.

3. Add green onions, red pepper, celery, tomatoes and parsley. Pour in dressing and toss to coat. Serve immediately or cover and refrigerate for up to 8 hours.

Nutrients per Serving

Calories	172
Carbohydrate	26 g
Fiber	4 g
Protein	5 g
Total fat	6 g
Saturated fat	1 g
Cholesterol	0 mg
Sodium	212 mg

America's Exchanges

1½	Starch
1	Vegetable
1	Fat

Canada's Choices

1	Carbohydrate
1	Fat

Potato Salad

||||||||||||||||||||||||||||||||||||||||||||||||||||||||||||||||||||||||||||||||||||||||||||||||||||||||||||||

Makes 4 servings
Serving size: ½ cup
(125 mL)

Allow time for the flavors
to blend and develop
in this salad, which is
popular for picnics and
other casual occasions.
Garnish it with sliced
red radishes when
they're in season.

Kitchen Tip
Choose round, waxy or
new potatoes for the nicest
texture. Baking or starchy
potatoes tend to crumble
and get mushy in potato
salad.

Nutrition Tip
If you count America's
Exchanges, remember that
potatoes are a Starchy
Vegetable in the Starch
group; if you count Canada's
Choices, they belong in the
Grains and Starches section
of the Carbohydrate group.

2	medium potatoes (1 lb/500 g)	2
1	bay leaf	1
¼ cup	chopped onion	60 mL
2 tbsp	chopped celery	30 mL
¼ cup	Tangy Salad Cream (see recipe, page 124)	60 mL
½ tsp	prepared mustard	2 mL
¼ tsp	celery seeds	1 mL
¼ tsp	salt	1 mL
¼ tsp	freshly ground black pepper	1 mL

1. Place potatoes and bay leaf in a saucepan and add enough cold water to cover. Bring to a boil over high heat; reduce heat and boil gently for 15 to 20 minutes or until just tender. Drain and let cool slightly. Peel potatoes and cut into small pieces.

2. In a large bowl, combine potatoes, onion and celery.

3. In a small bowl, whisk together salad cream, mustard and celery seeds. Pour over potato mixture and toss gently to coat. Season with salt and pepper. Refrigerate for at least 2 hours, to blend the flavors, or for up to 1 day.

Nutrients per Serving	
Calories	103
Carbohydrate	21 g
Fiber	2 g
Protein	2 g
Total fat	1 g
Saturated fat	0 g
Cholesterol	13 mg
Sodium	191 mg

America's Exchanges	
1½	Starches

Canada's Choices	
1	Carbohydrate

Warm German Potato Salad

Traditionally, German-style potato salads are made with a vinaigrette dressing that soaks nicely into the warm potatoes, and are served warm. Whether you serve it warm, at room temperature or chilled, you will be not be disappointed.

Kitchen Tips

Adding some of the dressing while the potatoes are warm allows them to absorb all the flavor, making them extra-delicious.

The salad can be cooled completely, covered and refrigerated for up to 1 day. Cover and refrigerate the remaining dressing separately. Let stand at room temperature for 30 minutes to take the chill off, then toss with the remaining dressing.

Nutrients per Serving	
Calories	154
Carbohydrate	22 g
Fiber	2 g
Protein	2 g
Total fat	7 g
Saturated fat	1 g
Cholesterol	0 mg
Sodium	231 mg

2 lbs	small new potatoes	1 kg
1	carrot, sliced	1
½ tsp	salt	2 mL
2	green onions, chopped	2
1	red, yellow or orange bell pepper, chopped	1
3 tbsp	chopped fresh parsley	45 mL
Vinaigrette		
1	clove garlic, minced	1
¼ tsp	salt	1 mL
¼ tsp	freshly ground black pepper	1 mL
¼ cup	extra virgin olive oil	60 mL
2 tbsp	red wine vinegar	30 mL

1. Scrub potatoes and cut in half (or into quarters, if larger). Place in a large saucepan and add enough cold water to cover by at least 1 inch (2.5 cm). Bring to a boil over high heat. Reduce heat and boil gently for about 13 minutes or until potatoes are almost tender. Add carrots and boil for 2 minutes or until potatoes are tender and carrots are tender-crisp. Drain, transfer to a large bowl and toss with salt. Let cool slightly while preparing vinaigrette.

2. *Vinaigrette:* In a small bowl, whisk together garlic, salt, pepper, oil and vinegar.

3. Add green onions, red pepper and parsley to potatoes. Pour in half the vinaigrette and toss gently to coat. Let cool until lukewarm (or cool completely). Just before serving, add the remaining vinaigrette and toss again.

America's Exchanges	
1	Starch
1	Vegetable
1	Fat

Canada's Choices	
1	Carbohydrate
1½	Fats

Sesame Ginger Brown Rice Salad

This Asian-inspired salad, made with nutritious brown rice and vegetables, can be enjoyed warm, at room temperature or chilled. Leftovers are terrific for lunch. Serve with grilled chicken, pork or shrimp for a complete meal.

Kitchen Tip

Toasting sesame seeds brings out their nutty flavor. Toast seeds in a small dry skillet over medium heat, stirring constantly, for 3 to 4 minutes or until golden brown and fragrant. Immediately transfer to a small bowl and let cool.

1 cup	long-grain brown rice	250 mL
1/2 tsp	salt	2 mL
4 tsp	vegetable oil, divided	20 mL
1 tbsp	reduced-sodium soy sauce	15 mL
1 tbsp	freshly squeezed lemon juice	15 mL
1/2 tsp	liquid honey	2 mL
1	stalk celery, diced	1
1	carrot, diced	1
1	red bell pepper, finely chopped	1
1 1/2 tsp	minced gingerroot	7 mL
1/2 cup	thawed frozen green peas	125 mL
2	green onions, sliced	2
2 tbsp	sesame seeds, toasted (see tip, at left)	30 mL

1. In a medium saucepan, combine rice, salt and 2 cups (500 mL) water. Bring to a boil over high heat. Reduce heat to low, cover and simmer for 45 minutes or until rice is tender and most of the liquid is absorbed. Remove from heat and let stand, covered, for 10 minutes. Fluff with a fork.

2. Meanwhile, in a small bowl, whisk together 2 tsp (10 mL) of the oil, soy sauce, lemon juice and honey. Set aside.

Nutrients per Serving

Calories	139
Carbohydrate	23 g
Fiber	2 g
Protein	3 g
Total fat	4 g
Saturated fat	0 g
Cholesterol	0 mg
Sodium	236 mg

America's Exchanges	
1 1/2	Starches
1	Fat

Canada's Choices	
1	Carbohydrate
1	Fat

Nutrition Tip

Brown rice is the whole grain with the outer bran layer and germ intact. It is more nutritious than white rice and requires a longer cooking time. Brown rice can also be cooked in a large amount of gently boiling water until tender, then drained, or prepared in a rice cooker.

Variations

Replace 1 tsp (5 mL) of the vegetable oil in the soy sauce mixture with toasted sesame oil and add $1/2$ tsp (5 mL) Asian chili hot sauce (or to taste).

Substitute cooked shelled edamame (green soybeans) for the green peas

3. In a large skillet, heat the remaining oil over medium heat. Sauté celery, carrot, red pepper and ginger for 3 minutes or until just starting to soften. Remove from heat and stir in peas.

4. In a serving bowl, combine rice, vegetable mixture and soy sauce mixture, tossing gently to coat. Serve warm or let cool completely. To serve cold, let cool to room temperature, cover and refrigerate for at least 4 hours or for up to 1 day.

5. Just before serving, gently stir in green onions and sesame seeds.

Chickpea Garden Green Salad

Chickpeas, also called garbanzo beans, are creamy yellow beans with a nutlike taste that goes well with crisp vegetables. You'll find them dried and in cans at the supermarket.

Kitchen Tip

You can also shake the dressing ingredients together in a small jar.

2 cups	shredded lettuce	500 mL
1¼ cups	rinsed drained canned or cooked chickpeas	300 mL
½ cup	sliced celery	125 mL
¼ cup	chopped green bell pepper	60 mL
¼ cup	chopped sweet onion, such as Spanish, Vidalia or other mild onion	60 mL
2 tbsp	chopped fresh parsley	30 mL
2 tbsp	freshly squeezed lemon juice	30 mL
2 tsp	vegetable oil	10 mL
Pinch	garlic powder	Pinch
	Freshly ground black pepper	
⅛ tsp	salt (or less)	0.5 mL

1. In a salad bowl, combine lettuce, chickpeas, celery, green pepper and onion.

2. In a small bowl, whisk together parsley, lemon juice, oil and garlic powder. Pour over salad and toss to coat. Season to taste with pepper and up to ⅛ tsp (0.5 mL) salt.

Nutrients per Serving

Calories	107
Carbohydrate	16 g
Fiber	3 g
Protein	4 g
Total fat	3 g
Saturated fat	0 g
Cholesterol	0 mg
Sodium	227 mg

America's Exchanges	
1	Starch
½	Fat

Canada's Choices	
1	Carbohydrate
½	Fat

Four-Bean Salad

This hearty salad is best if made at least a day ahead to allow the flavors to blend.

Kitchen Tip

You can replace the frozen green and yellow wax beans with fresh when they're in season. Boil them for about 3 minutes, until tender-crisp, then rinse under cold water until cool.

Nutrition Tip

Four-bean salads are often made entirely with canned beans, which are very high in sodium. By replacing the canned green and yellow wax beans and lima beans with frozen, you reduce the sodium by over 200 mg per serving.

3 cups	frozen cut green and yellow wax beans	750 mL
1¹/₂ cups	frozen baby lima beans	375 mL
1	can (14 oz/398 mL) red kidney beans, drained and rinsed	1
1 cup	chopped celery	250 mL
¹/₂ cup	thinly sliced sweet onion, such as Spanish, Vidalia or other mild onion	125 mL
¹/₃ cup	chopped green bell pepper	75 mL

Dressing

¹/₂ cup	vegetable oil	125 mL
¹/₄ cup	white vinegar	60 mL
2 tsp	granulated sugar	10 mL
1 tsp	dry mustard	5 mL
1 tsp	dried thyme	5 mL
¹/₄ tsp	salt	1 mL
¹/₄ tsp	freshly ground black pepper	1 mL
Pinch	garlic powder	Pinch

1. In a pot of boiling water, cook green and yellow beans and lima beans according to package directions (adding them to the pot accordingly if cooking times are different). Drain and rinse under cold water until cool. Drain well.

2. In a large bowl, combine green beans, wax beans, kidney beans, lima beans, celery, onion and green pepper.

3. *Dressing:* In a small bowl, whisk together oil, vinegar, sugar, mustard, thyme, salt, pepper and garlic powder.

4. Pour dressing over bean mixture and toss to coat. Cover and refrigerate, stirring occasionally, for at least 1 day, to blend the flavors, or for up to 2 days. Drain off excess liquid before serving.

Nutrients per Serving

Calories	160
Carbohydrate	19 g
Fiber	6 g
Protein	6 g
Total fat	7 g
Saturated fat	1 g
Cholesterol	0 mg
Sodium	205 mg

America's Exchanges	
1	Other Carbohydrate
1	Lean Meat
1	Fat

Canada's Choices	
¹/₂	Carbohydrate
¹/₂	Meat & Alternatives
1	Fat

Crunchy Tuna Salad in Pepper Cups

Each serving of this main course salad sits in its own cup, so it is easy to serve on a luncheon or party plate. Waist-watchers will love it because it is low in fat and calories.

Kitchen Tip

To peel tomatoes, blanch ripe tomatoes in a pot of boiling water for 30 to 60 seconds, depending on ripeness (less ripe will need longer). Using a slotted spoon, transfer tomatoes to a bowl of ice water and let stand until chilled. Drain. Using a paring knife, cut out core and peel off skins.

Nutrition Tip

Tuna is an economical source of protein and, like salmon and other coldwater fish, it contains healthy omega-3 fatty acids.

Nutrients per Serving	
Calories	127
Carbohydrate	11 g
Fiber	2 g
Protein	10 g
Total fat	5 g
Saturated fat	1 g
Cholesterol	15 mg
Sodium	286 mg

2	large, nicely shaped green bell peppers	2
1/4 cup	light mayonnaise	60 mL
1/4 cup	plain yogurt	60 mL
1/2 tsp	grated lemon zest	2 mL
1 tbsp	freshly squeezed lemon juice	15 mL
1/8 tsp	salt	0.5 mL
Pinch	freshly ground black pepper	Pinch
2	tomatoes, peeled, seeded and chopped	2
1	can (6 oz/170 g) water-packed flaked tuna, drained	1
1 cup	coarsely chopped iceberg lettuce	250 mL
1/4 cup	sliced green onions	60 mL
4	crisp lettuce leaves	4

1. Cut green peppers in half crosswise to form shells; carefully remove core and seeds. Bring a large saucepan of water to a boil over high heat. Add peppers, cut side up. Cover and boil for 3 minutes or until tender-crisp. Using a slotted spoon, remove peppers and turn upside down to drain. Refrigerate until ready to use.

2. In a bowl, combine mayonnaise, yogurt, lemon zest, lemon juice, salt and pepper. Add tomatoes, tuna, chopped lettuce and green onions; fold gently to coat. Spoon into pepper shells, piling high. Refrigerate for at least 2 hours, until well chilled, or for up to 8 hours.

3. Place each pepper on a lettuce leaf.

America's Exchanges	
1	Vegetable
1/2	Other Carbohydrate
1	Lean Meat

Canada's Choices	
1	Meat & Alternatives
1/2	Fat

Tuna Salad

Tuna salad makes a great sandwich when teamed with whole wheat bread. Or, for a light luncheon or supper, present it with fresh tomato wedges and cucumber rings and warm-from-the-oven whole wheat biscuits.

Kitchen Tip
To grate the lemon zest, use the fine side of a box cheese grater or a Microplane-style grater. If you use a five-hole zester, chop the zest into smaller pieces with a knife.

Variation
Substitute a 7$\frac{1}{2}$-oz (213 g) can of salmon for the tuna.

1	can (6 oz/170 g) water-packed chunk tuna, drained	1
$\frac{1}{3}$ cup	2% cottage cheese	75 mL
$\frac{1}{2}$ cup	finely chopped celery	125 mL
$\frac{1}{4}$ cup	finely chopped onion	60 mL
2 tbsp	finely chopped fresh parsley	30 mL
$\frac{1}{2}$ tsp	grated lemon zest	2 mL
$\frac{1}{4}$ tsp	dried tarragon (optional)	1 mL
2 tbsp	Tangy Salad Cream (see recipe, page 124)	30 mL

1. In a bowl, using a fork, mash together tuna and cottage cheese. Stir in celery, onion, parsley, lemon zest, tarragon (if using) and salad cream until well blended.

Nutrients per Serving	
Calories	70
Carbohydrate	3 g
Fiber	0 g
Protein	11 g
Total fat	1 g
Saturated fat	0 g
Cholesterol	17 mg
Sodium	207 mg

America's Exchanges	
2	Lean Meats

Canada's Choices	
1$\frac{1}{2}$	Meat & Alternatives

Tangy Salad Cream

||||||||||||||||||||||||||||||||||||||||||||||||||||||||||||||||||||||||||||||||||||||||||||||||||||||||||||||||||||||||||||

**Makes about
¾ cup (175 mL)**
Serving size: 2 tbsp
(30 mL)

This creamy, smooth salad dressing is a tasty, economical substitute for store-bought dressings and can be used to perk up many recipes.

Nutrition Tip
This homemade dressing contains less than half the sodium of a commercial whipped dressing.

2 tbsp	granulated sugar	30 mL
1	egg	1
⅓ cup	cider vinegar	75 mL
1 tbsp	all-purpose flour	15 mL
1 tsp	dry mustard	5 mL
⅛ tsp	salt	0.5 mL
⅛ tsp	freshly ground black pepper	0.5 mL
2 tsp	margarine or butter	10 mL

1. In a small, heavy saucepan, whisk together sugar, egg, ⅔ cup (150 mL) water and vinegar. Whisk in flour, mustard, salt and pepper. Cook over medium heat, whisking constantly, for about 5 minutes or until smooth and thickened (it will thicken further upon refrigeration). Whisk in margarine until smooth.

2. Pour into a jar, cover tightly and store in the refrigerator for up to 2 weeks.

Nutrients per Serving	
Calories	42
Carbohydrate	5 g
Fiber	0 g
Protein	1 g
Total fat	2 g
Saturated fat	0 g
Cholesterol	27 mg
Sodium	60 mg

America's Exchanges	
½	Fat
1	Free Food

Canada's Choices	
½	Fat
1	Extra

Herb Dressing

||||||||||||||||||||||||||||||||||||||||||||||||||||||||||||||||||||||||||||||||||||||||||||||||||||||||||||||||||||||||||||||||||||||||||||||||||||||||||

**Makes 1½ cups
(375 mL)**
Serving size: 2 tbsp
(30 mL)

You can shake up a jar of this dressing in 5 minutes from start to finish. It is one of the most versatile dressings to have on hand: you can toss it with greens or drizzle it over hot or cold asparagus spears or any chilled crisply cooked vegetables.

Kitchen Tip

The flavor of onion tends to get stronger as the dressing is stored, so omit it if you prefer a milder flavor.

Nutrition Tip

By making your own salad dressing, you can greatly reduce your sodium intake. Two tablespoons (30 mL) of this dressing contain less than 100 mg of sodium. You will find two to four times this amount in the same quantity of a commercial dressing.

Nutrients per Serving	
Calories	14
Carbohydrate	2 g
Fiber	0 g
Protein	1 g
Total fat	0 g
Saturated fat	0 g
Cholesterol	1 mg
Sodium	82 mg

1½ cups	buttermilk	375 mL
1 tbsp	chopped fresh parsley	15 mL
1 tbsp	finely chopped onion (see tip, at left)	15 mL
½ tsp	garlic powder	2 mL
½ tsp	dried thyme	2 mL
½ tsp	dried tarragon	2 mL
¼ tsp	salt	1 mL
¼ tsp	freshly ground black pepper	1 mL
1 tsp	white vinegar	5 mL
¼ tsp	Worcestershire sauce	1 mL

1. In a jar, combine buttermilk, parsley, onion, garlic powder, thyme, tarragon, salt and pepper. Cover tightly and shake briskly.

2. Add vinegar and Worcestershire sauce; shake again. Refrigerate for at least 2 hours to blend the flavors. Shake well before using. Store in the refrigerator for up to 4 weeks.

America's Exchanges	
1	Free Food

Canada's Choices	
1	Extra

Slim 'n' Trim Italian Dressing

The combination of herbs and spices in this refreshing dressing adds punch to crisp greens and is terrific for marinating vegetables such as cucumbers, carrots and bell peppers.

Kitchen Tips

In place of store-bought chicken broth, you can use homemade Chicken Stock (page 78). You may need to add up to 1/8 tsp (0.5 mL) salt to bring out the flavors of the dressing. Taste the finished dressing and add just enough salt to perk up the flavor.

Extra dressing can be stored in the refrigerator for up to 5 days (without the garlic clove). If the dressing gels in the refrigerator, add a few drops of boiling water and shake or whisk to liquefy.

1	small clove garlic	1
1/3 cup	reduced-sodium chicken broth	75 mL
1 tbsp	vegetable oil	15 mL
1 tbsp	hot water	15 mL
1 tbsp	freshly squeezed lemon juice	15 mL
1 tbsp	cider vinegar or wine vinegar	15 mL
Pinch	freshly ground black pepper	Pinch
Pinch	curry powder	Pinch
Pinch	dried thyme	Pinch
Pinch	dried oregano	Pinch
Pinch	dried parsley	Pinch

1. In a jar, combine garlic, broth, oil, hot water, lemon juice, vinegar, pepper, curry powder, thyme, oregano and parsley. Cover tightly and shake briskly. Refrigerate for at least 30 minutes to blend the flavors. Remove garlic. Shake well before using.

Nutrients per Serving	
Calories	34
Carbohydrate	1 g
Fiber	0 g
Protein	0 g
Total fat	3 g
Saturated fat	0 g
Cholesterol	0 mg
Sodium	46 mg

America's Exchanges	
1/2	Fat

Canada's Choices	
1/2	Fat

Raspberry Vinaigrette

||||||||||||||||||||||||||||||||||||||||||||||||||||||||||||||||||||||||||||||||||||||||||||||||||||||||||||||||||||||||||

**Makes ⅔ cup
(150 mL)**
Serving size: 1 tbsp
(15 mL)

When raspberries are in
season, freeze them so
you have them on hand
to prepare this light,
refreshing salad dressing
any time of the year.

Kitchen Tips
To make sure the raspberry
flavor is not overpowered,
use a mild-flavored
vegetable oil, such as canola,
grapeseed or sunflower.

Serve over dark green
lettuce, such as spinach,
romaine or leaf lettuce. For
an added punch, sprinkle the
salad with fresh raspberries.

Variation
Stir in 1 to 2 tsp (5 to 10 mL)
chopped fresh mint after
puréeing and straining the
vinaigrette.

Nutrients per Serving

Calories	66
Carbohydrate	2 g
Fiber	0 g
Protein	0 g
Total fat	7 g
Saturated fat	0 g
Cholesterol	0 mg
Sodium	56 mg

● **Blender**

⅔ cup	fresh or frozen raspberries (thawed if frozen)	150 mL
¼ tsp	salt	1 mL
¼ tsp	freshly ground black pepper	1 mL
⅓ cup	vegetable oil	75 mL
4 tsp	red wine vinegar	20 mL
2 tsp	liquid honey	10 mL
¼ tsp	Dijon or dry mustard	1 mL

1. In blender, combine raspberries, salt, pepper, oil, vinegar, honey and mustard; purée until smooth. If desired, strain through a fine-mesh sieve to remove any seeds. Use immediately or transfer to an airtight container and refrigerate for up to 2 days.

America's Exchanges	
1	Fat

Canada's Choices	
1½	Fat

All-Purpose Balsamic Vinaigrette

||||||||||||||||||||||||||||||||||||||||||||||||||||||||||||||||||||||||||||||||||||||||||||||||||||||||||||||||||

6 tbsp	balsamic vinegar	90 mL
2 tsp	liquid honey (see tip, at left)	10 mL
1 tsp	Dijon mustard	5 mL
¼ cup	extra virgin olive oil	60 mL
	Freshly ground black pepper	
¼ tsp	salt (or less)	1 mL

Makes about
²/₃ cup (150 mL)
Serving size: 1 tbsp
(15 mL)

Just like wine, balsamic vinegar is available in a wide range of prices. Purchase the best bottle you can for this vinaigrette.

Kitchen Tips

Balsamic vinegars vary in sweetness. If you have a sweet one, add 1 tsp (5 mL) honey to start, then add oil. Taste and gradually add up to 1 tsp (5 mL) more honey, if desired.

This vinaigrette is lovely on arugula, Boston lettuce, romaine or mixed salad greens. Or try it on a pasta salad or a grilled chicken or beef salad.

Variation

Garlic Balsamic Vinaigrette: Add 1 pressed or finely minced clove of garlic.

1. In a small bowl or measuring cup, whisk together vinegar, honey and mustard. Gradually whisk in oil until well blended. Season to taste with pepper and up to ¼ tsp (1 mL) salt. Use immediately or transfer to an airtight container and refrigerate for up to 1 week. Let warm to room temperature and shake or whisk well before serving.

Nutrients per Serving

Calories	55
Carbohydrate	3 g
Fiber	0 g
Protein	0 g
Total fat	5 g
Saturated fat	1 g
Cholesterol	0 mg
Sodium	67 mg

America's Exchanges	
1	Fat

Canada's Choices	
1	Fat

Tomato French Dressing

Tomato paste makes a rich-tasting base for this delicious dressing. Vary the herb combinations to suit your own palate.

Kitchen Tips

Extra tomato paste can be divided into small portions on squares of plastic wrap, wrapped tightly and frozen in a freezer bag or airtight container for up to 6 months.

If you enjoy the flavor of olive oil, use extra virgin in this recipe. For a milder flavor, use a light olive oil or canola oil instead.

2 tsp	granulated sugar	10 mL
1 tsp	dried cilantro or parsley	5 mL
1 tsp	dried basil	5 mL
½ tsp	dry mustard	2 mL
¼ tsp	garlic powder	1 mL
⅛ tsp	salt	0.5 mL
Pinch	freshly ground black pepper	Pinch
3 tbsp	no-salt-added tomato paste	45 mL
2 tbsp	white wine vinegar	30 mL
2 tbsp	olive oil	30 mL
¼ tsp	Worcestershire sauce	1 mL

1. In a jar, combine sugar, cilantro, basil, mustard, garlic powder, salt, pepper, tomato paste, vinegar, oil, Worcestershire sauce and ½ cup (125 mL) water. Cover tightly and shake briskly. Refrigerate for at least 2 hours to blend the flavors. Store in the refrigerator for up to 4 weeks. Let stand at room temperature for 15 minutes and shake well before using.

Nutrients per Serving	
Calories	42
Carbohydrate	3 g
Fiber	0 g
Protein	0 g
Total fat	3 g
Saturated fat	0 g
Cholesterol	0 mg
Sodium	45 mg

America's Exchanges	
½	Fat

Canada's Choices	
½	Fat

Thousand Island Dressing

‖‖

**Makes about
1 cup (250 mL)**
Serving size: 2 tbsp
(30 mL)

Not only is this a tangy
dressing for greens,
but it also makes a
succulent sauce for hot
or cold vegetables, fish
and meat. Or try it as a
sandwich spread in place
of butter or mayonnaise.

½ cup	Tomato French Dressing (see recipe, page 129)	125 mL
¼ cup	low-fat plain yogurt	60 mL
1 tbsp	chopped pickle relish	15 mL
1 tbsp	chopped drained capers	15 mL

1. In a bowl, whisk together dressing, yogurt, relish
   and capers. Use immediately or store in an airtight
   container in the refrigerator for up to 1 week.

Nutrients per Serving

Calories	31
Carbohydrate	3 g
Fiber	0 g
Protein	1 g
Total fat	2 g
Saturated fat	0 g
Cholesterol	0 mg
Sodium	123 mg

America's Exchanges	
½	Fat

Canada's Choices	
½	Fat

Tofu Mayonnaise

||||||||||||||||||||||||||||||||||||||||||||||||||||||||||||||||||||||||||||||||||||||||||||||||||||||||||||||||||||||||||||||||

**Makes 1½ cups
(375 mL)**
Serving size: 2 tbsp
(30 mL)

Enjoy the richness of mayonnaise with a fraction of the calories in our smooth, mayonnaise-like dressing made with tofu as the base.

Nutrition Tips

Most vinegars contain negligible amounts of sodium. When choosing rice vinegar, however, be sure to buy the natural (sometimes called "unseasoned") variety. Avoid seasoned rice vinegar, which can contain significant amounts of sodium.

Commercial salad dressings and condiments are often high in sodium. Two tablespoons (30 mL) of this dressing contains less than half the sodium found in a typical commercial salad dressing.

Nutrients per Serving	
Calories	14
Carbohydrate	1 g
Fiber	0 g
Protein	1 g
Total fat	1 g
Saturated fat	0 g
Cholesterol	0 mg
Sodium	125 mg

● **Blender or food processor**

1 cup	mashed drained tofu	250 mL
1 tsp	dried parsley	5 mL
½ tsp	garlic powder	2 mL
½ tsp	salt	2 mL
2 tbsp	white vinegar or natural rice vinegar	30 mL
1 tsp	Dijon mustard	5 mL
1 tsp	sodium-reduced soy sauce	5 mL

1. In blender, combine tofu, parsley, garlic powder, salt, vinegar, mustard and soy sauce. Process for about 1 minute or until smooth. Store in an airtight container in the refrigerator for up to 4 weeks.

America's Exchanges	
1	Free Food

Canada's Choices	
1	Extra

Supreme Salad Seasoning

||||||||||||||||||||||||||||||||||||||||||||||||||||||||||||||||||||||||||||||||||||||||||||||||||||||||||||||||||||||||||

Just a pinch or two
of this seasoning mix
sprinkled on green salads
gives them added zest.
It can also be used to
season other dishes,
such as stews, casseroles,
soups and sauces.

Kitchen Tip

Toasting sesame seeds
brings out their nutty flavor.
Toast seeds in a small
dry skillet over medium
heat, stirring constantly,
for 3 to 4 minutes or until
golden brown and fragrant.
Immediately transfer to a
small bowl and let cool.

$1/3$ cup	freshly grated Parmesan cheese	75 mL
$1/4$ cup	sesame seeds, toasted (see tip, at left)	60 mL
2 tbsp	paprika	30 mL
1 tbsp	poppy seeds	15 mL
2 tsp	dried parsley	10 mL
1 tsp	dried onion flakes	5 mL
1 tsp	garlic powder	5 mL
1 tsp	celery seeds	5 mL
$1/2$ tsp	freshly ground black pepper	2 mL
$1/4$ tsp	salt	1 mL

1. In a jar, combine Parmesan, sesame seeds, paprika, poppy seeds, parsley, onion flakes, garlic powder, celery seeds, pepper and salt. Cover tightly and shake until well mixed. Store in the refrigerator for up to 4 months.

Nutrients per Serving	
Calories	20
Carbohydrate	1 g
Fiber	0 g
Protein	1 g
Total fat	1 g
Saturated fat	0 g
Cholesterol	1 mg
Sodium	46 mg

America's Exchanges	
1	Free Food

Canada's Choices	
1	Extra

Vegetables

Asparagus Rice Pilaf

This elegant rice dish makes a wonderful side dish for chicken, pork or beef.

Kitchen Tip

In place of the homemade chicken stock, you can use 1½ cups (375 mL) store-bought reduced-sodium chicken broth plus 1 cup (250 mL) water. If you do this, omit the salt in the recipe.

Nutrition Tip

Homemade stock gives this pilaf terrific flavor without added salt. Even reduced-sodium broth can contribute a lot of sodium to a recipe: 1 cup (250 mL) of commercial ready-to-use reduced-sodium broth contains about ¼ tsp (1 mL) of salt, equivalent to 600 mg of sodium.

8 oz	asparagus	250 g
1 tbsp	margarine or butter	15 mL
1	small onion, chopped	1
1 cup	long-grain white rice	250 mL
2½ cups	hot Chicken Stock (see recipe, page 78)	625 mL
2 tbsp	freshly grated Parmesan cheese, divided	30 mL
	Freshly ground black pepper	
¼ tsp	salt (or less)	1 mL

1. Snap off butt ends of asparagus and cut stems into ½-inch (1 cm) pieces. Set tips aside.

2. In a saucepan, melt margarine over medium heat. Sauté asparagus stems and onion for 5 minutes or until onion is softened.

3. Stir in rice and stock; bring to a boil. Reduce heat to low, cover and simmer for 10 minutes. Add asparagus tips and simmer for 5 minutes. Stir in 1 tbsp (15 mL) of the Parmesan. Season to taste with pepper and up to ¼ tsp (1 mL) salt. Cover and let stand for 5 minutes. Fluff with a fork and sprinkle with the remaining Parmesan.

Nutrients per Serving

Calories	155
Carbohydrate	26 g
Fiber	1 g
Protein	6 g
Total fat	3 g
Saturated fat	1 g
Cholesterol	2 mg
Sodium	169 mg

America's Exchanges	
2	Starches
½	Fat

Canada's Choices	
1½	Carbohydrates
½	Fat

Green Beans with Water Chestnuts

||||||||||||||||||||||||||||||||||||||||||||||||||||||||||||||||||||||||||||||||||||||||||||||||||||||||

Tender-crisp green beans with a touch of Asian flair are sure to brighten up any weekday meal.

Nutrition Tips

If using store-bought chicken broth, look for one with the lowest amount of sodium. As you compare nutrition labels, keep in mind that some broths are ready-to-use, while some are condensed and need to be diluted with an equal amount of water. Make sure you're comparing the same amount of the same type of product.

Water chestnuts are usually, but not always, canned without salt. Be sure to choose a brand that does not contain salt.

Variation

Substitute trimmed thin asparagus spears for the green beans.

Nutrients per Serving	
Calories	37
Carbohydrate	8 g
Fiber	2 g
Protein	2 g
Total fat	0 g
Saturated fat	0 g
Cholesterol	0 mg
Sodium	117 mg

1	small clove garlic, finely chopped	1
1 tsp	finely chopped gingerroot	5 mL
½ cup	reduced-sodium chicken broth or Chicken Stock (see recipe, page 78)	125 mL
12 oz	green beans, cut in half lengthwise	375 g
⅓ cup	thinly sliced drained canned water chestnuts	75 mL
1 tsp	reduced-sodium soy sauce	5 mL
	Freshly ground black pepper	

1. In a skillet, combine garlic, ginger and broth; bring to a boil over medium-high heat. Add green beans and water chestnuts. Sprinkle with soy sauce. Cover tightly and steam for 7 to 8 minutes or until vegetables are tender-crisp. If moisture has not evaporated, uncover, increase heat and shake pan to evaporate remaining liquid. Season to taste with pepper. Serve hot.

America's Exchanges	
1	Vegetable

Canada's Choices	
1	Extra

Orangey Harvard Beets

||||||||||||||||||||||||||||||||||||||||||||||||||||||||||||||||||||||||||||||||||||||||||||||||||

Beets always brighten up the dinner plate, and this side dish has an intriguing sweet-sour taste with a hint of orange.

Kitchen Tip

To grate the orange zest, use the fine side of a box cheese grater or a Microplane-style grater. If you use a five-hole zester, chop the zest into smaller pieces with a knife.

1	can (14 oz/398 mL) diced or sliced beets, with juice	1
1 tsp	grated orange zest	5 mL
2 tsp	white vinegar	10 mL
1 tsp	cornstarch	5 mL
1 tbsp	freshly squeezed orange juice	15 mL

1. In a saucepan, combine beets with juice, orange zest and vinegar; bring to a boil over medium-high heat.

2. In a small bowl, whisk together cornstarch and orange juice to make a smooth paste. Stir into beets and cook, stirring, for about 2 minutes or until liquid thickens and coats beets with a smooth, thin sauce.

Nutrients per Serving

Calories	36
Carbohydrate	9 g
Fiber	1 g
Protein	1 g
Total fat	0 g
Saturated fat	0 g
Cholesterol	0 mg
Sodium	148 mg

America's Exchanges	
1	Vegetable

Canada's Choices	
1	Extra

Sautéed Broccoli and Red Peppers

Jam-packed with nutrients, this yummy vegetable side dish is perfect with chicken, pork chops or broiled salmon. For a vegetarian main dish, prepare the variation with chickpeas (below).

Kitchen Tip

Do not discard the broccoli stalks — they have plenty of flavor and crunch. Peel away the thick outer layer and shred the stalks with a food processor or on the coarse side of a box grater. Add to a cabbage slaw or vegetable soup, or sprinkle into a mixed salad.

Variation

Add 1 cup (250 mL) drained rinsed cooked or canned chickpeas and sauté for 1 minute before adding the oregano and vinegar.

Nutrients per Serving	
Calories	69
Carbohydrate	8 g
Fiber	2 g
Protein	2 g
Total fat	4 g
Saturated fat	1 g
Cholesterol	0 mg
Sodium	170 mg

1 tbsp	olive oil	15 mL
1	red onion, chopped	1
1	clove garlic, minced	1
1/4 tsp	salt	1 mL
	Freshly ground black pepper	
3 cups	small broccoli florets	750 mL
1	red bell pepper, chopped	1
1/2 tsp	dried oregano	2 mL
2 tbsp	red wine vinegar	30 mL

1. In a large nonstick skillet, heat oil over medium-high heat. Sauté onion, garlic, salt and black pepper to taste for about 4 minutes or until onion is softened.

2. Stir in broccoli and red pepper; sauté for 4 to 5 minutes or until tender-crisp. Stir in oregano and vinegar; sauté for 1 minute.

America's Exchanges	
2	Vegetables
1/2	Fat

Canada's Choices	
1	Fat

Lubeck Cabbage

|||||||||||||||||||||||||||||||||||||||||||||||||||||||||||||||||||||||||||||||||||||||||||||||||||||||||||||||

Makes 4 servings
Serving size: ⅔ cup
(150 mL)

This German side dish can be cooked on the stovetop or in the oven (see variation, below). The mild, mellow flavor will surprise and delight your taste buds. For variety, use red cabbage.

Nutrition Tip

If using store-bought chicken broth, look for one with the lowest amount of sodium. As you compare nutrition labels, keep in mind that some broths are ready-to-use, while some are condensed and need to be diluted with an equal amount of water. Make sure you're comparing the same amount of the same type of product.

Variation

To cook this dish in the oven, combine the ingredients in an 8-cup (2 L) casserole dish. Cover and bake in a 325°F (160°C) oven for 1½ to 2 hours or until cabbage is tender

Nutrients per Serving	
Calories	33
Carbohydrate	7 g
Fiber	2 g
Protein	1 g
Total fat	0 g
Saturated fat	0 g
Cholesterol	0 mg
Sodium	54 mg

⅓ cup	reduced-sodium chicken broth or Chicken Stock (see recipe, page 78)	75 mL
⅓ cup	dry white wine	75 mL
2	whole allspice berries	2
½ tsp	cumin or caraway seeds (optional)	2 mL
1	small sweet onion, such as Spanish, Vidalia or other mild onion, thinly sliced	1
½	apple, peeled and thinly sliced	½
4 cups	shredded cabbage	1 L

1. In a heavy saucepan, combine broth, wine, allspice and cumin seeds (if using). Stir in onion, apple and cabbage; bring to a boil over high heat. Reduce heat to low, cover tightly and simmer for 1½ to 2 hours or until cabbage is tender. If moisture has not evaporated, uncover, increase heat and shake pan to evaporate remaining liquid.

America's Exchanges	
1	Vegetable

Canada's Choices	
1	Extra

Herbed Cauliflower Gratin

Makes 4 servings

Flavorful and easy to prepare, this gratin is special enough for entertaining. When you use flavor-packed aged Cheddar cheese, you need only a small amount.

Kitchen Tip

Look for precut cauliflower in the produce section of the grocery store. It's a great time saver, and you can often buy just the amount you need.

Variations

In place of Cheddar, try Swiss cheese.

Use 1 tsp (5 mL) chopped fresh basil or thyme in place of dried.

Try a combination of broccoli and cauliflower.

In place of cauliflower, use 4 cups (1 L) frozen chunky mixed vegetables, thawed, and omit step 1.

Nutrients per Serving	
Calories	148
Carbohydrate	14 g
Fiber	2 g
Protein	9 g
Total fat	7 g
Saturated fat	4 g
Cholesterol	21 mg
Sodium	309 mg

- Preheat oven to 375°F (190°C)
- 6-cup (1.5 L) shallow casserole dish, greased

4 cups	cauliflower florets	1 L
1¼ cups	2% milk	300 mL
2 tbsp	all-purpose flour	30 mL
½ tsp	dry mustard	2 mL
½ tsp	dried basil or thyme	2 mL
¼ tsp	salt	1 mL
¼ tsp	freshly ground black pepper	1 mL
½ cup	shredded aged (old) Cheddar cheese, divided	125 mL
½ cup	fresh whole wheat bread crumbs	125 mL
1 tbsp	chopped fresh parsley (optional)	15 mL

1. In a medium saucepan of boiling water, cook cauliflower for 3 to 4 minutes or until just tender; drain and set aside.

2. In the same saucepan, whisk milk into flour until blended; whisk in mustard, basil, salt and pepper. Cook over medium-high heat, whisking constantly, for 3 to 5 minutes or until boiling and thickened. Remove from heat and stir in all but 2 tbsp (30 mL) of the cheese. Gently stir in cauliflower. Pour evenly into prepared casserole dish.

3. In a small bowl, combine the remaining cheese, bread crumbs and parsley (if using). Sprinkle evenly over cauliflower mixture.

4. Bake in preheated oven for 20 minutes or until sauce is bubbling and topping is golden brown. Let stand for 5 minutes.

America's Exchanges	
½	Starch
1	Vegetable
1	Lean Meat
½	Fat

Canada's Choices	
½	Carbohydrate
1	Meat & Alternatives
1	Fat

Thyme-Scented Carrots

||||||||||||||||||||||||||||||||||||||||||||||||||||||||||||||||||||||||||||||||||||||||||||||||||||

Makes 4 servings
Serving size: 3/4 cup
(175 mL)

These carrots are simple enough to prepare for everyday meals, yet they are sure to impress dinner guests, too.

Kitchen Tips

Leave packaged carrots in their bags and refrigerate them in the vegetable crisper. To avoid bitter carrots, keep them in a separate compartment from apples.

The secret to even cooking is to cut the carrots into pieces of the same size.

Variation

Substitute 3 sprigs of fresh thyme for the dried thyme and finely chopped shallots for the onion. Discard thyme sprigs before serving. Garnish each serving with a fresh thyme sprig, if desired.

3½ cups	thinly sliced carrots (sliced on the diagonal)	875 mL
¼ cup	finely chopped onion	60 mL
1 tbsp	butter or margarine	15 mL
½ tsp	dried thyme	2 mL
¼ tsp	salt	1 mL
	Freshly ground black pepper	

1. In a large nonstick skillet, combine carrots, onion, butter, thyme, salt, pepper to taste and ½ cup (125 mL) water. Bring to a boil over medium-high heat. Reduce heat and boil gently, stirring occasionally, for 7 to 9 minutes or until carrots are tender-crisp and water has evaporated.

Nutrients per Serving	
Calories	69
Carbohydrate	10 g
Fiber	3 g
Protein	1 g
Total fat	3 g
Saturated fat	2 g
Cholesterol	8 mg
Sodium	232 mg

America's Exchanges	
2	Vegetables
½	Fat

Canada's Choices	
½	Fat

Crispy Baked Parsnips

Crispy on the outside, soft and flavorful inside, these parsnips offer a change of pace from everyday vegetables.

- **Preheat oven to 425°F (220°C)**
- **Steamer basket**
- **Rimmed baking sheet, lightly greased**

1 lb	parsnips (about 4 medium), peeled and cut into $2\frac{1}{2}$-inch (6 cm) sticks	500 g
2 tbsp	1% milk	30 mL
1 tsp	vegetable oil	5 mL
$\frac{1}{4}$ cup	dry bread crumbs	60 mL
$\frac{1}{4}$ tsp	salt	1 mL
Pinch	freshly ground black pepper	Pinch

1. Place parsnips in a steamer basket set in a pot of boiling water over medium-high heat. Cover and steam for about 10 minutes or until tender-crisp. Transfer parsnips to a plate and let cool slightly.

2. In a bowl, combine milk and oil. Place bread crumbs on a plate. Dip parsnip pieces in milk mixture, then coat with bread crumbs. Season with salt and pepper. Spread out on prepared baking sheet.

3. Bake in preheated oven for 20 minutes or until crisp and light brown.

Nutrients per Serving	
Calories	112
Carbohydrate	22 g
Fiber	3 g
Protein	2 g
Total fat	2 g
Saturated fat	0 g
Cholesterol	1 mg
Sodium	209 mg

America's Exchanges	
$1\frac{1}{2}$	Starches

Canada's Choices	
1	Carbohydrate
$\frac{1}{2}$	Fat

Confetti Peas

|||||||||||||||||||||||||||||||||||||||||||||||||||||||||||||||||||||||||||||||||||||||||||||||||||||||||||||||||

Makes 4 servings
Serving size: ½ cup
(125 mL)

Prepare this dish as a colorful, flavorful change from plain buttered peas. You'll be pleasantly surprised by the flavor, seeing as not even a speck of butter is added.

Nutrition Tip

If using store-bought chicken broth, look for one with the lowest amount of sodium. As you compare nutrition labels, keep in mind that some broths are ready-to-use, while some are condensed and need to be diluted with an equal amount of water. Make sure you're comparing the same amount of the same type of product.

½ cup	chopped red bell pepper	125 mL
½ cup	chopped celery	125 mL
⅓ cup	chopped onion	75 mL
½ cup	reduced-sodium chicken broth or Chicken Stock (see recipe, page 78), divided	125 mL
1½ cups	frozen green peas	375 mL
	Freshly ground black pepper	
⅛ tsp	salt (or less)	0.5 mL

1. In a skillet, over medium heat, combine red pepper, celery, onion and ⅓ cup (75 mL) of the broth. Cook, stirring, for 3 minutes.

2. Add peas and the remaining stock. Cook, stirring, for 5 to 6 minutes or until vegetables are tender and liquid has evaporated. Season to taste with pepper and up to ⅛ tsp (0.5 mL) salt.

Nutrients per Serving	
Calories	55
Carbohydrate	10 g
Fiber	3 g
Protein	4 g
Total fat	0 g
Saturated fat	0 g
Cholesterol	0 mg
Sodium	193 mg

America's Exchanges	
½	Starch

Canada's Choices	
1	Extra

Scalloped Tomatoes

This easy vegetable side dish takes just a few minutes to prepare.

1	can (19 oz/540 mL) no-salt-added tomatoes, with juice	1
$1/4$ cup	chopped onion	60 mL
$1/4$ cup	chopped green or red bell pepper	60 mL
2 tbsp	chopped fresh parsley	30 mL
$1/2$ cup	Seasoned Bread Crumbs (see recipe, page 72)	125 mL
$1/4$ tsp	salt (or less)	1 mL
	Freshly ground black pepper	

1. Drain juice from tomatoes into a skillet; reserve tomatoes. Add onion, green pepper and parsley to skillet. Boil, stirring, over medium heat for about 4 minutes or until vegetables are tender and most of the liquid has evaporated.

2. Reserve 1 tbsp (15 mL) bread crumbs. Stir the remaining bread crumbs and the reserved tomatoes into the skillet. Cover and boil for about 8 minutes or until heated through. Stir in up to $1/4$ tsp (1 mL) salt and season to taste with pepper. Serve sprinkled with the reserved bread crumbs.

Nutrients per Serving	
Calories	73
Carbohydrate	14 g
Fiber	2 g
Protein	3 g
Total fat	1 g
Saturated fat	0 g
Cholesterol	1 mg
Sodium	251 mg

America's Exchanges	
$1/2$	Starch
1	Vegetable

Canada's Choices	
$1/2$	Carbohydrate

Lentil-Stuffed Tomatoes

||||||||||||||||||||||||||||||||||||||||||||||||||||||||||||||||||||||||||||||||||||||||||||||||||||||||||||||||

Makes 4 servings

Prepare these tomatoes to serve as a side dish with oven-cooked meals. They can be stuffed up to 4 hours in advance, refrigerated, then heated (allow a longer heating time in this case).

Nutrition Tip

The amount of salt in canned legumes varies from brand to brand, so be sure to check the sodium value in the Nutrition Facts table. Draining and rinsing them before use removes about 50% of the sodium.

- **Preheat oven to 400°F (200°C)**
- **6- or 12-cup muffin pan**

4	firm tomatoes	4
1/4 cup	finely chopped celery	60 mL
1 tbsp	finely chopped onion	15 mL
1 tbsp	finely chopped green bell pepper	15 mL
1/2 tsp	curry powder	2 mL
1 cup	rinsed drained canned brown lentils	250 mL
1 tbsp	freshly grated Parmesan cheese	15 mL

1. Core tomatoes and cut a thin slice from the top of each. Scoop pulp and juice into a skillet and mash pulp. Place tomato shells cut side down on a paper towel to drain.

2. Add celery, onion, green pepper and curry powder to tomato pulp and juice. Cook, stirring, over medium heat for about 5 minutes or until vegetables are tender. Add lentils and cook, stirring, until mixture is thickened.

3. Spoon lentil mixture into tomato shells. Sprinkle with Parmesan. Place stuffed tomatoes in 4 muffin cups. Set muffin pan on a baking sheet.

4. Bake in preheated oven for 10 minutes or until heated through.

Nutrients per Serving	
Calories	86
Carbohydrate	15 g
Fiber	4 g
Protein	6 g
Total fat	1 g
Saturated fat	0 g
Cholesterol	1 mg
Sodium	221 mg

America's Exchanges	
1/2	Starch
1	Vegetable

Canada's Choices	
1/2	Carbohydrate
1/2	Meat & Alternatives

Crunchy Tuna Salad in Pepper Cups (page 122)

Lentil-Stuffed Tomatoes (page 144)

Lemon Almond
Sautéed Greens (page 146)

Beef Steak with Herb Garnish (page 155)

Crispy Baked Fish (page 175)

Caribbean Stewed
Chicken (page 169)

Curried Pork and Fruit (page 198)

Chicken and Snow Pea Stir-Fry (page 204)

Zucchini with Tomato Sauce

Makes 4 servings

Zucchini cooks very quickly and tastes best when it still has some crunch, so do not overcook it. Serve this colorful dish as an accompaniment to roast meat or poultry.

Kitchen Tip

Warm the baking dish in a 200°F (100°C) oven for 5 to 10 minutes, or fill it with hot water and let stand for 15 minutes; drain well and pat dry before adding the zucchini to make sure the zucchini doesn't cool down too much.

Nutrition Tip

Part-skim mozzarella contains one-third less fat than regular mozzarella. Lower-fat versions of many cheeses are available. Typically, they contain up to 7 g of fat per oz (30 g), compared with 10 g of fat for the same amount of regular cheese.

- Preheat broiler
- 8-inch (20 cm) square baking dish, warmed

2 tsp	margarine or butter	10 mL
1	small clove garlic, finely chopped	1
2 tbsp	chopped green onion	30 mL
1 tbsp	all-purpose flour	15 mL
¼ tsp	salt	1 mL
Pinch	freshly ground black pepper	Pinch
¾ cup	reduced-sodium tomato juice	175 mL
4	small zucchini, trimmed and cut in half lengthwise	4
1 cup	shredded part-skim mozzarella cheese	250 mL

1. In a small saucepan, melt margarine over medium heat. Sauté garlic and green onion until softened. Stir in flour, salt and pepper until smooth. Gradually stir in tomato juice and bring to a boil; boil, stirring, for 3 to 4 minutes or until thickened.

2. Meanwhile, in a pot of boiling water, cook zucchini for about 2 minutes or until tender-crisp. Drain and place cut side up in baking dish. Drizzle tomato sauce over zucchini, then sprinkle with mozzarella.

3. Broil for about 5 minutes or until cheese is melted.

Nutrients per Serving

Calories	134
Carbohydrate	9 g
Fiber	2 g
Protein	10 g
Total fat	7 g
Saturated fat	4 g
Cholesterol	19 mg
Sodium	379 mg

America's Exchanges	
1	Vegetable
1	Lean Meat
1	Fat

Canada's Choices	
1	Meat & Alternatives
1	Fat
1	Extra

Lemon Almond Sautéed Greens

|||||||||||||||||||||||||||||||||||||||||||||||||||||||||||||||||||||||||||||||||||||||||||||||||||||||||||||||||

Perk up your meal and boost your vitamin C and fiber with this quick, tasty, lemon-scented side dish. It's sure to become a favorite!

Kitchen Tips
Wash greens well in a colander under cold running water. Drain, leaving the water clinging to the leaves. There's no need to spin or pat them dry.

One medium bunch of Swiss chard or an 8-oz (250 g) package of fresh spinach is just the right amount for this recipe. Avoid baby spinach, as it's too tender and cooks too quickly — save it for salads.

1 tbsp	vegetable oil	15 mL
1	clove garlic, minced	1
6 cups	lightly packed chopped Swiss chard (or 8 cups/2 L trimmed spinach)	1.5 L
1 cup	shredded cabbage	250 mL
1 tsp	grated lemon zest	5 mL
¼ tsp	salt	1 mL
¼ tsp	freshly ground black pepper	1 mL
1½ tsp	freshly squeezed lemon juice	7 mL
2 tbsp	sliced almonds, toasted (see tip, page 103)	30 mL

1. In a large, deep skillet or wok, heat oil over medium-high heat. Sauté garlic for 30 seconds or until fragrant. Add Swiss chard, cabbage, lemon zest, salt and pepper; sauté for about 2 minutes or until chard is slightly wilted.

2. Stir in 1 tbsp (15 mL) water, cover and boil, stirring occasionally, for about 2 minutes or until vegetables are just tender.

3. Stir in lemon juice and sauté, uncovered, for 1 to 2 minutes or until vegetables are tender and most of the water has evaporated. Serve sprinkled with almonds.

Nutrients per Serving

Calories	65
Carbohydrate	4 g
Fiber	2 g
Protein	2 g
Total fat	5 g
Saturated fat	0 g
Cholesterol	0 mg
Sodium	249 mg

America's Exchanges

1	Vegetable
1	Fat

Canada's Choices

1	Fat

Popeye Pie

Makes 6 servings

Even finicky eaters will decide they like spinach when you serve this pie. Like other dark green leafy vegetables, spinach is a valuable source of folate, iron and potassium (bet Popeye didn't know that!).

Kitchen Tip

You can use a package of frozen chopped spinach instead of fresh, if you prefer. Skip step 1 and simply thaw the spinach and press out excess liquid.

- **Preheat oven to 375°F (190°C)**
- **9-inch (23 cm) glass pie plate, well greased**

1	package (8 oz/250 g) spinach, trimmed	1
1/3 cup	finely chopped celery	75 mL
1/4 cup	finely chopped onion	60 mL
2 tbsp	freshly grated Parmesan cheese	30 mL
1/2 tsp	ground nutmeg	2 mL
1/4 tsp	salt	1 mL
2	eggs, well beaten	2
1 cup	2% milk	250 mL

1. Rinse spinach and shake off excess water. Place in a heavy saucepan over low heat, cover and steam for 5 to 7 minutes or until wilted. Drain, chop and press out excess liquid.

2. In a large bowl, combine celery, onion, Parmesan, nutmeg, salt, eggs and milk. Fold in spinach. Pour into prepared pie plate.

3. Bake in preheated oven for 45 minutes or until a tester inserted in the center comes out clean. Cut into wedges and serve warm.

Nutrients per Serving

Calories	75
Carbohydrate	5 g
Fiber	1 g
Protein	5 g
Total fat	4 g
Saturated fat	2 g
Cholesterol	67 mg
Sodium	191 mg

America's Exchanges	
1	Vegetable
1	Lean Meat

Canada's Choices	
1	Meat & Alternatives
1	Extra

Skinny Scalloped Potatoes

Makes 6 servings
Serving size: ¾ cup
(175 mL)

Potatoes have more charm, more flavor and more dietary fiber when their skins are left on.

- **Preheat oven to 350°F (180°C)**
- **6-cup (1.5 L) shallow casserole dish, lightly greased**

2 cups	Basic White Sauce (see recipe, page 58)	500 mL
4	potatoes, sliced	4
2	onions, sliced	2

1. Spread a thin layer of sauce in prepared casserole dish. Arrange half the potatoes on top, overlapping as necessary. Top with half the onions. Spread half the remaining sauce evenly over top. Repeat with the remaining potatoes, onions and sauce.

2. Cover and bake in preheated oven for 40 minutes. Uncover and bake for about 20 minutes or until potatoes are tender and top is browned.

Nutrients per Serving	
Calories	191
Carbohydrate	35 g
Fiber	3 g
Protein	6 g
Total fat	3 g
Saturated fat	1 g
Cholesterol	7 mg
Sodium	236 mg

America's Exchanges	
2	Starches
1	Vegetable
½	Fat

Canada's Choices	
2	Carbohydrates
½	Fat

Baked Stuffed Potatoes

|||||||||||||||||||||||||||||||||||||||||||||||||||||||||||||||||||||||||||||||||||||||||||||||||||||||||||||||||||||||||||||||||||

Baked potatoes are always a favorite, and you'll love them even more with a cheese and herb stuffing.

Kitchen Tips
The skins will be softer if you wrap the potatoes in foil before baking.

Prepare through step 2 up to 1 day in advance and store, covered, in the refrigerator. Allow a slightly longer reheating time.

Variation
Substitute an equal amount of chopped fresh chives or dill pickle for the parsley.

● **Preheat oven to 400°F (200°C)**

4	small baking potatoes (about 1 lb/500 g)	4
½ cup	2% cottage cheese	125 mL
2 tbsp	chopped fresh parsley	30 mL
2 tbsp	freshly grated Parmesan cheese	30 mL
	Paprika (optional)	

1. Prick potatoes with a fork. Wrap individually in foil, if desired (see tip, at left). Bake in preheated oven for 35 minutes or until tender. Remove from oven, leaving oven on. Unwrap potatoes, if necessary, and cut a small slice off the top of each. Scoop potato flesh into a bowl; reserve shells.

2. Mash potato with cottage cheese, ⅓ cup (75 mL) water, parsley and Parmesan until smooth. Spoon mixture back into potato shells. Place on a baking sheet and sprinkle with paprika (if using).

3. Bake for 10 to 15 minutes or until heated through.

Nutrients per Serving

Calories	122
Carbohydrate	20 g
Fiber	2 g
Protein	7 g
Total fat	2 g
Saturated fat	1 g
Cholesterol	5 mg
Sodium	169 mg

America's Exchanges	
1	Starch
1	Lean Meat

Canada's Choices	
1	Carbohydrate
½	Meat & Alternatives

Baked Sweet Potato Fries

Makes 4 servings

Baked fries are a terrific alternative to the deep-fried variety, and when they're made with sweet potatoes, you get added vitamins and fiber — and they taste great, too!

Kitchen Tip

Sweet potatoes are sometimes incorrectly labeled "yams." True yams are larger than sweet potatoes and have fewer nutrients. Be sure to pick up sweet potatoes with orange-colored flesh. Store at room temperature for up to 1 week.

- **Preheat oven to 400°F (200°C)**
- **Large baking sheet, lined with parchment paper**

1	large sweet potato (about 1 lb/500 g)	1
1 tbsp	olive oil, divided	15 mL
¼ tsp	salt	1 mL
	Freshly ground black pepper	

1. Peel sweet potato and rinse. Cut in half crosswise, then cut lengthwise into sticks about ½ inch (1 cm) square. Place on prepared baking sheet. Drizzle with oil and sprinkle with salt and pepper. Spread out in a single layer, leaving space between each fry.

2. Bake for about 30 minutes, flipping sweet potatoes halfway through, until browned and tender.

Nutrients per Serving

Calories	116
Carbohydrate	20 g
Fiber	3 g
Protein	2 g
Total fat	4 g
Saturated fat	1 g
Cholesterol	0 mg
Sodium	177 mg

America's Exchanges	
1	Starch
1	Fat

Canada's Choices	
1	Carbohydrate
1	Fat

Scalloped Sweet Potatoes

|||||||||||||||||||||||||||||||||||||||||||||||||||||||||||||||||||||||||||||||||||||||||||||||||||||||||||||||||||||||||||||||||||

Sweet potatoes are packed with nutrients, and you're sure to enjoy them in this easy, tasty scalloped dish.

Kitchen Tip
Many of the recipes in this book use 1% milk. Some, however, need a higher-fat milk to work properly. This recipe uses 2% milk to prevent the sauce from curdling.

Variations
Add ¼ cup (60 mL) finely chopped onion with the sweet potatoes.

After baking, sprinkle with ½ cup (125 mL) shredded Cheddar or Gouda cheese; broil until cheese is browned.

- **Preheat oven to 350°F (180°C)**
- **8-cup (2 L) shallow casserole dish, greased**

1½ cups	2% milk	375 mL
3 tbsp	all-purpose flour	45 mL
½ tsp	dried thyme or oregano	2 mL
½ tsp	dry mustard	2 mL
¼ tsp	salt	1 mL
¼ tsp	freshly ground black pepper	1 mL
1½ lbs	sweet potatoes, peeled and thinly sliced (about 4 cups/1 L)	750 g

1. In a measuring cup, whisk together milk, flour, thyme, mustard, salt and pepper.

2. Place sweet potatoes in a large pot and pour milk mixture over top. Bring just to a boil over medium-high heat, occasionally stirring gently. Reduce heat to low and simmer, stirring occasionally, for 10 minutes or until sweet potatoes are almost tender.

3. Spread evenly in prepared casserole dish. Bake in preheated oven for 20 minutes or until bubbling and sweet potatoes are tender. Let stand for 5 minutes before serving.

Nutrients per Serving

Calories	184
Carbohydrate	36 g
Fiber	4 g
Protein	6 g
Total fat	2 g
Saturated fat	1 g
Cholesterol	7 mg
Sodium	225 mg

America's Exchanges	
2½	Starches

Canada's Choices	
2	Carbohydrates
½	Fat

Mix 'n' Mash Vegetables

||||||||||||||||||||||||||||||||||||||||||||||||||||||||||||||||||||||||||||||||||||||||||||||||||||||||||||||||||

Makes 4 servings

Here is a chance to create something different out of traditional winter vegetables. Your guests will have quite a time guessing the ingredients.

Kitchen Tip

For a very smooth texture, purée the turnip mixture in a food processor or with an immersion blender. For a coarser texture, a regular potato masher will do.

Nutrition Tip

When choosing a margarine, look for a non-hydrogenated soft margarine. These are low in saturated fat and do not contain trans fat. Avoid hard margarines, which contain high amounts of saturated and trans fat.

1½ cups	chopped turnip or rutabaga	375 mL
1½ cups	chopped carrot	375 mL
1 cup	chopped peeled sweet potato	250 mL
2 tsp	margarine or butter	10 mL
¼ tsp	salt	1 mL
	Freshly ground black pepper	

1. In a pot of boiling water, cook turnip, carrot and sweet potato for about 20 minutes or until tender. Drain well and transfer to a bowl.

2. Mash or whip turnip mixture until smooth. Stir in margarine and salt. Season to taste with pepper.

Nutrients per Serving	
Calories	80
Carbohydrate	15 g
Fiber	3 g
Protein	1 g
Total fat	2 g
Saturated fat	0 g
Cholesterol	0 mg
Sodium	210 mg

America's Exchanges	
1	Starch

Canada's Choices	
½	Carbohydrate
½	Fat

Meat, Poultry and Fish

Calgary Pot Roast

|||||||||||||||||||||||||||||||||||||||||||||||||||||||||||||||||||||||||||||||||||||||||||||||||||||||||||||||||||

Makes 10 servings

Pot roast is always a hit, and it is easy to prepare. Braising it in tomato sauce guarantees tender, flavorful beef.

Nutrition Tips

Trim excess visible fat from meats and remove fat from the pan juices of cooked meats before serving.

Canned foods often contain a lot of salt. In this recipe, you can reduce the sodium per serving by about 100 mg by using no-salt-added tomato sauce.

- Preheat oven to 325°F (160°C)
- 13- by 9-inch (33 by 23 cm) glass baking dish, lightly greased

1 tsp	dry mustard	5 mL
½ tsp	salt	2 mL
3¼ lb	boneless lean beef brisket, cross rib, chuck or blade roast, trimmed	1.625 kg
½ cup	chopped onion	125 mL
1	can (7½ oz/213 mL) tomato sauce	1
2 tbsp	white wine or red wine vinegar	30 mL
½ tsp	dried thyme	2 mL
¼ tsp	freshly ground black pepper	1 mL

1. Rub dry mustard and salt all over beef. Place in prepared baking dish. Top with onion.

2. In a bowl, combine tomato sauce, vinegar, thyme and pepper; pour over roast.

3. Cover tightly and bake in preheated oven for 3 hours or until meat is fork-tender.

Nutrients per Serving

Calories	183
Carbohydrate	3 g
Fiber	0 g
Protein	23 g
Total fat	8 g
Saturated fat	3 g
Cholesterol	60 mg
Sodium	273 mg

America's Exchanges	
3	Lean Meats

Canada's Choices	
3	Meat & Alternatives

Beef Steak with Herb Garnish

||||||||||||||||||||||||||||||||||||||||||||||||||||||||||||||||||||||||||||||||||||||||||||||||||||||||||||||||||||||||

Makes 4 servings

Steak is flavorful, so you can serve it with simple accompaniments, such as a baked potato and a crisp green vegetable. Be sure to make the herb garnish early to give the flavors time to blend.

Variation

Instead of pan-frying, you can place steaks on a broiler pan and broil about 5 inches (12.5 cm) from the heat or grill on a preheated barbecue grill over medium-high heat.

1	small clove garlic, very finely chopped	1
2 tbsp	finely chopped green onion	30 mL
2 tbsp	finely chopped fresh parsley	30 mL
1/4 tsp	salt	1 mL
Pinch	freshly ground black pepper	Pinch
2 tbsp	freshly squeezed lemon juice	30 mL
2 tsp	vegetable oil	10 mL
	Vegetable cooking spray	
1 1/4 lbs	boneless beef tenderloin (filet) or sirloin steak(s), about 1 inch (2.5 cm) thick	625 g

1. In a glass bowl, combine garlic, green onion, parsley, salt, pepper, lemon juice and oil; let stand at room temperature for at least 2 hours or for up to 8 hours.

2. Heat a heavy skillet over medium-high heat and spray with cooking spray. Add steak(s) and fry, turning once, for about 5 minutes for medium-rare, or to desired doneness. Transfer to a platter and let stand for 5 minutes.

3. Spoon herb garnish over each serving.

Nutrients per Serving

Calories	224
Carbohydrate	1 g
Fiber	0 g
Protein	29 g
Total fat	10 g
Saturated fat	4 g
Cholesterol	69 mg
Sodium	209 mg

America's Exchanges	
4	Lean Meats

Canada's Choices	
4	Meat & Alternatives

Minute Steak Extraordinaire

||||||||||||||||||||||||||||||||||||||||||||||||||||||||||||||||||||||||||||||||||||||||||||||||||||||||

Minute steaks are always thin, so they cook quickly. Here, they become a superb dish for a last-minute meal when you wish to serve something fancy.

1 lb	beef minute steaks	500 g
1	clove garlic, cut in half	1
1/4 tsp	salt	1 mL
	Freshly ground black pepper	
1 tbsp	butter	15 mL
1 tbsp	brandy	15 mL
1/4 cup	finely chopped fresh parsley	60 mL
1/3 cup	dry white wine	75 mL
1/3 cup	evaporated 2% milk	75 mL

1. Rub steaks with cut surfaces of garlic clove. Sprinkle with salt and season to taste with pepper. In a heavy skillet, melt butter over medium heat. Cook steaks for about 2 minutes per side for medium, or to desired doneness. Transfer steaks to a platter and keep warm.

2. Add brandy to skillet and cook, stirring, for 1 minute, scraping up any brown bits from bottom of pan. Add parsley and wine; cook, stirring, for 2 minutes. Reduce heat and stir in milk. Return steaks to sauce, spooning sauce over meat. Serve immediately.

Nutrients per Serving	
Calories	157
Carbohydrate	2 g
Fiber	0 g
Protein	21 g
Total fat	5 g
Saturated fat	3 g
Cholesterol	50 mg
Sodium	194 mg

America's Exchanges	
3	Lean Meats

Canada's Choices	
3	Meat & Alternatives

Braised Steak and Green Pepper

||||||||||||||||||||||||||||||||||||||||||||||||||||||||||||||||||||||||||||||||||||||||||||||||||||||

Makes 6 servings

In this recipe, the green pepper should still have some crunch for maximum flavor and texture. If you are not a green pepper lover, you can use a red bell pepper or chunks of zucchini instead.

Kitchen Tip

In place of the homemade beef stock, you can use store-bought reduced-sodium beef broth. If you do this, omit the salt in the recipe.

2 tbsp	all-purpose flour	30 mL
1/2 tsp	salt	2 mL
1/4 tsp	freshly ground black pepper	1 mL
1 1/4 lbs	lean boneless beef round steak, cut into 1/4-inch (0.5 cm) strips	625 g
1 tbsp	vegetable oil	15 mL
1 3/4 cups	Beef Stock (see recipe, page 76)	425 mL
1 cup	canned no-salt-added diced tomatoes, juice drained and reserved	250 mL
1	onion, sliced	1
1	clove garlic, finely chopped	1
1	large green bell pepper, cut into strips	1
1 1/2 tsp	Worcestershire sauce	7 mL

1. In a large, shallow bowl, combine flour, salt and pepper. Dredge beef in seasoned flour, shaking off excess, and place on a clean plate. Discard any excess flour mixture.

2. In a large saucepan, heat half the oil over medium-high heat. Cook beef in batches, stirring, for 3 to 4 minutes or until browned on all sides, adding oil as needed between batches. Transfer browned beef to a plate. Drain off fat.

3. Return all beef and any accumulated juices to the saucepan. Add stock, tomato juice, onion and garlic; reduce heat to low, cover and simmer for 1 1/2 hours or until meat is fork-tender.

4. Add tomatoes, green pepper and Worcestershire sauce. Cook, stirring, for 4 to 5 minutes or until bubbling and peppers are tender-crisp.

Nutrients per Serving

Calories	172
Carbohydrate	8 g
Fiber	1 g
Protein	23 g
Total fat	5 g
Saturated fat	1 g
Cholesterol	44 mg
Sodium	264 mg

America's Exchanges	
1	Vegetable
3	Lean Meats

Canada's Choices	
3	Meat & Alternatives

Beef Burgundy

||||||||||||||||||||||||||||||||||||||||||||||||||||||||||||||||||||||||||||||||||||||||||||||||||||||||||||||||||||||||||||||

Beef burgundy is best made a day in advance so all the flavors have time to blend. Refrigerate it, then reheat it at serving time.

2	slices bacon	2
1 tbsp	vegetable oil	15 mL
2 cups	coarsely chopped onions	500 mL
2 lbs	lean boneless stewing beef, trimmed and cut into 1-inch (2.5 cm) cubes	1 kg
2 tbsp	all-purpose flour	30 mL
¹⁄₂ tsp	salt	2 mL
¹⁄₂ tsp	dried thyme or marjoram (or a mixture of both)	2 mL
¹⁄₄ tsp	freshly ground black pepper	1 mL
¹⁄₄ tsp	garlic powder	1 mL
1¹⁄₂ cups	dry red wine	375 mL
1¹⁄₂ cups	Beef Stock (see recipe, page 76)	375 mL
1 tbsp	tomato paste	15 mL
8 oz	mushrooms, cut into chunks	250 g
¹⁄₄ tsp	salt (or less)	1 mL
	Freshly ground black pepper	

1. In a deep pot, over medium-high heat, cook bacon until crisp. Transfer bacon to a plate lined with paper towels and blot to absorb fat; set aside. Drain off fat from skillet.

2. Add oil to skillet. Sauté onions for about 3 minutes or until softened. Using a slotted spoon, transfer onions to another plate.

3. Add beef to skillet, in batches, and cook, stirring, for 4 to 5 minutes or until browned on all sides. Transfer browned beef to a plate. Drain off fat from skillet.

Nutrients per Serving	
Calories	222
Carbohydrate	8 g
Fiber	1 g
Protein	24 g
Total fat	10 g
Saturated fat	3 g
Cholesterol	49 mg
Sodium	338 mg

America's Exchanges	
2	Vegetables
3	Lean Meats

Canada's Choices	
3	Meat & Alternatives

Kitchen Tips

In place of the homemade beef stock, you can use store-bought reduced-sodium beef broth. If you do this, omit the salt in the recipe.

When you refrigerate a recipe that contains liquid, fat often rises to the surface, even if you have first thoroughly trimmed the meat. Skim this fat off before reheating

4. Return beef and any accumulated juices to skillet. Stir in flour, $\frac{1}{2}$ tsp (2 mL) salt, thyme, pepper and garlic powder; cook, stirring, for 1 minute. Crumble bacon and return to the pan. Stir in reserved onions, wine, stock and tomato paste. Reduce heat to low, cover, leaving lid slightly ajar, and simmer for 2 hours or until beef is fork-tender.

5. Stir in mushrooms. Taste and adjust seasoning with up to $\frac{1}{4}$ tsp (1 mL) salt and pepper to taste; simmer for 20 minutes or until mushrooms are tender.

Salisbury Steak
with Mushroom Sauce

1¼ lbs	lean ground beef	625 g
1	egg, beaten	1
1	clove garlic, finely chopped	1
½ cup	finely chopped onion	125 mL
¼ cup	cracker crumbs or dry bread crumbs	60 mL
½ tsp	salt	2 mL
Pinch	freshly ground black pepper	Pinch
1 tsp	prepared mustard	5 mL
	Vegetable cooking spray	
1½ cups	hot Mushroom Sauce (see recipe, page 64)	375 mL

(see recipe, page 64)

Makes 6 servings

Salisbury steak elevates ground beef to a more elegant level, and both kids and adults will enjoy it.

Nutrition Tip
Use the Nutrition Facts table to compare different varieties of crackers. Look for ones that are lower in fat and sodium, and avoid those containing trans fat. Crackers made from whole grains are higher in fiber.

1. In a large bowl, combine beef, egg, garlic, onion, cracker crumbs, salt, pepper and mustard; mix thoroughly. Divide into 6 portions and shape each into a ½-inch (1 cm) thick patty.

2. Heat a large skillet over medium heat and lightly coat with cooking spray. Cook patties in batches, turning once, for 10 to 12 minutes or until evenly browned and no longer pink in the center. Transfer patties to a warm serving platter and spoon mushroom sauce over top.

Nutrients per Serving

Calories	202
Carbohydrate	6 g
Fiber	1 g
Protein	20 g
Total fat	10 g
Saturated fat	4 g
Cholesterol	81 mg
Sodium	439 mg

America's Exchanges	
1	Vegetable
3	Lean Meats

Canada's Choices	
3	Meat & Alternatives
1	Extra

Cheeseburger Patties Deluxe

|||||||||||||||||||||||||||||||||||||||||||||||||||||||||||||||||||||||||||||||||||||||||||||||||||||||||

Makes 4 servings

These patties will be a favorite during barbecue season. Serve as a main course with vegetables and potato salad, or as a burger on a toasted bun (remember to count the Starch Exchanges or Carbohydrate Choices).

Kitchen Tip

Instead of barbecuing, place patties on a broiler pan and broil about 5 inches (12.5 cm) from the heat, turning once, for about 8 minutes per side or until meat is no longer pink in the center.

Nutrition Tip

The meat serving here is larger than most in this book, so save this recipe for special occasions. It's hard to make these "stuffed" patties smaller!

Variation

Try another reduced-fat cheese, such as provolone or Cheddar, or add some finely snipped basil or other fresh herbs.

Nutrients per Serving

Calories	266
Carbohydrate	5 g
Fiber	1 g
Protein	27 g
Total fat	15 g
Saturated fat	6 g
Cholesterol	114 mg
Sodium	398 mg

• **Preheat barbecue grill to medium-high**

1 lb	lean ground beef	500 g
1	egg, beaten	1
1/4 cup	quick-cooking rolled oats	60 mL
1/2 tsp	salt	2 mL
Pinch	freshly ground black pepper	Pinch
2	green onions, finely chopped	2
1/2 cup	shredded reduced-fat Swiss or mozzarella cheese	125 mL

1. In a large bowl, combine beef, egg, oats, salt and pepper; mix thoroughly. Divide into 8 portions and shape each into a 1/4-inch (0.5 cm) thick patty. Top each of 4 patties with one-quarter each of the green onions and cheese. Cover each with another patty and pinch the edges together to form 4 firm burgers.

2. Grill burgers, turning once, for 8 to 10 minutes per side or until meat is no longer pink in the center. (Do not overcook, or the cheese will leak out.)

America's Exchanges	
4	Lean Meats
1/2	Fat
1	Free Food

Canada's Choices	
4	Meat & Alternatives
1/2	Fat
1	Extra

Veggie Meatloaf

Makes 6 servings

Vegetables add fiber and flavor when mixed into a meatloaf. You can use lean ground pork instead of the beef, if you prefer.

Kitchen Tips

Finely chopping or shredding the vegetables ensures that the meatloaf will hold together well for slicing. If the veggie pieces are too big, the meatloaf may crumble.

In place of store-bought beef broth, you can use homemade Beef Stock (page 76). Because there's no salt in the homemade stock, you may want to add up to $\frac{1}{4}$ tsp (1 mL) more salt to the beef mixture.

- Preheat oven to 350°F (180°C)
- Food processor (optional)
- 13- by 9-inch (33 by 23 cm) metal baking pan

2	carrots, coarsely chopped	2
1	stalk celery, coarsely chopped	1
1	small onion, coarsely chopped	1
1 cup	reduced-sodium beef broth, divided	250 mL
1	egg, beaten	1
$\frac{1}{4}$ cup	dry bread crumbs	60 mL
1 tbsp	dried parsley	15 mL
$\frac{3}{4}$ tsp	salt	3 mL
$\frac{1}{2}$ tsp	freshly ground black pepper	2 mL
1 lb	lean ground beef	500 g

1. In food processor, combine carrots, celery and onion; pulse until finely chopped (or shred by hand).

2. In a skillet, combine carrot mixture and $\frac{1}{2}$ cup (125 mL) of the broth. Cook over medium heat, stirring, for 7 minutes or until vegetables are tender-crisp. Let cool slightly.

3. In a large bowl, combine the remaining broth, egg, bread crumbs, parsley, salt and pepper. Add carrot mixture and beef; mix thoroughly. Form into a firm 2-inch (5 cm) thick loaf. Place in baking pan.

4. Bake in preheated oven for 50 minutes or until a meat thermometer inserted in the center of the loaf registers 170°F (77°C). Immediately transfer meatloaf to a warm serving platter (so it will not absorb the fat in the pan).

Nutrients per Serving

Calories	170
Carbohydrate	7 g
Fiber	1 g
Protein	16 g
Total fat	8 g
Saturated fat	3 g
Cholesterol	71 mg
Sodium	488 mg

America's Exchanges	
1	Vegetable
2	Lean Meats
$\frac{1}{2}$	Fat

Canada's Choices	
2	Meat & Alternatives
$\frac{1}{2}$	Fat
1	Extra

Meatballs

Makes 24 meatballs
Serving size: 4 meatballs

You'll find many uses for these meatballs, so keep some in your freezer to use in sauces or to make emergency snacks or meals. Simply heat as they are or in a savory or spicy sauce.

Kitchen Tips
Wetting your hands with cold water will make forming the meatballs easier.

Place baked meatballs on a baking sheet lined with parchment paper or waxed paper and freeze until solid. Transfer to a freezer bag or airtight container and store in the freezer for up to 3 months.

Variations
Vary the flavor by using other herbs or by adding 2 tbsp (30 mL) finely chopped or shredded onion.

Substitute lean ground pork or lamb for the beef.

Nutrients per Serving

Calories	155
Carbohydrate	3 g
Fiber	0 g
Protein	15 g
Total fat	8 g
Saturated fat	3 g
Cholesterol	71 mg
Sodium	276 mg

- **Preheat oven to 325°F (160°C)**
- **Rimmed baking sheet with a rack**

1	egg	1
$1/4$ cup	dry bread crumbs	60 mL
1 tbsp	dried parsley	15 mL
1 tsp	dried oregano or Italian seasoning	5 mL
$1/2$ tsp	salt	2 mL
$1/4$ tsp	freshly ground black pepper	1 mL
1 lb	lean ground beef	500 g

1. In a large bowl, beat together egg and $2/3$ cup (150 mL) water. Stir in bread crumbs, parsley, oregano, salt and pepper. Add beef and mix thoroughly; let stand for 3 minutes. Form into $1\frac{1}{2}$-inch (4 cm) meatballs using about 2 tbsp (30 mL) meat mixture per meatball.

2. Place meatballs on rack on baking sheet. Bake in preheated oven for 35 minutes or until no longer pink in the center.

America's Exchanges			Canada's Choices	
2	Lean Meats		2	Meat & Alternatives
$1/2$	Fat		$1/2$	Fat
1	Free Food		1	Extra

Spicy Luncheon Roll

||||||||||||||||||||||||||||||||||||||||||||||||||||||||||||||||||||||||||||||||||||||||||||||||||||||||||||||||||||||||

Makes 6 servings

This homemade deli meat is perfect for picnics, brown bag lunches and cold buffets.

Variation
You can use all ground beef or all ground pork instead of a mixture.

- Cheesecloth
- Large saucepan or Dutch oven with rack

1	slice bacon, finely chopped	1
8 oz	lean ground beef	250 g
8 oz	lean ground pork	250 g
1/4 cup	fresh whole wheat bread crumbs	60 mL
1	egg, beaten	1
1/2 tsp	salt	2 mL
1/4 tsp	freshly ground black pepper	1 mL
1/4 tsp	ground nutmeg	1 mL
1/4 cup	reduced-sodium beef broth	60 mL
2	drops hot pepper sauce	2
	Hot water	
1	bay leaf	1

1. In a small skillet, sauté bacon over medium heat until fat is released and bacon starts to brown but isn't crisp. Drain off fat. Transfer bacon to a large bowl and let cool.

2. Add beef, pork, bread crumbs, egg, salt, pepper, nutmeg, broth and hot pepper sauce to bacon; mix thoroughly. Form into a firm 8- by 2½-inch (20 by 6 cm) roll. Wrap roll in cheesecloth, tying ends securely with kitchen twine.

3. Place roll on rack in saucepan and add enough hot water to cover. Add bay leaf, cover and bring to a boil over high heat. Reduce heat to low and simmer for 1½ hours or until a meat thermometer inserted in the center of the loaf registers 170°F (77°C). Lift roll from water and let drain. Remove cloth. Serve hot as a meatloaf or let cool, cover and refrigerate for at least 8 hours, until chilled, or for up to 2 days and serve sliced as luncheon meat.

Nutrients per Serving	
Calories	150
Carbohydrate	1 g
Fiber	0 g
Protein	15 g
Total fat	9 g
Saturated fat	3 g
Cholesterol	75 mg
Sodium	308 mg

America's Exchanges	
2	Lean Meats
1/2	Fat

Canada's Choices	
2	Meat & Alternatives
1/2	Fat

Brown 'n' Serve Sausage

||||||||||||||||||||||||||||||||||||||||||||||||||||||||||||||||||||||||||||||||||||||||||||||||||||||||||||||||||||||||||||

Your butcher will probably be happy to trim and grind pork shoulder, loin or leg for top-notch pork, which makes these sausages so good. The two-step cooking procedure ensures the removal of most of the fat.

Kitchen Tips

Always crush or rub dried herbs before use to release the aroma and enhance the flavor.

Wetting your hands with cold water will make forming the rolls easier.

Prepare the sausages through step 2, let cool, then place in an airtight container and store in the refrigerator for up to 5 days or in the freezer for up to 2 months. Proceed with step 3, adding about 2 minutes to the cooking time if cooking from frozen.

1 lb	lean ground pork	500 g
1/4 cup	cracker crumbs	60 mL
1 tsp	salt	5 mL
1 tsp	dried sage	5 mL
1/2 tsp	dried thyme	2 mL
1/2 tsp	dried oregano	2 mL
1/4 tsp	freshly ground black pepper	1 mL
Pinch	ground cloves	Pinch
	Vegetable cooking spray	

1. In a large bowl, combine pork and cracker crumbs. Stir in 1/4 cup (60 mL) water, salt, sage, thyme, oregano, pepper and cloves; mix thoroughly. Divide into 12 portions and form each into a sausage-shaped roll or a flat patty.

2. Lightly spray a large skillet with cooking spray. Place rolls in cold skillet. Cook over medium heat, turning often, for about 4 minutes per side or until just beginning to brown and no longer pink inside. Transfer sausages to a plate lined with paper towels and blot to absorb fat.

3. Return sausages to a clean cold skillet. Cook over medium heat, turning once or twice, for about 4 minutes or until sausages are brown and crisp.

Nutrients per Serving

Calories	70
Carbohydrate	1 g
Fiber	0 g
Protein	7 g
Total fat	4 g
Saturated fat	1 g
Cholesterol	23 mg
Sodium	231 mg

America's Exchanges	
1	Lean Meat

Canada's Choices	
1	Meat & Alternatives

Stuffing-Topped Pork Chops

Makes 2 servings

The vegetable and herb stuffing baked on top turns these pork chops into an elegant main course.

Kitchen Tip

To make fresh bread crumbs, grate whole wheat bread or rolls on the coarse side of a box grater or tear into pieces and pulse in a food processor. Extra bread crumbs can be frozen in a freezer bag or airtight container for up to 3 months.

- **Preheat oven to 325°F (160°C)**
- **8-inch (20 cm) square glass baking dish, greased**

1 cup	shredded zucchini	250 mL
1/3 cup	shredded carrot	75 mL
2 tsp	vegetable oil	10 mL
1 tbsp	finely chopped onion	15 mL
1/4 cup	fresh whole wheat bread crumbs	60 mL
1/4 tsp	dried sage	1 mL
1/4 tsp	dried rosemary	1 mL
2	1/2-inch (1 cm) thick boneless pork loin chops (each 4 oz/125 g), trimmed	2
1/4 tsp	dry mustard	1 mL

1. In a small bowl, combine zucchini and carrot.

2. In a small skillet, heat oil over medium-high heat. Sauté onion for 3 minutes. Add bread crumbs, sage and rosemary; sauté until crispy. Stir into zucchini mixture.

3. Rub pork chops with mustard and place in prepared baking dish. Spoon zucchini mixture on top of pork chops, dividing evenly and packing lightly.

4. Cover and bake in preheated oven for 10 minutes. Uncover and bake for 10 to 15 minutes or until a meat thermometer inserted in the center of the chops registers 160°F (71°C).

Nutrients per Serving

Calories	233
Carbohydrate	7 g
Fiber	2 g
Protein	23 g
Total fat	12 g
Saturated fat	3 g
Cholesterol	62 mg
Sodium	88 mg

America's Exchanges	
1	Vegetable
3	Lean Meats
1/2	Fat

Canada's Choices	
3	Meat & Alternatives
1/2	Fat
1	Extra

Gourmet Lamb with Pork

||||||||||||||||||||||||||||||||||||||||||||||||||||||||||||||||||||||||||||||||||||||||||||||||||||||||||||||||||||||||||||||||||||||||

Makes 16 servings

Guests will wonder what the mysterious ingredients are in this luxurious roast, served with velouté sauce.

Kitchen Tip

If you're comfortable with boning large pieces of meat, you can bone and stuff the lamb yourself. However, phoning an independent butcher and placing an order to have them do it is much easier!

Variation

If you enjoy mint with your lamb, use some dried mint in the mixed dried herbs for the rub or add 1 tbsp (15 mL) chopped fresh mint to the hot velouté sauce.

- Preheat oven to 325°F (160°C)
- Roasting pan with rack

7 lb	leg of lamb (see step 1, below)	3.5 kg
1½ lbs	pork tenderloin (about 2 small)	750 g
1 tsp	mixed dried herbs (basil, marjoram, oregano)	5 mL
½ tsp	freshly ground black pepper	2 mL
¼ tsp	garlic powder	1 mL
1 cup	Velouté Sauce (see recipe, page 60)	250 mL

1. Ask your butcher to bone a leg of lamb and replace the bone with pork tenderloins. Have the roast rolled and tied securely.

2. Crush herbs in the palm of your hand and rub into the surface of the lamb. Sprinkle with pepper and garlic powder. Place on rack in roasting pan.

3. Roast in preheated oven for 2½ to 3 hours or until a meat thermometer inserted in the center of the pork registers 155°F (68°C). Transfer to a cutting board, tent with foil and let stand for 10 minutes before carving.

4. Cut roast crosswise into thin slices. Serve drizzled with velouté sauce.

Nutrients per Serving	
Calories	239
Carbohydrate	1 g
Fiber	0 g
Protein	37 g
Total fat	9 g
Saturated fat	4 g
Cholesterol	119 mg
Sodium	101 mg

America's Exchanges	
5	Lean Meats

Canada's Choices	
5	Meat & Alternatives

Liver, Tomatoes and Green Onions

Liver is very nutritious, but it is also high in cholesterol, so it should be eaten no more than once a week. The secret to success when cooking liver is to avoid overcooking it. For an economical meal, use beef, pork or lamb liver.

Nutrition Tip

Iron combines with protein to form hemoglobin, a part of red blood cells that is essential in transporting oxygen and carbon dioxide through the body. Sources of iron include liver, kidneys, lean meats, egg yolks, dark green leafy vegetables, dried peas, lentils and beans, and enriched or whole-grain breads and cereals.

1 tbsp	all-purpose flour	15 mL
1/4 tsp	salt	1 mL
1/4 tsp	freshly ground black pepper	1 mL
8 oz	beef, pork, lamb or calf's liver, cut into 1-inch (2.5 cm) strips	250 g
2 tsp	vegetable oil, divided	10 mL
1 tsp	butter or margarine	5 mL
2	green onions, chopped	2
1	tomato, chopped	1
1 tbsp	freshly squeezed lemon juice	15 mL

1. In a large, shallow bowl, combine flour, salt and pepper. Dredge liver in seasoned flour, shaking off excess, and place on a clean plate. Discard any excess flour mixture.

2. In a large skillet, heat 1 tsp (5 mL) oil and butter over medium heat. Cook liver in batches, stirring, for 5 minutes or until just slightly pink inside and tender. Transfer to a serving dish and keep warm. Wipe out skillet.

3. Add the remaining oil to skillet and sauté green onions and tomato for 2 minutes or until heated through. Add to cooked liver and sprinkle with lemon juice.

Nutrients per Serving

Calories	241
Carbohydrate	12 g
Fiber	2 g
Protein	24 g
Total fat	11 g
Saturated fat	3 g
Cholesterol	333 mg
Sodium	382 mg

America's Exchanges	
1	Vegetable
1/2	Other Carbohydrate
3	Lean Meats

Canada's Choices	
1/2	Carbohydrate
3	Meat & Alternatives
1/2	Fat

Caribbean Stewed Chicken

|||||||||||||||||||||||||||||||||||||||||||||||||||||||||||||||||||||||||||||||||||||||||||||||||||||||||||||||||||||

Serve this beautifully seasoned stew with Fluffy Dumplings (page 71) for a praise-winning dinner.

Kitchen Tip

Extra liquid from the stew can be stored in an airtight container in the refrigerator for up to 3 days or in the freezer for up to 6 months. When ready to use, skim off any fat that has risen to the top. Reheat and pour over grilled chicken or fish or use as the base for a curry dish.

Nutrition Tip

A serving of this recipe made with chicken thighs has 6 g of fat. By using chicken breasts, you can reduce it to 2 g per serving.

Nutrients per Serving

Calories	193
Carbohydrate	4 g
Fiber	1 g
Protein	23 g
Total fat	9 g
Saturated fat	2 g
Cholesterol	86 mg
Sodium	281 mg

1	large onion, chopped	1
1	large tomato, coarsely chopped	1
1 tbsp	chopped fresh parsley	15 mL
½ tsp	dried thyme	2 mL
½ tsp	dried rosemary	2 mL
¼ tsp	ground ginger	1 mL
¼ tsp	ground cinnamon	1 mL
2 tbsp	freshly squeezed lime or lemon juice	30 mL
2 lbs	skinless bone-in chicken thighs or breasts	1 kg
½ tsp	salt	2 mL
¼ tsp	freshly ground black pepper	1 mL
1 tbsp	vegetable oil	15 mL
2 tbsp	all-purpose flour	30 mL
¼ tsp	ground nutmeg	1 mL

1. In a glass bowl, combine onion, tomato, parsley, thyme, rosemary, ginger, cinnamon and lime juice. Add chicken, turning to coat evenly. Cover and refrigerate for 2 hours.

2. Remove chicken from marinade, discarding marinade. Place chicken in a Dutch oven or pot and add 3 cups (750 mL) water, salt and pepper. Cover and bring to a boil over high heat. Reduce heat to low and simmer for 1½ hours or until chicken is tender.

3. In a small saucepan, heat oil over medium heat. Stir in flour and nutmeg until blended. Remove 1½ cups (375 mL) liquid from stew and strain. Gradually stir into flour mixture and cook, stirring, for about 2 minutes or until thickened.

4. Place chicken pieces on a warm platter. Serve drizzled with sauce. (Strain remaining liquid from stew for later use.)

America's Exchanges	
3	Lean Meats
1	Free Food

Canada's Choices	
3	Meat & Alternatives

Chicken Paprika

||||||||||||||||||||||||||||||||||||||||||||||||||||||||||||||||||||||||||||||||||||||||||||||||

This slimmed-down version of an old Hungarian favorite has all the flavor of the traditional dish, but less fat.

Nutrition Tip

When choosing a margarine, look for a non-hydrogenated soft margarine. These are low in saturated fat and do not contain trans fat. Avoid hard margarines, which contain high amounts of saturated and trans fat.

1 tsp	vegetable oil	5 mL
1 tsp	margarine or butter	5 mL
1 cup	chopped onion	250 mL
2 tsp	paprika	10 mL
½ tsp	salt	2 mL
Pinch	freshly ground black pepper	Pinch
1½ lbs	skinless bone-in chicken breasts or legs	750 g
1	small green bell pepper, cut into chunks	1
1 tbsp	all-purpose flour	15 mL
½ cup	2% milk	125 mL
⅓ cup	light sour cream	75 mL

1. In a heavy skillet, heat oil and margarine over medium heat. Sauté onion for 5 minutes. Stir in paprika, salt and pepper. Add chicken and cook until lightly browned on both sides. (Do not let onion burn.)

2. Add ¾ cup (175 mL) water, reduce heat to low, cover and simmer for 1 hour or until chicken is tender. Add green pepper and simmer for 5 minutes.

3. In a jar, combine flour and milk. Cover tightly and shake until thoroughly mixed. Stir into liquid around chicken. Cook, stirring, for 2 to 3 minutes or until thickened. Stir in sour cream and simmer until heated through (do not let boil).

Nutrients per Serving	
Calories	228
Carbohydrate	10 g
Fiber	1 g
Protein	32 g
Total fat	6 g
Saturated fat	2 g
Cholesterol	83 mg
Sodium	404 mg

America's Exchanges	
½	Other Carbohydrate
4	Lean Meats

Canada's Choices	
4	Meat & Alternatives
1	Extra

Baked Chicken with Wine Sauce

||||||||||||||||||||||||||||||||||||||||||||||||||||||||||||||||||||||||||||||||||||||||||||||||||||||||||||||||||||||||

Makes 4 servings

Chicken never lacks loyal supporters. A wine-flavored sauce adds flavor that makes this dish suitable for a gourmet.

Kitchen Tip

In place of the homemade chicken stock, you can use store-bought reduced-sodium chicken broth. If you do this, omit the salt in the recipe.

- **Preheat oven to 425°F (220°C)**
- **13- by 9-inch (33 by 23 cm) shallow baking pan**

1¼ lbs	boneless skinless chicken thighs or breasts	625 g
¼ cup	Seasoned Bread Crumbs (see recipe, page 72)	60 mL
2 tsp	vegetable oil	10 mL
1 tbsp	cornstarch	15 mL
1¼ cups	Chicken Stock (see recipe, page 78)	300 mL
⅓ cup	port wine or dry sherry	75 mL
½ tsp	salt (or less)	2 mL

1. If using thighs, roll up chicken and fasten with a toothpick (leave breasts flat). Place bread crumbs on a plate. Rinse chicken under cold water and shake off excess water. Coat with bread crumbs.

2. Spread oil in baking pan. Arrange chicken in pan. Bake in preheated oven for 25 minutes. Turn chicken over and bake for 10 to 20 minutes or until coating is golden, juices run clear when thighs are pierced and breasts are no longer pink inside.

3. Meanwhile, in a small bowl, whisk together cornstarch and 2 tbsp (30 mL) of the stock; set aside.

4. In a saucepan, combine the remaining stock and wine; bring to a boil over high heat. Boil for about 10 minutes or until sauce is reduced by about one-quarter. Stir in cornstarch mixture and cook, stirring, until sauce is clear and slightly thickened. Taste and gradually add up to ½ tsp (2 mL) salt. Serve over hot chicken.

Nutrients per Serving

Calories	260
Carbohydrate	8 g
Fiber	0 g
Protein	30 g
Total fat	10 g
Saturated fat	2 g
Cholesterol	104 mg
Sodium	448 mg

America's Exchanges	
½	Other Carbohydrate
4	Lean Meats

Canada's Choices	
½	Carbohydrate
4	Meat & Alternatives

Herbed Chicken

|||||||||||||||||||||||||||||||||||||||||||||||||||||||||||||||||||||||||||||||||||||||||||||||||||||||||||||||||||

Makes 2 servings

Serve this versatile, tasty chicken over toast or in crêpes, tortillas or popovers. Make it ahead and reheat just before serving. It's handy to have in the freezer for emergencies.

Kitchen Tip

To freeze, portion chicken mixture into airtight containers, let cool, then cover and freeze for up to 3 months. Let thaw overnight in the refrigerator or defrost in the microwave. Reheat in a saucepan over medium heat, stirring often, until bubbling.

12 oz	bone-in skin-on chicken breasts	375 g
1 tsp	dried marjoram	5 mL
¼ tsp	salt	1 mL
1	stalk celery, chopped	1
1	small onion, chopped	1
1 tbsp	instant skim milk powder	15 mL
1 tsp	cornstarch	5 mL
Pinch	freshly ground black pepper	Pinch

1. Place chicken in a saucepan and add 2 cups (500 mL) water, marjoram and salt. Bring to a boil over high heat. Reduce heat and simmer for about 25 minutes or until chicken is no longer pink inside.

2. Transfer chicken to a cutting board and let cool slightly. Strain broth into a bowl and refrigerate until fat sets on top; remove and discard fat. Remove skin and bones from chicken; discard skin and bones. Cut chicken into bite-size pieces; set aside.

3. In a heavy saucepan, bring ¼ cup (60 mL) of the skimmed broth to a boil over medium-high heat. Add celery and onion; boil, stirring, for about 4 minutes or until tender.

4. In a bowl, whisk together the remaining broth, milk powder, cornstarch and pepper until smooth. Stir into celery mixture and cook, stirring, over medium heat for about 3 minutes or until sauce is slightly thickened. Add chicken and cook, stirring, until heated through.

Nutrients per Serving

Calories	160
Carbohydrate	6 g
Fiber	1 g
Protein	28 g
Total fat	2 g
Saturated fat	1 g
Cholesterol	70 mg
Sodium	383 mg

America's Exchanges

1	Vegetable
4	Lean Meats

Canada's Choices

4	Meat & Alternatives

Chicken Italiano

Makes 4 servings

Young people give this Italian-style recipe top marks.

Kitchen Tips

Warm the baking dish in a 200°F (100°C) oven for 5 to 10 minutes or fill it with hot water and let stand for 15 minutes; drain well and pat dry before adding chicken.

If you can't find a 14-oz (398 mL) can of tomatoes, use a 28-oz (796 mL) can, purée the tomatoes without the herbs, then measure 1¾ cups (425 mL) and stir in basil, tarragon, salt and pepper. Transfer extra puréed tomatoes to an airtight container and refrigerate for up to 3 days or freeze for up to 6 months.

- Preheat broiler
- Blender or food processor
- 8-inch (20 cm) square glass baking dish, warmed

1	can (14 oz/398 mL) no-salt-added tomatoes, with juice	1
½ tsp	dried basil	2 mL
½ tsp	dried tarragon	2 mL
½ tsp	salt	2 mL
¼ tsp	freshly ground black pepper	1 mL
2 tsp	margarine, vegetable oil or butter	10 mL
1	clove garlic, finely chopped	1
1½ lbs	skinless bone-in chicken breasts	750 g
2 tbsp	chopped fresh parsley (or 2 tsp/10 mL dried parsley)	30 mL
½ cup	shredded mozzarella cheese	125 mL

1. In blender, combine tomatoes, basil, tarragon, salt and pepper; purée until smooth.

2. In a large skillet, melt margarine over medium heat. Sauté garlic for 1 minute. Add chicken and cook, turning once or twice, for about 5 minutes or until golden on both sides. Turn chicken fleshy side down and cover with tomato mixture; bring to a boil. Reduce heat and simmer for 15 minutes or until no longer pink inside.

3. Remove chicken and place fleshy side up in baking dish. Stir parsley into sauce and spoon over chicken. Sprinkle with mozzarella. Broil for 1 minute or until cheese is melted.

Nutrients per Serving

Calories	225
Carbohydrate	5 g
Fiber	1 g
Protein	34 g
Total fat	7 g
Saturated fat	3 g
Cholesterol	89 mg
Sodium	448 mg

America's Exchanges

1	Vegetable
4	Lean Meats

Canada's Choices

4	Meat & Alternatives

Broiled Fillets Almandine

Makes 4 servings

Always popular in restaurants, this is a distinctive way to serve fish fillets, and one of the best. It is a fish dinner to make you proud, and it is unbelievably quick and easy to prepare.

Nutrition Tips

Catfish and trout are higher in fat than tilapia. If you use these fish, count an additional Fat Exchange or Choice per serving.

When choosing a margarine, look for a non-hydrogenated soft margarine. These are low in saturated fat and do not contain trans fat. Avoid hard margarines, which contain high amounts of saturated and trans fat.

- **Preheat broiler, with rack placed 6 inches (15 cm) from heat**
- **Broiler pan or shallow baking dish**

1 lb	skinless fish fillets, such as tilapia, catfish or trout	500 g
2 tbsp	melted margarine or butter	30 mL
¼ cup	sliced almonds	60 mL
½ tsp	salt	2 mL
¼ tsp	freshly ground white pepper	1 mL
	Juice of ½ lemon	

1. Place fish, skinned side up, on broiler pan. Broil for about 6 minutes. Turn each fillet.

2. In a bowl, combine margarine, almonds, salt, white pepper and lemon juice. Spoon evenly over fish. Broil for about 3 minutes or until fish is opaque and flakes easily when tested with a fork and almonds are toasted.

Nutrients per Serving

Calories	211
Carbohydrate	2 g
Fiber	1 g
Protein	25 g
Total fat	11 g
Saturated fat	1 g
Cholesterol	36 mg
Sodium	403 mg

America's Exchanges	
3	Lean Meats
1	Fat

Canada's Choices	
3½	Meat & Alternatives

Crispy Baked Fish

|||||||||||||||||||||||||||||||||||||||||||||||||||||||||||||||||||||||||||||||||||||||||||||||||||||||||||||||

Makes 4 servings

This baked fish has all the flavor and texture of fried fish, but without the fat necessary for frying. It is an excellent way to cook either fresh or frozen fillets.

Kitchen Tip

Before purchasing fish, always learn what you can about sustainability and fishing practices. Ask your fishmonger or check online resources.

- **Preheat oven to 450°F (230°C)**
- **Baking sheet, lightly greased**

1 lb	skinless haddock or halibut fillets	500 g
2 tbsp	Tangy Salad Cream (see recipe, page 124)	30 mL
½ cup	Seasoned Bread Crumbs (see recipe, page 72)	125 mL

1. Pat fish with paper towels to remove excess liquid. Brush with salad cream. Coat with crumb mixture, pressing crumbs into fish. Arrange on prepared baking sheet. Discard any excess crumbs.

2. Bake in preheated oven for 15 to 20 minutes or until coating is crispy and fish is opaque and flakes easily when tested with a fork.

Nutrients per Serving	
Calories	142
Carbohydrate	6 g
Fiber	0 g
Protein	23 g
Total fat	2 g
Saturated fat	1 g
Cholesterol	73 mg
Sodium	158 mg

America's Exchanges	
½	Starch
3	Lean Meats

Canada's Choices	
½	Carbohydrate
3	Meat & Alternatives

Stuffed Baked Fillets

Makes 4 servings

For a finishing touch, serve these quick and easy stuffed fillets with Mushroom Sauce (page 64) or Velouté Sauce (page 60). For an even more special presentation, spread one-quarter of the filling on each of 4 long, thin fillets, roll up and secure with a toothpick; bake as directed.

Kitchen Tip

In place of store-bought chicken broth, you can use homemade Chicken Stock (page 78). You may need to add up to $\frac{1}{8}$ tsp (0.5 mL) more salt to bring out the flavors of the sauce. Taste the finished sauce and add just enough salt to perk up the flavor.

- Preheat oven to 425°F (220°C)
- 8-inch (20 cm) square glass baking dish, greased

3	green onions, finely chopped	3
$\frac{1}{2}$ cup	finely chopped celery	125 mL
$\frac{1}{3}$ cup	finely chopped red or green bell pepper	75 mL
$\frac{2}{3}$ cup	reduced-sodium chicken broth, divided	150 mL
3 tbsp	dry bread crumbs	45 mL
2 tbsp	chopped fresh parsley	30 mL
2 tbsp	chopped walnuts or almonds	30 mL
$\frac{1}{2}$ tsp	salt	2 mL
$\frac{1}{2}$ tsp	grated lemon zest	2 mL
1 tbsp	freshly squeezed lemon juice	15 mL
1 lb	skinless fish fillets, such as haddock, tilapia or catfish	500 g
	Paprika (optional)	

1. In a small skillet, combine green onions, celery, red pepper and half the broth. Cover and simmer over medium heat for about 7 minutes or until vegetables are tender. Stir in bread crumbs, parsley, walnuts, salt, lemon zest and lemon juice.

2. Arrange half the fish in prepared baking dish. Top with vegetable mixture, then the remaining fish. Pour the remaining broth over fish. Sprinkle to taste with paprika (if using).

3. Cover loosely and bake in preheated oven for 20 minutes or until fish is opaque and flakes easily when tested with a fork.

Nutrients per Serving	
Calories	157
Carbohydrate	7 g
Fiber	1 g
Protein	24 g
Total fat	4 g
Saturated fat	0 g
Cholesterol	65 mg
Sodium	514 mg

America's Exchanges	
$\frac{1}{2}$	Other Carbohydrate
3	Lean Meats

Canada's Choices	
3	Meat & Alternatives
1	Extra

Poached Fish

Makes 4 servings

Onion, lemon and bay leaf flavor white fish for an appealing entrée that's as easy on the cook as it is on the figure.

Kitchen Tips

Before purchasing fish, always learn what you can about sustainability and fishing practices. Ask your fishmonger or check online resources.

This cooking time is for fillets that are about 1 inch (2.5 cm) thick; if you have thinner fillets, check earlier for doneness.

1	onion, chopped	1
6	whole black peppercorns	6
4	slices lemon	4
3	sprigs parsley	3
1	bay leaf	1
1 tsp	salt	5 mL
1 lb	skinless white fish fillets, such as haddock or halibut	500 g

1. In a large skillet, combine onion, peppercorns, lemon, parsley, bay leaf, salt and $1\frac{1}{2}$ cups (375 mL) water. Bring to a boil over high heat. Arrange fish in a single layer in pan; reduce heat to low, cover and simmer for 10 to 12 minutes or until fish is opaque and flakes easily when tested with a fork.

2. Using a slotted spoon, transfer fish to a serving platter, along with onions and lemon slices, if desired.

Nutrients per Serving

Calories	111
Carbohydrate	3 g
Fiber	1 g
Protein	22 g
Total fat	1 g
Saturated fat	0 g
Cholesterol	65 mg
Sodium	312 mg

America's Exchanges	
3	Lean Meats

Canada's Choices	
3	Meat & Alternatives

Creole Fish Bake

||||||||||||||||||||||||||||||||||||||||||||||||||||||||||||||||||||||||||||||||||||||||||||||||||||||||

Makes 4 servings

Only minutes are required to prepare this one-dish meal. Select the fish best suited to your family's taste and budget.

Nutrition Tip

When purchasing store-bought chicken broth, look for one with the lowest amount of sodium. As you compare nutrition labels, keep in mind that some broths are ready-to-use, while some are condensed and need to be diluted with an equal amount of water. Make sure you're comparing the same amount of the same type of product.

- **Preheat oven to 400°F (200°C)**
- **8-inch (20 cm) square glass baking dish**

1	small onion, finely chopped	1
1	can (14 oz/398 mL) no-salt-added diced tomatoes, with juice	1
1 cup	frozen mixed vegetables	250 mL
1/3 cup	chopped fresh parsley	75 mL
1/2 tsp	dried thyme	2 mL
1/2 tsp	salt	2 mL
1/2 tsp	freshly ground black pepper	2 mL
1/2 cup	reduced-sodium chicken broth or water	125 mL
1 lb	frozen white fish fillets, partially thawed and cut into 1-inch (2.5 cm) chunks	500 g
4	lemon wedges	4

1. In baking dish, combine onion, tomatoes with juice, mixed vegetables, parsley, thyme, salt, pepper and broth. Arrange fish on vegetable mixture.

2. Bake in preheated oven for 25 to 30 minutes or until fish is opaque and flakes easily when tested with a fork.

3. Serve in shallow bowls, garnished with lemon wedges.

Nutrients per Serving	
Calories	160
Carbohydrate	12 g
Fiber	3 g
Protein	24 g
Total fat	2 g
Saturated fat	0 g
Cholesterol	60 mg
Sodium	485 mg

America's Exchanges	
2	Vegetables
3	Lean Meats

Canada's Choices	
3	Meat & Alternatives
1	Extra

Salmon Broccoli Loaf

||||||||||||||||||||||||||||||||||||||||||||||||||||||||||||||||||||||||||||||||||||||||||||||||||||||||||

The flavor and color provided by canned salmon and vitamin C–rich broccoli make this loaf popular with people of all ages.

Nutrition Tip

Cottage cheese has traditionally contained a lot of salt, with about 400 mg (17% DV) in $\frac{1}{2}$ cup (125 mL). Some brands now contain less. Be sure to check the Nutrition Facts table when shopping and choose the one that's lowest in sodium.

- **Preheat oven to 350°F (180°C)**
- **8- by 4-inch (20 by 10 cm) loaf pan, well greased**

$1\frac{1}{2}$ cups	finely chopped fresh or frozen broccoli	375 mL
2	eggs	2
1	can ($7\frac{1}{2}$ oz/213 g) salmon, with liquid	1
1 cup	2% cottage cheese	250 mL
$\frac{1}{4}$ cup	chopped onion	60 mL
2 tbsp	dry bread crumbs	30 mL
$\frac{1}{2}$ tsp	salt	2 mL
1	small tomato, cut into 5 slices	1
$\frac{1}{4}$ cup	freshly grated Parmesan cheese	60 mL

1. In a saucepan of boiling water, blanch broccoli for 2 minutes or until bright green. Drain well and let cool slightly.

2. In a bowl, whisk eggs until blended. Stir in broccoli, salmon, cottage cheese, onion, bread crumbs and salt until well blended.

3. Overlap tomato slices in bottom of prepared loaf pan. Sprinkle with Parmesan. Spoon salmon mixture over tomatoes.

4. Bake in preheated oven for 1 hour or until a tester inserted in the center comes out clean. Let cool for 5 minutes, then turn out onto a serving platter and cut into 6 slices.

Nutrients per Serving	
Calories	164
Carbohydrate	8 g
Fiber	1 g
Protein	16 g
Total fat	7 g
Saturated fat	3 g
Cholesterol	78 mg
Sodium	519 mg

America's Exchanges	
1	Vegetable
2	Lean Meats

Canada's Choices	
2	Meat & Alternatives
1	Extra

Pacific Salmon Pie

IIIIIIIIIIIIIIIIIIIIIIIIIIIIIIIIIIIIIIIIIIIIIIIIIIIIIIIIIIIIIIIIIIIIIIIIIIIIIIIIIIIIIIIIIIIIIIIIIIIIIIIIIIIIIIIIIIIIIIIIIIIIIIIIII

Makes 6 servings

Salmon and Swiss cheese are baked together in this rice-crusted pie that's as good cold as it is hot.

Kitchen Tip

To serve cold, let pie cool completely, wrap and refrigerate for at least 8 hours, until chilled, or for up to 2 days.

- **Preheat oven to 375°F (190°C)**
- **9-inch (23 cm) glass pie plate, greased**

¼ tsp	salt	1 mL
½ cup	long-grain white rice	125 mL
2 tsp	margarine or butter	10 mL
1 cup	finely chopped celery	250 mL
¼ cup	finely chopped onion	60 mL
2	eggs, beaten, divided	2
Pinch	freshly ground black pepper	Pinch
½ cup	shredded Swiss cheese	125 mL
1	can (7½ oz/213 g) salmon, with liquid, flaked	1
½ cup	skim milk	125 mL
Pinch	curry powder	Pinch
Pinch	ground nutmeg	Pinch
Pinch	ground cinnamon	Pinch

1. In a saucepan, bring 1½ cups (375 mL) water and salt to a boil over high heat. Add rice and return to a boil. Reduce heat to low, cover and simmer for about 15 minutes or until liquid is absorbed and rice is almost tender.

2. In a skillet, melt margarine over medium-high heat. Sauté celery and onion for 4 minutes or until softened.

Nutrients per Serving

Calories	204
Carbohydrate	15 g
Fiber	1 g
Protein	13 g
Total fat	10 g
Saturated fat	4 g
Cholesterol	81 mg
Sodium	325 mg

America's Exchanges	
1	Starch
2	Lean Meats
1	Fat

Canada's Choices	
1	Carbohydrate
1½	Meat & Alternatives
1	Fat

3. Stir half the eggs and pepper into rice. Press rice onto bottom and sides of prepared pie plate to form a crust. Sprinkle half the cheese over rice. Spread half the celery mixture and all of the salmon on top. Top with the remaining celery mixture and cheese.

4. In a bowl, whisk together the remaining eggs, milk, curry powder, nutmeg and cinnamon. Pour over ingredients in pie plate.

5. Bake in preheated oven for 30 to 35 minutes or until a tester inserted in the center comes out clean. Let cool for 5 minutes, then cut into 6 wedges.

Tuna Impromptu

||||||||||||||||||||||||||||||||||||||||||||||||||||||||||||||||||||||||||||||||||||||||||||||||||||||||||

Canned tuna makes a great foundation for incredibly quick and easy dishes such as this one.

Kitchen Tip

To peel tomatoes, blanch ripe tomatoes in a pot of boiling water for 30 to 60 seconds, depending on ripeness (less ripe will need longer). Using a slotted spoon, transfer tomatoes to a bowl of ice water and let stand until chilled. Drain. Using a paring knife, cut out core and peel off skins.

2 tsp	vegetable oil	10 mL
4	eggs, lightly beaten	4
2	stalks celery, chopped	2
2	green onions, chopped	2
1	can (6 oz/170 g) water-packed chunk tuna, drained	1
½ tsp	dried tarragon	2 mL
1	large tomato, peeled and chopped	1
¼ tsp	salt (or less)	1 mL
	Freshly ground black pepper	

1. In a heavy skillet, heat 1 tsp (5 mL) oil over medium heat. Pour in eggs and cook until set (do not stir). Flip eggs and cook for 30 seconds. Remove from pan, chop and set aside.

2. Add the remaining oil to the skillet. Sauté celery and green onions for about 3 minutes or until tender-crisp. Add tuna and tarragon; sauté for 2 minutes. Stir in tomato and eggs; sauté until heated through. Taste and add up to ¼ tsp (1 mL) salt. Season to taste with pepper. Serve immediately.

Nutrients per Serving	
Calories	145
Carbohydrate	3 g
Fiber	1 g
Protein	14 g
Total fat	8 g
Saturated fat	2 g
Cholesterol	199 mg
Sodium	343 mg

America's Exchanges	
2	Lean Meats
½	Fat

Canada's Choices	
2	Meat & Alternatives
½	Fat

One-Dish Meals

Easy Oven Stew

Makes 4 servings
Serving size: $3/4$ cup
(175 mL)

Call this one "stay-away stew" if you wish. Let it cook in the oven while you are busy or out for the afternoon. You can also make this stew in a slow cooker; just reduce the stock to $1/2$ cup (125 mL).

Kitchen Tip
In place of the homemade beef stock, you can use store-bought reduced-sodium beef broth. If you do this, omit the salt in the recipe.

- **Preheat oven to 275°F (140°C)**
- **10-cup (2.5 L) casserole dish**

1 lb	lean stewing beef, cut into bite-size pieces	500 g
2	onions, cut into wedges	2
1 cup	sliced carrots	250 mL
1	bay leaf	1
$1/2$ tsp	salt	2 mL
Pinch	freshly ground black pepper	Pinch
$1/4$ cup	no-salt-added tomato paste	60 mL
$1\frac{3}{4}$ cups	Beef Stock (see recipe, page 76), divided	425 mL
2 tbsp	all-purpose flour	30 mL
$3/4$ cup	frozen green peas	175 mL

1. In casserole dish, combine beef, onions, carrots, bay leaf, salt, pepper, tomato paste and $1\frac{1}{2}$ cups (375 mL) of the stock; stir well.

2. Cover and bake in preheated oven for $3\frac{1}{2}$ hours, stirring once or twice, until beef is almost fork-tender.

3. In a small bowl, whisk flour into remaining stock until smooth (or shake in a jar with a lid). Stir into baking dish, along with peas; cover and bake for about 20 minutes or until beef is fork-tender and stew is slightly thickened.

Nutrients per Serving

Calories	246
Carbohydrate	18 g
Fiber	4 g
Protein	27 g
Total fat	7 g
Saturated fat	3 g
Cholesterol	47 mg
Sodium	426 mg

America's Exchanges

2	Vegetables
$1/2$	Other Carbohydrate
3	Lean Meats

Canada's Choices

$1/2$	Carbohydrate
3	Meat & Alternatives

Chili Con Carne

Warm up a frosty evening with a steaming bowl of chili. Serve some crunchy carrot and celery sticks on the side.

Kitchen Tip

Plan ahead! Make a double batch of this chili, portion into airtight containers, leaving 1 inch (2.5 cm) of headspace, and let cool. Cover and freeze for up to 3 months. Thaw overnight in the refrigerator or defrost in the microwave before reheating.

Nutrition Tip

Canned foods often contain a lot of salt. We have reduced the sodium in this recipe by using no-salt-added canned tomatoes and by draining and rinsing the kidney beans. You can further reduce the sodium (by about 300 mg per serving) by using no-salt-added tomato sauce.

Nutrients per Serving	
Calories	281
Carbohydrate	25 g
Fiber	7 g
Protein	24 g
Total fat	10 g
Saturated fat	4 g
Cholesterol	51 mg
Sodium	549 mg

1½ lbs	lean ground beef	750 g
1	large green bell pepper, chopped	1
1 cup	chopped onion	250 mL
2	cans (each 19 oz/540 mL) no-salt-added diced tomatoes, with juice	2
1	can (14 oz/398 mL) tomato sauce	1
1	clove garlic, finely chopped	1
1	bay leaf	1
1 to 1½ tsp	chili powder	5 to 7 mL
½ tsp	dried oregano	2 mL
Pinch	ground cloves	Pinch
Pinch	freshly ground black pepper	Pinch
2 cups	rinsed drained canned kidney beans	500 mL

1. In a large, heavy pot, over medium-high heat, cook beef, green pepper and onion, breaking beef up with the back of a spoon, for about 8 minutes or until beef is no longer pink. Drain off fat.

2. Stir in tomatoes, tomato sauce, garlic, bay leaf, 1 tsp (5 mL) chili powder, oregano, cloves and pepper. Reduce heat to low, cover, leaving lid slightly ajar, and simmer, stirring occasionally, for 1 hour.

3. Stir in beans. Taste and add the remaining chili powder, if desired. Simmer for 20 minutes. Discard bay leaf.

America's Exchanges	
2	Vegetables
1	Other Carbohydrate
3	Lean Meats

Canada's Choices	
½	Carbohydrate
3	Meat & Alternatives

Lasagna

||||||||||||||||||||||||||||||||||||||||||||||||||||||||||||||||||||||||||||||||||||||||||||||||||||||||||||||||||||||||||||||||||||||||||||||||||||||||||||

This version of a favorite meal-in-a-dish is excellent with a green salad.

- **Preheat oven to 350°F (180°C)**
- **13- by 9-inch (33 by 23 cm) baking dish, greased**

½ cup	freshly grated Parmesan cheese	125 mL
1 cup	Basic White Sauce (see recipe, page 58)	250 mL
9	lasagna noodles	9
1 lb	lean ground beef	500 g
1	package (10 oz/300 g) frozen chopped spinach, thawed, drained and squeezed dry	1
2 cups	shredded part-skim mozzarella cheese	500 mL
3 cups	Spaghetti Sauce (see recipe, page 66)	750 mL

1. Reserve 1 tbsp (15 mL) Parmesan for topping. Stir remainder into white sauce; set aside.

2. In a pot of boiling water, cook noodles according to package directions (omitting salt) just until tender. Drain and separate.

3. Meanwhile, in a skillet, over medium-high heat, cook beef, breaking it up with the back of a spoon, for about 8 minutes or until no longer pink. Drain off fat.

Nutrients per Serving

Calories	323
Carbohydrate	29 g
Fiber	3 g
Protein	24 g
Total fat	13 g
Saturated fat	6 g
Cholesterol	48 mg
Sodium	530 mg

America's Exchanges

1	Vegetable
1½	Other Carbohydrates
3	Lean Meats
1	Fat

Canada's Choices

1½	Carbohydrates
2½	Meat & Alternatives
1	Fat

Nutrition Tip

Part-skim mozzarella contains one-third less fat than regular mozzarella. Lower-fat versions of many cheeses are available. Typically, they contain up to 7 g of fat per oz (30 g), compared with 10 g of fat for the same amount of regular cheese.

4. Spread ¾ cup (175 mL) spaghetti sauce in bottom of prepared baking dish. Top with 3 lasagna noodles, half the spinach, half the beef and one-third of the Parmesan sauce. Spread ¾ cup (175 mL) spaghetti sauce over top. Repeat layers of noodles, spinach, beef, Parmesan sauce and spaghetti sauce. Top with the remaining noodles, the remaining Parmesan sauce, mozzarella, the remaining spaghetti sauce and the reserved Parmesan.

5. Cover with foil and bake in preheated oven for 35 minutes. Uncover and bake for 10 minutes or until lightly browned. Let stand for 5 minutes before serving.

Enchiladas

||||||||||||||||||||||||||||||||||||||||||||||||||||||||||||||||||||||||||||||||||||||||||||||||||||||||||||||||

Makes 6 servings
Serving size:
2 enchiladas with sauce

The herbs and peppers make this south-of-the-border favorite a flavorful but not too spicy one-dish meal suitable for the whole family.

Nutrition Tip
This recipe calls for the homemade tortillas in this book. You can also use 6-inch (15 cm) commercial tortillas. Because these are thicker than the homemade ones, add 1 Starch Exchange or Carbohydrate Choice per serving.

- Preheat oven to 350°F (180°C)
- 13- by 9-inch (33 by 23 cm) glass baking dish, lightly greased

1 lb	lean ground beef	500 g
1	clove garlic, finely chopped	1
2	green bell peppers, chopped	2
1	small onion, chopped	1
¼ cup	chopped fresh cilantro or parsley	60 mL
½ tsp	salt	2 mL
¼ tsp	freshly ground black pepper	1 mL
¼ tsp	chili powder	1 mL
2 tbsp	freshly squeezed lime or lemon juice	30 mL
1½ cups	2% cottage cheese	375 mL
2 tbsp	freshly grated Parmesan cheese	30 mL
12	Whole Wheat Flour Tortillas (see recipe, page 68)	12
½ cup	shredded part-skim mozzarella cheese	125 mL

Tomato Sauce

2	firm tomatoes, seeded and chopped	2
1	green bell pepper, chopped	1
2 tbsp	chopped onion	30 mL
1 tbsp	chopped fresh cilantro or parsley	15 mL

1. In a large skillet, over medium-high heat, cook beef and garlic, breaking beef up with the back of a spoon, for about 8 minutes or until beef is no longer pink. Drain off fat.

Nutrients per Serving

Calories	335
Carbohydrate	25 g
Fiber	3 g
Protein	29 g
Total fat	13 g
Saturated fat	5 g
Cholesterol	52 mg
Sodium	557 mg

America's Exchanges

1½	Starches
1	Vegetable
3	Lean Meats
1	Fat

Canada's Choices

1	Carbohydrate
3½	Meat & Alternatives
½	Fat

2. Stir in green peppers, onion, cilantro, salt, pepper, chili powder, 2 cups (500 mL) water and lime juice. Reduce heat and simmer, stirring occasionally, for about 15 minutes or until liquid is reduced by half. Stir in cottage cheese and Parmesan; simmer for 5 minutes.

3. Spoon about 2 tbsp (30 mL) beef mixture down the center of each tortilla. Roll tortilla around filling and place, seam side down, in a single layer in prepared baking dish. Pour remaining beef mixture over enchiladas.

4. Bake in preheated oven for 15 minutes.

5. *Sauce:* Meanwhile, in a small saucepan, combine tomatoes, green pepper, onion, cilantro and $1/4$ cup (60 mL) water. Cook over medium heat, stirring often, for about 7 minutes or until vegetables are tender.

6. Sprinkle mozzarella over enchiladas and top with sauce. Bake for 5 minutes or until cheese is melted.

Tacos

Makes 6 servings
Serving size: 2 tacos

Tacos have a delightful contrast of flavors and textures, with crisp fresh vegetables and a tasty meat and bean filling.

Nutrition Tip
This recipe calls for the homemade taco shells in this book. You can also use 6-inch (15 cm) commercial taco shells. Because these are thicker than the homemade ones, add 1 Starch Exchange or Carbohydrate Choice per serving.

8 oz	lean ground beef	250 g
2 tbsp	finely chopped onion	30 mL
2 tbsp	finely chopped green bell pepper	30 mL
1 tsp	chili powder	5 mL
½ tsp	salt	2 mL
¼ tsp	freshly ground black pepper	1 mL
¼ tsp	Worcestershire sauce (optional)	1 mL
2	drops hot pepper sauce	2
1	can (5½ oz/156 mL) no-salt-added tomato paste	1
1	can (14 to 19 oz/398 to 540 mL) kidney beans, drained and rinsed	1
12	Soft Taco Shells (see variation, page 69)	12
3 cups	assorted chopped vegetables (lettuce, tomatoes, cucumber, celery)	750 mL
½ cup	shredded Cheddar cheese	125 mL

1. In a large saucepan, over medium-high heat, cook beef, onion and green pepper, breaking beef up with the back of a spoon, for about 8 minutes or until beef is no longer pink. Drain off fat.

2. Stir in chili powder, salt, pepper, Worcestershire sauce (if using) and hot pepper sauce until well blended. Stir in tomato paste, beans and ¼ cup (60 mL) water. Reduce heat and simmer, stirring occasionally, for 20 minutes or until very thick.

3. Fill each taco shell with ¼ cup (60 mL) beef filling. Top each with ¼ cup (60 mL) vegetables and sprinkle with 2 tsp (10 mL) cheese.

Nutrients per Serving

Calories	281
Carbohydrate	33 g
Fiber	7 g
Protein	17 g
Total fat	10 g
Saturated fat	4 g
Cholesterol	30 mg
Sodium	558 mg

America's Exchanges

2	Vegetables
1	Other Carbohydrate
2	Lean Meats
½	Fat

Canada's Choices

1½	Carbohydrates
2	Meat & Alternatives
½	Fat

Burger Pizza

|||||||||||||||||||||||||||||||||||||||||||||||||||||||||||||||||||||||||||||||||||||||||||||||||||||||||

Makes 8 servings

For this recipe, favorite meatloaf ingredients are combined, then shaped like a pizza crust and topped with an assortment of toppings. Serve tossed greens and a few carrot sticks on the side.

Nutrition Tip

If you replace the lean ground beef in this recipe with extra-lean, you can reduce the amount of fat per serving by 4 grams.

- Preheat oven to 350°F (180°C)
- Rimmed baking sheet or pizza pan, lined with foil

1 lb	lean ground beef	500 g
5	unsalted-top saltine crackers, crushed	5
¼ cup	finely chopped onion	60 mL
¼ cup	finely chopped celery	60 mL
½ tsp	dried oregano	2 mL
1	egg	1
1 tsp	prepared mustard	5 mL
1 tsp	Worcestershire sauce	5 mL
6	mushrooms, sliced	6
1	tomato, sliced	1
½	green bell pepper, cut into thin slices	½
	Freshly ground black pepper	
1 cup	shredded part-skim mozzarella cheese	250 mL
1 tbsp	freshly grated Parmesan cheese	15 mL

1. In a large bowl, combine beef, crackers, onion, celery, oregano, egg, mustard and Worcestershire sauce; mix thoroughly.

2. Transfer to prepared baking sheet and pat into a 10-inch (25 cm) patty. Form a ridge around the edge. Scatter mushrooms, tomato and green pepper over top. Season to taste with pepper. Top with mozzarella and Parmesan.

3. Bake in preheated oven for 15 to 20 minutes or until meat is no longer pink inside. Let stand for 5 minutes. Cut into 8 wedges.

Nutrients per Serving	
Calories	184
Carbohydrate	4 g
Fiber	1 g
Protein	16 g
Total fat	12 g
Saturated fat	5 g
Cholesterol	67 mg
Sodium	160 mg

America's Exchanges	
2	Lean Meats
1	Fat
1	Free Food

Canada's Choices	
2	Meat & Alternatives
1	Fat

Pizza Lovers' Pizza

Makes 4 servings

This hearty meatless pizza has a juicy and delicious topping that lives up to the wonderful aroma it produces as it cooks.

• 12-inch (30 cm) pizza pan, greased

Dough

1 tsp	granulated sugar	5 mL
1/2 cup	warm water	125 mL
1 1/2 tsp	instant (quick-rising) yeast	7 mL
1 tbsp	olive oil	15 mL
1 1/4 cups	all-purpose flour, divided	300 mL
1/2 tsp	salt	2 mL

Topping

1/2 cup	Spaghetti Sauce (see recipe, page 66)	125 mL
4	green onions, chopped	4
1	small green bell pepper, coarsely chopped	1
1 cup	sliced mushrooms	250 mL
1 1/4 cups	shredded part-skim mozzarella cheese	300 mL

1. *Dough:* Dissolve sugar in warm water. Sprinkle yeast over water and let stand for 10 minutes or until frothy; stir well. Stir in oil.

2. In a bowl, combine 1/2 cup (125 mL) of the flour and salt. Add yeast mixture and beat vigorously until a sticky dough forms. Gradually stir in another 3/4 cup (175 mL) flour to make a stiff dough.

3. Transfer dough to a floured work surface and knead in enough of the remaining flour to make a smooth, not sticky dough. Continue kneading for 3 to 4 minutes or until dough is smooth. Cover and let rest for at least 10 minutes or for up to 30 minutes. Meanwhile, preheat oven to 375°F (190°C), with rack positioned in lower third.

Nutrients per Serving	
Calories	313
Carbohydrate	38 g
Fiber	3 g
Protein	16 g
Total fat	11 g
Saturated fat	5 g
Cholesterol	24 mg
Sodium	548 mg

America's Exchanges	
2	Starches
1	Vegetable
1	Lean Meat
1 1/2	Fats

Canada's Choices	
2	Carbohydrates
1 1/2	Meat & Alternatives
1	Fat

Variation

Replace ¼ to ½ cup (60 to 125 mL) of the all-purpose flour with whole wheat flour. Use it in the first addition of flour, using all-purpose for the second addition and for kneading.

4. Roll out dough to fit prepared pizza pan. Transfer to pan, forming a rim around the edge.

5. *Topping:* Spread spaghetti sauce evenly over dough. Arrange green onions, green pepper and mushrooms on top. Sprinkle evenly with mozzarella. Place foil around edge of pan to catch drippings, if desired.

6. Bake in lower third of oven for 20 to 25 minutes or until crust is golden brown and cheese is melted and bubbling. Cut into wedges

Country Supper Cabbage Rolls

Makes 24 cabbage rolls

Serving size:
3 cabbage rolls

Freezing the cabbage is an easy way to wilt the leaves, which makes them easier to remove from the core.

Kitchen Tips

Holding the frozen cabbage under warm water as you work may make it easier to remove the leaves.

Save any remaining cabbage to serve as a vegetable at another meal.

Portion extra baked cabbage rolls into airtight containers, let cool, cover and freeze for up to 3 months. Let thaw overnight in the refrigerator or defrost in the microwave before reheating.

Nutrients per Serving	
Calories	241
Carbohydrate	14 g
Fiber	2 g
Protein	17 g
Total fat	13 g
Saturated fat	5 g
Cholesterol	56 mg
Sodium	386 mg

- **8-cup (2 L) casserole dish**

1	head green cabbage	1
1 lb	lean ground pork	500 g
8 oz	lean ground beef	250 g
1/2 cup	long-grain white rice	125 mL
1/3 cup	chopped onion	75 mL
1	clove garlic, finely chopped (optional)	1
1 tsp	salt	5 mL
1/4 tsp	freshly ground black pepper	1 mL
1 cup	reduced-sodium tomato juice	250 mL

1. Place cabbage in freezer overnight to wilt leaves.

2. Preheat oven to 300°F (150°C).

3. Carefully remove 24 cabbage leaves from the frozen head, one at a time, cutting each from the core with a sharp knife. Trim the center rib on individual leaves to make the leaf the same thickness throughout, but do not remove the rib.

4. In a large bowl, combine pork, beef, rice, onion, garlic (if using), salt, pepper and 1/2 cup (125 mL) water; mix thoroughly.

5. Place about 5 tsp (25 mL) meat mixture on the rib end of each cabbage leaf. Roll up and tuck in sides. Pack cabbage rolls tightly into casserole dish, a single layer at a time, layering them with tomato juice. Pour 1/2 cup (125 mL) water over rolls.

6. Cover and bake in preheated oven for 2 hours. Reduce oven temperature to 250°F (120°C) and bake for 1 hour or until meat is no longer pink and rice is tender.

America's Exchanges	
1/2	Starch
1	Vegetable
2	Lean Meats
1	Fat

Canada's Choices	
1/2	Carbohydrate
2	Meat & Alternatives
1	Fat

Quick Quiche

‖‖

Makes 6 servings

Traditional quiche features a rich pastry crust. In this trimmer version, the pastry is omitted and a savory mixture of meat, vegetables and cheese serves as the crust.

Kitchen Tip

In place of fresh broccoli, you can use 2 cups (500 mL) frozen chopped broccoli. Skip step 1. Let it thaw and drain well, gently squeezing out liquid, then chop into small pieces.

- Preheat oven to 325°F (160°C)
- 9-inch (23 cm) glass pie plate, greased
- Blender or food processor (optional)

1½ cups	chopped broccoli	375 mL
½ cup	diced cooked chicken or turkey	125 mL
1½ cups	shredded Swiss cheese	375 mL
¼ cup	chopped onion	60 mL
½ cup	all-purpose flour	125 mL
1 tsp	baking powder	5 mL
½ tsp	salt	2 mL
Pinch	freshly ground black pepper	Pinch
Pinch	ground nutmeg	Pinch
2	eggs	2
2	egg whites	2
2 cups	1% milk	500 mL

1. In a saucepan of boiling water, blanch broccoli for 2 minutes or until bright green. Drain well and let cool slightly.

2. In a large bowl, combine broccoli, chicken, cheese and onion. Spread mixture in prepared pie plate.

3. In blender, combine flour, baking powder, salt, pepper, nutmeg, eggs, egg whites and milk; blend on high speed for 1 minute (or whisk vigorously in a bowl). Pour into pie plate.

4. Bake in preheated oven for 45 minutes or until a tester inserted in the center comes out clean. Let stand for 5 minutes, then cut into 6 wedges.

Nutrients per Serving

Calories	258
Carbohydrate	16 g
Fiber	1 g
Protein	20 g
Total fat	12 g
Saturated fat	7 g
Cholesterol	107 mg
Sodium	402 mg

America's Exchanges

½	Milk
1	Other Carbohydrate
2	Lean Meats
1	Fat

Canada's Choices

1	Carbohydrate
2	Meat & Alternatives
1	Fat

Shepherd's Pie

Makes 4 servings
Serving size: 1$\frac{1}{3}$ cups
(325 mL)

Use ground beef, pork or lamb to make this speedy family favorite. Alternatively, you can use 12 oz (375 g) cooked meat, such as leftover roast. Chop it into small pieces and skip the browning step.

- **Preheat oven to 375°F (190°C)**
- **6-cup (1.5 L) casserole dish**

2 cups	cubed peeled potatoes	500 mL
$\frac{1}{2}$ tsp	salt	2 mL
2 tbsp	freshly grated Parmesan cheese	30 mL
1 lb	lean ground beef, pork or lamb	500 g
1 tbsp	all-purpose flour	15 mL
$\frac{1}{2}$ tsp	celery salt	2 mL
2 cups	Beef Stock (see recipe, page 76)	500 mL
2 tsp	Worcestershire sauce	10 mL
2 tbsp	chopped onion	30 mL
1$\frac{1}{2}$ cups	frozen mixed vegetables	375 mL
1 cup	sliced mushrooms	250 mL

1. Place potatoes in a saucepan and add 6 cups (1.5 L) cold water (or more as necessary to cover); stir in salt. Bring to a boil over medium-high heat; reduce heat and boil gently for 15 to 20 minutes or until just tender. Drain, reserving 3 tbsp (45 mL) cooking liquid. Mash potatoes with reserved cooking liquid until fluffy; fold in Parmesan. Set aside.

2. Meanwhile, in a skillet, over medium-high heat, cook beef, breaking it up with the back of a spoon, for about 8 minutes or until no longer pink. Using a slotted spoon, transfer beef to a plate. Drain fat from skillet.

3. In a jar, combine flour, celery salt, stock and Worcestershire sauce. Cover tightly and shake until thoroughly mixed.

Nutrients per Serving

Calories	323
Carbohydrate	25 g
Fiber	3 g
Protein	28 g
Total fat	12 g
Saturated fat	5 g
Cholesterol	62 mg
Sodium	347 mg

America's Exchanges

1	Starch
2	Vegetables
3	Lean Meats
$\frac{1}{2}$	Fat

Canada's Choices

1	Carbohydrate
3	Meat & Alternatives
1	Fat

Kitchen Tip

In place of the homemade beef stock, you can use store-bought reduced-sodium beef broth. If you do this, use $1/4$ tsp (1 mL) celery seed in place of the celery salt.

4. Add stock mixture to skillet. Add onion, reduce heat to medium and cook, stirring, for 3 minutes. Add vegetables and bring to a boil. Cook, stirring, for 2 minutes. Return beef to skillet and stir in mushrooms; cook until heated through.

5. Spoon beef mixture into casserole dish and spread potato mixture evenly over top. Bake in preheated oven for 30 minutes or until potatoes are lightly browned and beef mixture is bubbling.

Curried Pork and Fruit

This curry has a mild spice level which is accented nicely with the fruit and works perfectly with the pork.

Kitchen Tips

Prepare this curry up to 1 day in advance. Transfer to a shallow container, let cool, cover and refrigerate. Reheat in a skillet over medium heat, stirring often, until bubbling. For the best flavor, add the peach or orange during the last 10 minutes of the reheating time.

Curries are traditionally served with rice. One-third cup (75 mL) of cooked rice counts as a Starch Exchange or Carbohydrate Choice. For added flavor, fiber and vitamins, use brown rice. You can cook rice without adding salt.

Nutrients per Serving	
Calories	253
Carbohydrate	14 g
Fiber	2 g
Protein	24 g
Total fat	11 g
Saturated fat	4 g
Cholesterol	71 mg
Sodium	365 mg

2 tbsp	white or cider vinegar	30 mL
½ tsp	salt	2 mL
¼ tsp	freshly ground black pepper	1 mL
1 lb	boneless lean pork shoulder or leg, cut into bite-size pieces	500 g
1	small clove garlic, finely chopped	1
1 tsp	finely chopped gingerroot	5 mL
1 tsp	curry powder	5 mL
¼ tsp	ground cinnamon	1 mL
¼ tsp	ground cloves	1 mL
2 tsp	vegetable oil	10 mL
1	onion, chopped	1
2 tbsp	all-purpose flour	30 mL
3 tbsp	raisins	45 mL
1	peach or orange, cut into chunks	1

1. In a glass bowl, combine vinegar, salt and pepper. Add pork and toss to coat.

2. In a heavy skillet, combine garlic, ginger, curry powder, cinnamon, cloves and oil. Heat over medium heat, stirring, just until mixture bubbles. Add onion and ⅓ cup (75 mL) water; cook, stirring, for 4 minutes.

3. Sprinkle flour over pork mixture and toss to coat. Add to skillet and cook, stirring, for about 4 minutes or until meat loses its pink color. Stir in raisins and ²⁄₃ cup (150 mL) water; bring to a boil. Reduce heat to low, cover and simmer, stirring occasionally, for 35 minutes or until pork is fork-tender (do not let boil).

4. Stir in peach, cover and simmer for 10 minutes.

America's Exchanges	
1	Fruit
3	Lean Meats
½	Fat

Canada's Choices	
½	Carbohydrate
3	Meat & Alternatives
½	Fat

Polynesian Pork

|||||||||||||||||||||||||||||||||||||||||||||||||||||||||||||||||||||||||||||||||||||||||||||||||||||||||||||||||||||||||||||||

Pork is one of the most versatile meats. Here, it pairs well with pineapple and green pepper in a quick, colorful exotic dish.

Kitchen Tip

Rice goes well with this recipe. One-third cup (75 mL) of cooked rice counts as a Starch Exchange or Carbohydrate Choice. For added flavor, fiber and vitamins, use brown rice. You can cook rice without adding salt; if you do add it, use no more than ¼ tsp (1 mL) per cup (250 mL) of dry rice. This will add about 75 mg of sodium per ⅓-cup (75 mL) serving.

1 tbsp	vegetable oil (or less)	15 mL
1½ lbs	boneless lean pork shoulder, loin or leg, cut into bite-size pieces	750 g
1	can (14 oz/398 mL) unsweetened pineapple chunks, with juice	1
1 tbsp	reduced-sodium soy sauce	15 mL
1 tsp	ground ginger	5 mL
¼ tsp	freshly ground black pepper	1 mL
2 tsp	cornstarch	10 mL
1 tbsp	cold water	15 mL
1	small green bell pepper, cut into chunks	1
2 tsp	unsweetened shredded coconut	10 mL

1. In a large pot, heat half the oil over medium-high heat. Cook pork in batches, stirring, for 3 to 4 minutes or until lightly browned on all sides, adding oil as needed between batches. Return all pork to the pot.

2. Drain pineapple and set chunks aside. In a bowl, combine pineapple juice, soy sauce, ginger and pepper. Pour over pork. Reduce heat to low, cover and simmer for 20 minutes.

3. In a small bowl, whisk together cornstarch and cold water. Stir into pan juices. Increase heat to medium-high and bring to a boil. Boil, stirring, for about 3 minutes or until sauce thickens. Stir in pineapple chunks and green pepper. Cook, stirring, for 2 to 3 minutes or until sauce coats and glazes pork. Serve garnished with coconut.

Nutrients per Serving

Calories	250
Carbohydrate	13 g
Fiber	1 g
Protein	23 g
Total fat	12 g
Saturated fat	4 g
Cholesterol	71 mg
Sodium	158 mg

America's Exchanges	
1	Fruit
3	Lean Meats
½	Fat

Canada's Choices	
1	Carbohydrate
3	Meat & Alternatives
½	Fat

Saucy Ham-Stuffed Potatoes

||||||||||||||||||||||||||||||||||||||||||||||||||||||||||||||||||||||||||||||||||||||||||||||||||||||||||||||||||||||||||||

Makes 4 servings

Ham and potatoes stuffed into baked potato shells make a dish pretty enough for company.

- Preheat oven to 400°F (200°C)
- Casserole dish

4	baking potatoes (1 1/2 lbs/750 g total)	4
8 oz	cooked reduced-sodium ham, coarsely chopped (about 2 cups/500 mL)	250 g
1/4 cup	dry white wine	60 mL
2 tsp	margarine or butter	10 mL
1/4 tsp	dried tarragon	1 mL
3 cups	sliced mushrooms	750 mL
2	green onions, finely chopped	2
2 tbsp	tomato paste	30 mL
1/3 cup	evaporated 2% milk	75 mL

1. Prick potatoes with a fork. Bake in preheated oven for 45 minutes or until tender.

2. Meanwhile, place ham in casserole dish, cover and heat in oven for 10 minutes.

3. In a skillet, combine 2 tbsp (30 mL) water, wine, margarine and tarragon. Add mushrooms, cover and bring to a boil over high heat; boil for 2 minutes. Using a slotted spoon, transfer mushrooms to a warm plate.

4. Add green onions, tomato paste and 6 tbsp (90 mL) water to skillet and boil, stirring, for 2 minutes.

Nutrients per Serving

Calories	250
Carbohydrate	37 g
Fiber	5 g
Protein	14 g
Total fat	5 g
Saturated fat	1 g
Cholesterol	31 mg
Sodium	509 mg

America's Exchanges

2	Starches
1	Vegetable
1	Lean Meat

Canada's Choices

2	Carbohydrates
1	Meat & Alternatives

Nutrition Tip

Reduced-sodium cold cuts and cured meats, such as ham and bacon, are available in well-stocked supermarkets. Remember, though, that reduced sodium does not mean low sodium, just that there is less (typically 25% to 30% less) than in the regular version of the same food. Always check the Nutrition Facts table for the serving size and the amount of sodium.

5. Cut baked potatoes in half lengthwise. Scoop out most of potato flesh, leaving just enough so the skin retains a shell shape; keep shells warm.

6. Mash potato and stir into skillet. Bring to a boil and cook, stirring, for 1 minute. Stir in ham, mushrooms and evaporated milk; cook, stirring constantly, until heated through. (Do not let boil.)

7. Divide ham mixture evenly among reserved potato shells. Serve immediately.

Ham and Asparagus Roll-Ups

||||||||||||||||||||||||||||||||||||||||||||||||||||||||||||||||||||||||||||||||||||||||||||||||||||||||||||||||||||||||||||||||||

Makes 6 servings
Serving size: 2 roll-ups
with sauce

In this quick, easy dish, sprightly green asparagus spears are rolled up inside slices of ham and blanketed with a delicious cheese sauce. It's especially good in early spring, when tender fresh asparagus is at its peak.

- **Preheat oven to 350°F (180°C)**
- **13- by 9-inch (33 by 23 cm) shallow glass baking dish**

24	fresh or frozen asparagus spears (thawed if frozen)	24
12	thin slices reduced-sodium deli ham	12
¾ cup	shredded Cheddar, Edam or Gouda cheese	175 mL
1 cup	Herb Sauce (see variation, page 58)	250 mL
¼ tsp	paprika	1 mL

1. If using fresh asparagus, in a pot of boiling water, blanch asparagus for 2 minutes or until bright green. For either fresh or frozen, drain well and pat dry.

2. Sprinkle about 1 tbsp (15 mL) Cheddar cheese over each ham slice. Roll up 2 asparagus spears inside each ham slice and arrange, seam side down, in baking dish. Pour herb sauce over roll-ups. Sprinkle with paprika.

3. Bake in preheated oven for 15 to 20 minutes or until bubbling.

Nutrients per Serving	
Calories	130
Carbohydrate	6 g
Fiber	1 g
Protein	10 g
Total fat	7 g
Saturated fat	4 g
Cholesterol	33 mg
Sodium	432 mg

America's Exchanges	
½	Other Carbohydrate
1	Lean Meat
1	Fat

Canada's Choices	
1½	Meat & Alternatives
½	Fat
1	Extra

Lamb Curry

||||||||||||||||||||||||||||||||||||||||||||||||||||||||||||||||||||||||||||||||||||||||||||||||

Makes 4 servings
Serving size: 1 cup
(250 mL)

Leftover lamb is best served warm, so why not turn it into a flavorful curry?

Kitchen Tips
In place of the homemade beef or chicken stock, you can use store-bought reduced-sodium beef or chicken broth. If you do this, omit the salt in the recipe.

Curries are traditionally served with rice. One-third cup (75 mL) of cooked rice counts as a Starch Exchange or Carbohydrate Choice. For added flavor, fiber and vitamins, use brown rice. You can cook rice without adding salt.

Variation
Substitute cooked pork or beef for the lamb.

4 tsp	vegetable oil	20 mL
1 cup	chopped onion	250 mL
1 to 2 tsp	curry powder	5 to 10 mL
2 tbsp	all-purpose flour	30 mL
2 cups	Beef Stock (see recipe, page 76) or Chicken Stock (see recipe, page 78)	500 mL
12 oz	boneless cooked lean lamb, cut into 1-inch (2.5 cm) cubes	375 g
½ tsp	salt	2 mL
¼ tsp	ground cinnamon	1 mL
Pinch	freshly ground black pepper	Pinch
1	small apple, peeled and chopped	1

1. In a skillet, heat 3 tsp (15 mL) oil over medium heat. Sauté onion for 5 minutes or until softened. Stir in curry powder and the remaining oil; sauté for 1 minute.

2. In a jar, combine flour and stock. Cover tightly and shake until thoroughly mixed. Pour over onion mixture and cook, stirring, for 5 minutes or until thickened.

3. Stir in lamb, salt, cinnamon and pepper; reduce heat to low, cover and simmer, stirring occasionally, for 20 minutes. Stir in apple, cover and simmer for 5 minutes.

Nutrients per Serving	
Calories	251
Carbohydrate	11 g
Fiber	1 g
Protein	27 g
Total fat	11 g
Saturated fat	3 g
Cholesterol	85 mg
Sodium	356 mg

America's Exchanges	
1	Other Carbohydrate
4	Lean Meats

Canada's Choices	
½	Carbohydrate
3	Meat & Alternatives
½	Fat

Chicken and Snow Pea Stir-Fry

||||||||||||||||||||||||||||||||||||||||||||||||||||||||||||||||||||||||||||||||||||||||||||||||||||||||||

Makes 4 servings

This quick stir-fry makes a complete and colorful meal. French-cut green beans or chopped broccoli can be substituted for the snow peas.

Kitchen Tip

Rice goes well with stir-fries. One-third cup (75 mL) of cooked rice counts as a Starch Exchange or Carbohydrate Choice. For added flavor, fiber and vitamins, use brown rice. You can cook rice without adding salt; if you do add it, use no more than $\frac{1}{4}$ tsp (1 mL) per cup (250 mL) of dry rice. This will add about 75 mg of sodium per $\frac{1}{3}$-cup (75 mL) serving.

2 tsp	cornstarch	10 mL
12 oz	boneless skinless chicken breasts, cut into bite-size pieces	375 g
2 tbsp	vegetable oil (or less), divided	30 mL
2	stalks celery, sliced on the diagonal	2
1	small onion, thinly sliced	1
$\frac{1}{2}$ cup	reduced-sodium chicken broth	125 mL
$\frac{1}{2}$ tsp	ground ginger	2 mL
4 oz	snow peas	125 g
2 tbsp	slivered almonds or drained canned sliced water chestnuts	30 mL
1 tbsp	reduced-sodium soy sauce	15 mL
$\frac{1}{4}$ tsp	salt (or less)	1 mL
	Freshly ground black pepper	

1. Place cornstarch in a bowl. Add chicken and toss to coat.

2. In a wok or large skillet, heat 2 tsp (10 mL) oil over medium-high heat. Stir-fry chicken in batches for 5 to 7 minutes or until golden on all sides, adding oil as needed between batches. Transfer chicken to a warm plate. Wipe out skillet.

3. Add 1 tsp (5 mL) oil to skillet. Stir-fry celery and onion for 4 minutes or until softened. Stir in broth and ginger; reduce heat and simmer for 4 minutes. Return chicken and any accumulated juices to pan and stir in snow peas, almonds and soy sauce; cover and simmer for 2 minutes. Taste and season with up to $\frac{1}{4}$ tsp (1 mL) salt. Season to taste with pepper.

Nutrients per Serving	
Calories	207
Carbohydrate	7 g
Fiber	2 g
Protein	22 g
Total fat	10 g
Saturated fat	1 g
Cholesterol	50 mg
Sodium	411 mg

America's Exchanges	
1	Vegetable
3	Lean Meats

Canada's Choices	
3	Meat & Alternatives

Fruited Chicken Crêpes

|||||||||||||||||||||||||||||||||||||||||||||||||||||||||||||||||||||||||||||||||||||||||||||||||||||||||||||||||||||||||||||||||||||

Makes 2 servings

When both the crêpes and the filling are prepared ahead, a special meal can be put together in no time at all. Reheat the filling and spoon it into warm crêpes.

Kitchen Tips

Toast almonds in a small dry skillet over medium heat, stirring constantly, for about 3 minutes or until golden and fragrant.

To make the filling ahead, transfer to a shallow container, let cool, cover and refrigerate for up to 2 days. Reheat in a saucepan over medium heat, stirring often, until bubbling.

3	dried apricots, coarsely chopped	3
1 tbsp	raisins	15 mL
$\frac{1}{2}$ tsp	ground cinnamon	2 mL
$\frac{1}{2}$ tsp	chili powder	2 mL
1$\frac{1}{4}$ cups	Chicken Stock (see recipe, page 78)	300 mL
1$\frac{1}{4}$ cups	chopped cooked chicken	300 mL
2	warm Crêpes (see recipe, page 70)	2
1 tbsp	slivered almonds, toasted (see tip, at left)	15 mL

1. In a saucepan, combine apricots, raisins, cinnamon, chili powder and stock. Bring to a boil over high heat. Reduce heat and simmer, stirring occasionally, for about 15 minutes or until liquid is reduced by half and is slightly thickened. Stir in chicken and simmer for 5 minutes.

2. Place crêpes on warm serving plates. Divide filling between crêpes, reserving a small amount for the top. Roll up crêpes and spoon reserved filling over top. Garnish with almonds. Serve immediately.

Nutrients per Serving

Calories	290
Carbohydrate	21 g
Fiber	2 g
Protein	33 g
Total fat	8 g
Saturated fat	2 g
Cholesterol	125 mg
Sodium	133 mg

America's Exchanges	
$\frac{1}{2}$	Starch
1	Other Carbohydrate
4	Lean Meats

Canada's Choices	
1	Carbohydrate
4	Meat & Alternatives

Turkey Tetrazzini

||||||||||||||||||||||||||||||||||||||||||||||||||||||||||||||||||||||||||||||||||||||||||||||||||||||||||||||||||||||||||||||||||||||||||||||

Makes 8 servings
Serving size: 1 cup
(250 mL)

When you have no turkey leftovers on hand, you can simmer economical turkey parts to provide the cooked turkey for this tetrazzini, a popular dish for both family meals and entertaining.

Kitchen Tip

In place of the homemade chicken stock, you can use store-bought reduced-sodium chicken broth. If you do this, reduce the salt to 1 tsp (5 mL).

- **Preheat oven to 350°F (180°C)**
- **10-cup (2.5 L) casserole dish, lightly greased**

8 oz	spaghetti or thin noodles	250 g
2 tbsp	margarine or butter, divided	30 mL
8 oz	mushrooms, sliced	250 g
1 tbsp	freshly squeezed lemon juice	15 mL
6 tbsp	all-purpose flour	90 mL
2½ cups	Chicken Stock (see recipe, page 78) or turkey stock	625 mL
1 cup	2% milk	250 mL
2 tbsp	chopped fresh parsley (or 2 tsp/10 mL dried parsley)	30 mL
1½ tsp	salt	7 mL
½ tsp	ground nutmeg	2 mL
½ tsp	onion powder	2 mL
Pinch	paprika	Pinch
Pinch	freshly ground white pepper	Pinch
¼ cup	dry sherry	60 mL
4 cups	chopped cooked turkey	1 L
¼ cup	freshly grated Parmesan cheese	60 mL

1. In a pot of boiling water, cook spaghetti according to package directions (omitting salt) until almost tender. Drain and set aside.

2. Meanwhile, in a skillet, heat 2 tsp (10 mL) of the margarine over medium-high heat. Sauté mushrooms for 5 minutes or until lightly browned. Sprinkle with lemon juice. Remove from heat and set aside.

Nutrients per Serving

Calories	332
Carbohydrate	32 g
Fiber	2 g
Protein	29 g
Total fat	9 g
Saturated fat	3 g
Cholesterol	58 mg
Sodium	590 mg

America's Exchanges	
2	Starches
3	Lean Meats

Canada's Choices	
2	Carbohydrates
3	Meat & Alternatives

Nutrition Tip

When choosing a margarine, look for a non-hydrogenated soft margarine. These are low in saturated fat and do not contain trans fat. Avoid hard margarines, which contain high amounts of saturated and trans fat.

3. In a medium saucepan, melt the remaining margarine over medium heat. Stir in flour until smooth. Gradually add stock and milk, stirring briskly to remove any lumps; bring to a boil, stirring. Stir in parsley, salt, nutmeg, onion powder, paprika, white pepper and sherry; boil, stirring, for 2 to 3 minutes or until thickened.

4. Pour enough sauce into prepared casserole dish to coat the bottom. Layer mushrooms, spaghetti and turkey over sauce. Pour the remaining sauce over turkey. Sprinkle with Parmesan.

5. Bake in preheated oven for 30 to 40 minutes or until bubbling.

Light and Fresh Chicken à la King

Makes 6 servings

This lighter, one-pot version of a classic recipe is sure to become your favorite way to reinvent leftover chicken.

Kitchen Tips

In place of the homemade chicken stock, you can use store-bought reduced-sodium chicken broth. If you do this, omit the salt in step 1.

Two large cooked chicken breasts will make about 3 cups (750 mL) shredded chicken.

Variation

You can use leftover cooked turkey and turkey stock in place of the chicken.

	Nutrients per Serving	
Calories		298
Carbohydrate		29 g
Fiber		4 g
Protein		28 g
Total fat		8 g
Saturated fat		2 g
Cholesterol		86 mg
Sodium		428 mg

1 tbsp	vegetable oil	15 mL
4	carrots, thinly sliced	4
1	small onion, chopped	1
8 oz	mushrooms, sliced	250 g
3/4 tsp	salt (or less), divided	3 mL
1/4 tsp	freshly ground black pepper	1 mL
2 cups	Chicken Stock (see recipe, page 78)	500 mL
4 oz	broad egg noodles	125 g
3 cups	coarsely shredded cooked chicken (about 12 oz/375 g)	750 mL
1 cup	frozen green peas, thawed	250 mL
1 tbsp	all-purpose flour	15 mL
1 cup	2% milk	250 mL
2 tbsp	freshly squeezed lemon juice	30 mL
	Chopped fresh parsley	

1. In a large pot, heat oil over medium-high heat. Sauté carrots, onion, mushrooms, 1/2 tsp (2 mL) of the salt and the pepper for about 10 minutes or until mushrooms release their liquid and start to brown.

2. Stir in stock and bring to a boil, scraping up brown bits from bottom. Stir in noodles; reduce heat to low, cover and simmer for 5 min or until noodles are almost tender.

3. Stir chicken and peas into pot. Whisk flour into milk and stir into pot. Increase heat to medium and simmer, stirring often, for about 5 minutes or until chicken is hot and sauce is slightly thickened. Stir in lemon juice. Taste and add up to 1/4 tsp (1 mL) more salt. Garnish with parsley. Serve immediately.

America's Exchanges	
1	Starch
2	Vegetables
3	Lean Meats

Canada's Choices	
1 1/2	Carbohydrates
3	Meat & Alternatives

Meatless Dishes

Mushroom Omelet

4	eggs, lightly beaten	4
¼ cup	shredded Swiss cheese	60 mL
1 tbsp	chopped fresh basil or parsley (or 1 tsp/5 mL dried parsley)	15 mL
¼ tsp	freshly ground white pepper	1 mL
⅛ tsp	salt	0.5 mL
1 tsp	vegetable oil	5 mL
1	small onion, chopped	1
8 oz	mushrooms, sliced	250 g

The secrets to a good omelet are beating the eggs just until frothy and cooking over medium heat. Mushroom omelets are perfect for a breakfast party, brunch or a quick, light supper.

Kitchen Tip

A flexible, heatproof silicone spatula is the perfect tool for omelet-making, allowing you to gently lift the fragile eggs as they set without cutting or breaking them and making it easier to remove the omelet from the pan.

1. In a bowl, whisk together eggs, cheese, basil, white pepper and salt. Set aside.

2. In an omelet pan or nonstick skillet, heat oil over medium heat. Sauté onion for 2 minutes. Add mushrooms and sauté for 3 minutes.

3. Pour egg mixture over mushroom mixture. Lift edges of omelet with a spatula as soon as egg starts to cook and tilt pan to allow uncooked egg to run underneath. Cook for 3 to 4 minutes or until set on top and golden on bottom. Run spatula around inside of skillet to loosen omelet. Fold omelet in half and turn out onto a warm serving platter.

Nutrients per Serving

Calories	271
Carbohydrate	10 g
Fiber	3 g
Protein	19 g
Total fat	17 g
Saturated fat	6 g
Cholesterol	387 mg
Sodium	302 mg

America's Exchanges	
2	Vegetables
2	Lean Meats
2	Fats

Canada's Choices	
2½	Meat & Alternatives
2	Fats

Vegetable Frittata

||||||||||||||||||||||||||||||||||||||||||||||||||||||||||||||||||||||||||||||||||||||||||

For this frittata, choose green vegetables that are in season for the best quality and the best price.

Nutrition Tips

If you use the optional garlic salt, it will add 120 mg of sodium per serving.

When purchasing a seasoning blend, be sure to check the sodium content. Some contain salt, though it's not always mentioned in the name as it is with garlic salt.

4	eggs	4
1 tbsp	chopped fresh parsley (or 1 tsp/5 mL dried parsley)	15 mL
½ tsp	dried oregano	2 mL
¼ tsp	garlic salt (optional)	1 mL
Pinch	freshly ground black pepper	Pinch
2 tsp	margarine or butter	10 mL
2	green onions, chopped	2
½ cup	chopped broccoli, asparagus or green beans	125 mL
½ cup	chopped celery	125 mL

1. In a bowl, whisk together eggs, parsley, oregano, garlic salt (if using), pepper and 1 tbsp (15 mL) water. Set aside.

2. In a heavy skillet, melt margarine over medium heat. Sauté green onions, broccoli and celery for 4 to 5 minutes or until tender-crisp.

3. Pour egg mixture over vegetable mixture and cook for 30 seconds. Cover and cook for 2 to 3 minutes or until set. Cut frittata in half and slide out of the skillet onto warmed plates.

Nutrients per Serving

Calories	198
Carbohydrate	5 g
Fiber	1 g
Protein	13 g
Total fat	14 g
Saturated fat	4 g
Cholesterol	372 mg
Sodium	313 mg

America's Exchanges

1	Vegetable
2	Lean Meats
1½	Fats

Canada's Choices

2	Meat & Alternatives
1½	Fats

Mock Egg Salad

||||||||||||||||||||||||||||||||||||||||||||||||||||||||||||||||||||||||||||||||||||||||||||||||||||||||||||||||

Real egg salad contains quite a bit of fat, thanks to the egg yolk. This version, made with chickpeas, provides protein and the taste of egg salad with almost no fat. Serve it stuffed in a tomato on a lettuce leaf, or open-faced on whole wheat toast, garnished with cucumber slices.

Kitchen Tip

A 19-oz (540 mL) can of chickpeas will yield 2 cups (500 mL) once drained and rinsed. If you have smaller cans, use two, drain and rinse, then measure the chickpeas. Any extra can be stored in an airtight container in the refrigerator for up to 3 days or frozen for up to 3 months. To cook from dried, soak and cook 1 cup (250 mL) dried chickpeas.

Nutrients per Serving	
Calories	92
Carbohydrate	15 g
Fiber	3 g
Protein	4 g
Total fat	2 g
Saturated fat	0 g
Cholesterol	9 mg
Sodium	211 mg

2 cups	rinsed drained canned or cooked chickpeas (see tip, at left)	500 mL
¼ cup	chopped celery	60 mL
½ tsp	dried basil	2 mL
¼ tsp	curry powder	1 mL
¼ tsp	garlic salt	1 mL
¼ cup	Tangy Salad Cream (see recipe, page 124)	60 mL

1. In a bowl, coarsely mash chickpeas. Stir in celery, basil, curry powder, garlic salt and dressing until well blended.

America's Exchanges	
1	Starch

Canada's Choices	
1	Carbohydrate
½	Meat & Alternatives

Spanish Bulgur

‖‖‖

Makes 8 servings
Serving size: 1 cup (250 mL)

Bulgur, chickpeas and soy nuts combine to provide a complete protein in Spanish bulgur, which tastes just as good as (or even better than) Spanish rice.

Kitchen Tip
In place of the homemade stock, you can use store-bought reduced-sodium vegetable or chicken broth. If you do this, reduce the salt to $\frac{1}{2}$ tsp (2 mL).

2 tbsp	vegetable oil	30 mL
1	clove garlic, finely chopped	1
1 cup	thinly sliced carrot	250 mL
$\frac{1}{2}$ cup	coarsely chopped onion	125 mL
$1\frac{1}{4}$ cups	coarse bulgur	300 mL
1	can (19 oz/540 mL) no-salt-added diced tomatoes, with juice	1
2 tsp	paprika	10 mL
1 tsp	dried tarragon or oregano	5 mL
1 tsp	salt	5 mL
Pinch	freshly ground black pepper	Pinch
$2\frac{1}{4}$ cups	hot Vegetable Stock (see recipe, page 79) or Chicken Stock (see recipe, page 78)	550 mL
1 cup	coarsely chopped celery	250 mL
1 cup	coarsely chopped green or red bell pepper	250 mL
1 cup	rinsed drained canned or cooked chickpeas	250 mL
$\frac{1}{2}$ cup	coarsely chopped soy nuts	125 mL

1. In a skillet, heat oil over medium heat. Sauté garlic, carrot and onion for 5 minutes. Add bulgur and sauté for about 3 minutes or until bulgur is coated with pan juices.

2. Stir in tomatoes with juice, paprika, tarragon, salt, pepper and stock; bring to a boil. Stir in celery and green pepper; reduce heat to low, cover and simmer for 15 minutes or until bulgur is almost tender.

3. Stir in chickpeas and soy nuts; cover and simmer for 5 minutes or until bulgur is tender and juices are absorbed. Remove from heat and let stand, covered, for 10 minutes. Fluff with a fork.

Nutrients per Serving

Calories	222
Carbohydrate	33 g
Fiber	7 g
Protein	9 g
Total fat	7 g
Saturated fat	1 g
Cholesterol	0 mg
Sodium	442 mg

America's Exchanges

1	Vegetable
$1\frac{1}{2}$	Other Carbohydrates
1	Lean Meat
1	Fat

Canada's Choices

$1\frac{1}{2}$	Carbohydrates
$\frac{1}{2}$	Meat & Alternatives
1	Fat

Lentil Burgers

Makes 5 servings

Lentil burgers are a tasty and inexpensive substitute for meat patties. You'll be surprised by how similar the flavor is. The addition of bread crumbs and cheese makes these burgers a complete protein.

Nutrition Tip

We often hear that we can get all the nutrients we need from a well-balanced diet. This is frequently untrue. For example, throughout most of North America, the sun is not strong enough for much of the year to provide adequate vitamin D, so we need a supplement. Unless you drink at least 2 cups (500 mL) of milk or fortified soy beverage each day, you likely need a calcium supplement. People over 50 need larger amounts of both vitamin D and calcium. If you are a vegan and do not drink fortified soy beverage, you will also need a vitamin B_{12} supplement.

1	can (19 oz/540 mL) brown lentils, drained and rinsed	1
$\frac{2}{3}$ cup	dry bread crumbs	150 mL
$\frac{1}{4}$ cup	finely chopped onion	60 mL
$\frac{1}{4}$ cup	finely chopped celery	60 mL
$\frac{1}{2}$ tsp	salt	2 mL
$\frac{1}{2}$ tsp	freshly ground black pepper	2 mL
1 tsp	Worcestershire sauce	5 mL
1 tbsp	vegetable oil	15 mL
$\frac{1}{2}$ cup	shredded Cheddar or Swiss cheese	125 mL

1. In a large bowl, mash lentils. Stir in bread crumbs, onion, celery, salt, pepper, $\frac{1}{3}$ cup (75 mL) water and Worcestershire sauce until well blended. Form into five $\frac{3}{4}$-inch (2 cm) thick patties.

2. In a skillet, heat oil over medium heat. Cook burgers for about 5 minutes per side or until browned on both sides. Top each with cheese.

Nutrients per Serving

Calories	196
Carbohydrate	23 g
Fiber	3 g
Protein	10 g
Total fat	7 g
Saturated fat	3 g
Cholesterol	12 mg
Sodium	465 mg

America's Exchanges	
$1\frac{1}{2}$	Other Carbohydrates
1	Lean Meat
1	Fat

Canada's Choices	
1	Carbohydrate
1	Meat & Alternatives
1	Fat

Bean-Stuffed Cabbage Rolls

||||||||||||||||||||||||||||||||||||||||||||||||||||||||||||||||||||||||||||||||||||||||||||||||||||||||||||||

Makes
16 cabbage rolls
Serving size:
4 cabbage rolls

In this delicious one-dish meal, black-eyed peas and barley create a savory filling that steams inside cabbage leaves.

Kitchen Tip
Holding the frozen cabbage under warm water as you work may make it easier to remove the leaves.

Nutrition Tips
To keep the sodium in check, cook the peas and barley without adding any salt. The salt added to the filling will make them flavorful enough.

A serving of this recipe is an excellent source of iron, supplying 25% of the Daily Value. It also contains significant amounts of thiamin, riboflavin, niacin, vitamin B_6, folate and pantothenic acid.

Nutrients per Serving

Calories	201
Carbohydrate	41 g
Fiber	10 g
Protein	10 g
Total fat	1 g
Saturated fat	0 g
Cholesterol	0 mg
Sodium	470 mg

- 8-cup (2 L) casserole dish

1	small head cabbage	1
2 cups	cooked black-eyed peas (see nutrition tip, at left), mashed	500 mL
1 cup	cooked barley (see nutrition tip, at left)	250 mL
1 cup	finely chopped celery	250 mL
1/2 cup	finely chopped onion	125 mL
1/2 tsp	salt	2 mL
1/2 tsp	dried basil	2 mL
Pinch	dried oregano	Pinch
Pinch	dried thyme	Pinch
2	drops hot pepper sauce	2
2 cups	reduced-sodium tomato juice	500 mL

1. Place cabbage in freezer overnight to wilt leaves.

2. Preheat oven to 350°F (180°C).

3. Carefully remove 16 cabbage leaves from frozen head, one at a time, cutting each from the core with a sharp knife. Trim the center rib on individual leaves to make the leaf the same thickness throughout, but do not remove the rib.

4. In a bowl, mash black-eyed peas and barley together. Stir in celery, onion, salt, basil, oregano, thyme and hot pepper sauce until well blended.

5. Place about 1/4 cup (60 mL) pea mixture on the rib end of each cabbage leaf. Roll up and tuck in sides. Pack cabbage rolls tightly into casserole dish. Pour tomato juice over rolls.

6. Cover and bake in preheated oven for 1 hour or until sauce is bubbling and cabbage rolls are hot in the center.

America's Exchanges	
2	Vegetables
1 1/2	Other Carbohydrates
1	Lean Meat

Canada's Choices	
2	Carbohydrates
1	Meat & Alternatives

Scalloped Soybeans

||||||||||||||||||||||||||||||||||||||||||||||||||||||||||||||||||||||||||||||||||||||||||||||||||||||||||||||||||||||

Makes 6 servings
Serving size: $2/3$ cup
(150 mL)

The soybeans absorb the flavor of the vegetables in this side dish, which makes a terrific accompaniment to a vegetarian meal that might otherwise be low in protein.

Kitchen Tip
You can substitute 3 cups (750 mL) rinsed drained canned soybeans for the dried. Skip steps 1 and 2.

Nutrition Tip
A serving of this recipe is an excellent source of iron, supplying 29% of the Daily Value. It also contains significant amounts of thiamin, riboflavin, niacin, vitamin B_6, and folate. But it has no vitamin B_{12}, found naturally only in animal-source foods. If you are a vegan and do not use fortified vegan products, you will need to take a vitamin B_{12} supplement.

Nutrients per Serving	
Calories	162
Carbohydrate	13 g
Fiber	6 g
Protein	13 g
Total fat	8 g
Saturated fat	1 g
Cholesterol	0 mg
Sodium	226 mg

- **6-cup (1.5 L) casserole dish**

1 cup	dried soybeans, rinsed	250 mL
1	onion, chopped	1
1 cup	chopped celery	250 mL
$1/2$ cup	finely chopped red or green bell pepper	125 mL
$1/2$ tsp	salt	2 mL
$1/2$ cup	no-salt-added tomato sauce	125 mL
$1/4$ cup	boiling water	60 mL
$1/4$ cup	fresh bread crumbs	60 mL
2 tsp	olive oil	10 mL

1. Place soybeans in a large bowl and add enough cold water to cover by at least 3 inches (7.5 cm). Cover and let stand at room temperature for at least 12 hours or for up to 24 hours.

2. Drain soybeans and rinse well; drain. In a saucepan, combine soybeans and 3 cups (750 mL) fresh water. Bring to a boil over high heat and boil for 10 minutes. Reduce heat to low, cover and simmer for $1\frac{1}{2}$ to 2 hours or until soybeans are softened. Drain.

3. Meanwhile, preheat oven to 350°F (180°C).

4. Pour soybeans into casserole dish. Stir in onion, celery, red pepper, salt, tomato sauce and boiling water.

5. In a bowl, combine bread crumbs and oil. Sprinkle over soybean mixture.

6. Bake in preheated oven for $1\frac{1}{2}$ to 2 hours or until soybeans are tender.

America's Exchanges	
1	Vegetable
$1/2$	Other Carbohydrate
2	Lean Meats

Canada's Choices	
$1\frac{1}{2}$	Meat & Alternatives
1	Extra

Tofu Chop Suey

Tofu supplies the protein, and tastes similar to chicken breasts, in this quick-to-prepare, colorful vegetarian main dish.

Kitchen Tip

All produce should be rinsed well under running water before it is prepared. After rinsing the bean sprouts, drain them well and pat them dry so they don't water down the flavor.

Nutrition Tip

Regular soy sauce typically contains about 900 mg of sodium per tbsp (15 mL) — over 30% of the Daily Value. You can significantly reduce the sodium content of recipes by using sodium-reduced soy sauce, which usually has 30% to 40% less sodium.

8 oz	firm or extra-firm tofu	250 g
¼ cup	reduced-sodium vegetable or chicken broth, divided	60 mL
2 tsp	vegetable oil	10 mL
¼ tsp	ground ginger	1 mL
1	small onion, coarsely chopped	1
¼	red bell pepper, cut into thin slices	¼
1 cup	sliced celery	250 mL
1½ cups	bean sprouts	375 mL
1 tbsp	reduced-sodium soy sauce	15 mL
⅛ tsp	salt (or less)	0.5 mL
	Freshly ground black pepper	

1. Drain tofu and cut into ¾-inch (2 cm) pieces. Place between layers of paper towels and weigh down with a dinner plate. Let stand for 10 minutes to compress and remove excess water.

2. In a skillet, heat 2 tbsp (30 mL) of the broth, oil and ginger over medium heat. Sauté onion, red pepper and celery for 3 minutes. Add bean sprouts and sauté for 1 minute.

3. Stir in the remaining broth, soy sauce and tofu; cook, stirring gently, for about 5 minutes or until vegetables are tender-crisp and liquid has evaporated. Taste and add up to ⅛ tsp (0.5 mL) salt. Season to taste with pepper.

Nutrients per Serving	
Calories	194
Carbohydrate	16 g
Fiber	3 g
Protein	13 g
Total fat	10 g
Saturated fat	1 g
Cholesterol	0 mg
Sodium	534 mg

America's Exchanges	
3	Vegetables
1	Lean Meat
1½	Fats

Canada's Choices	
1½	Meat & Alternatives
1	Fat
1	Extra

Noodles Romanoff

||||||||||||||||||||||||||||||||||||||||||||||||||||||||||||||||||||||||||||||||||||||||||||||||||||||||||||||||||||||||||||||||||||||||||||||||||

Serve these noodles in place of potatoes, or whenever you need to increase the protein in a meal. If you use whole wheat noodles in this recipe, you'll get added fiber, too.

Nutrition Tip
People of all ages need a regular supply of calcium. Milk, fortified soy beverage, yogurt, cheese and canned fish with bones (such as sardines and salmon) contain high amounts of calcium. Broccoli, carrots, green beans and dark green leafy vegetables also contain calcium, but in much lower amounts. Tofu varies in calcium content; check the Nutrition Facts table.

• **Food processor or blender (optional)**

1 cup	2% cottage cheese	250 mL
$1/2$ cup	1% milk	125 mL
2	green onions, chopped	2
$1/4$ cup	freshly grated Parmesan cheese	60 mL
1 tbsp	chopped fresh dill or parsley (or 1 tsp/5 mL dried dillweed)	15 mL
Pinch	freshly ground black pepper	Pinch
6 oz	wide or narrow egg noodles (about 4 cups/1 L)	175 g
	Additional freshly grated Parmesan cheese (optional)	

1. In food processor, combine cottage cheese and milk; process until very smooth (or whisk together in a bowl). Transfer to a bowl (if necessary) and stir in green onions, Parmesan, dill and pepper. Set aside.

2. In a pot of boiling water, cook noodles according to package directions (omitting salt) until just tender. Drain and return to saucepan. Fold in cheese mixture. Bring just to a simmer over medium-low heat, stirring gently (do not let boil). Serve immediately, sprinkled with additional Parmesan, if desired.

Nutrients per Serving	
Calories	131
Carbohydrate	18 g
Fiber	1 g
Protein	9 g
Total fat	3 g
Saturated fat	1 g
Cholesterol	27 mg
Sodium	174 mg

America's Exchanges	
1	Starch
1	Lean Meat

Canada's Choices	
1	Carbohydrate
1	Meat & Alternatives

Creamy Macaroni and Cheese

||||||||||||||||||||||||||||||||||||||||||||||||||||||||||||||||||||||||||||||||||||||||||||||||||||||||||

Makes 5 servings
Serving size: ³/₄ cup
(175 mL)

Old-fashioned macaroni and cheese can be as highly seasoned or as bland as you wish. The age, or ripeness, of the cheese will determine the strength of the flavor.

Kitchen Tip
For 1¹/₂ cups (375 mL) shredded Cheddar cheese, purchase 6 oz (175 g).

- Preheat oven to 350°F (180°C)
- 6-cup (1.5 L) casserole dish, lightly greased

1¹/₄ cups	elbow macaroni	300 mL
2 tsp	margarine or butter	10 mL
2 tbsp	all-purpose flour	30 mL
¹/₄ tsp	salt	1 mL
¹/₄ tsp	onion powder (optional)	1 mL
Pinch	freshly ground black pepper	Pinch
2 cups	1% milk	500 mL
2	drops hot pepper sauce	2
1¹/₂ cups	shredded aged (old) Cheddar cheese	375 mL
2 tbsp	dry bread crumbs	30 mL

1. In a pot of boiling water, cook macaroni according to package directions until almost tender. Drain and set aside.

2. Meanwhile, in a medium saucepan, melt margarine over medium heat. Whisk in flour, salt, onion powder (if using) and pepper. Gradually add milk, whisking constantly. Whisk in hot pepper sauce and bring to a simmer, whisking constantly. Remove from heat.

3. Reserve 2 tbsp (30 mL) Cheddar cheese for topping. Arrange half the macaroni in bottom of prepared casserole dish. Sprinkle with half the remaining Cheddar. Pour half the sauce over top. Repeat layers.

4. In a bowl, combine bread crumbs and reserved Cheddar. Sprinkle over top.

5. Bake in preheated oven for 30 minutes or until topping is lightly browned and sauce is bubbling.

Nutrients per Serving	
Calories	310
Carbohydrate	29 g
Fiber	1 g
Protein	16 g
Total fat	14 g
Saturated fat	8 g
Cholesterol	40 mg
Sodium	404 mg

America's Exchanges	
1¹/₂	Starches
¹/₂	Milk
1	Lean Meat
2	Fats

Canada's Choices	
2	Carbohydrates
1	Meat & Alternatives
2	Fats

Macaroni, Cheese and Tomatoes

|||||||||||||||||||||||||||||||||||||||||||||||||||||||||||||||||||||||||||||||||||||||||||||||||||||||||||||||||||||

Makes 5 servings
Serving size: 1 cup
(250 mL)

Tomatoes add a bright note to macaroni and cheese, an easy lunch or supper dish beloved by people of all ages.

- **Preheat oven to 350°F (180°C)**
- **6-cup (1.5 L) casserole dish, greased**

1 cup	elbow macaroni	250 mL
1	can (19 oz/540 mL) no-salt-added tomatoes, with juice	1
½ tsp	dried basil or dillweed	2 mL
Pinch	freshly ground black pepper	Pinch
½ tsp	prepared mustard	2 mL
1 cup	shredded Cheddar cheese	250 mL
½ cup	corn flakes cereal, crushed	125 mL

1. In a pot of boiling water, cook macaroni according to package directions until almost tender. Drain and set aside.

2. In a large bowl, break up tomatoes in their juice. Stir in basil, pepper and mustard. Gently stir in macaroni and Cheddar cheese. Spoon into casserole dish and sprinkle with corn flakes.

3. Bake in preheated oven for 30 minutes or until browned and bubbling.

Nutrients per Serving

Calories	198
Carbohydrate	22 g
Fiber	2 g
Protein	9 g
Total fat	8 g
Saturated fat	5 g
Cholesterol	24 mg
Sodium	179 mg

America's Exchanges	
1	Vegetable
1	Other Carbohydrate
1	Lean Meat
1	Fat

Canada's Choices	
1	Carbohydrate
1	Meat & Alternatives
1	Fat

Breads, Muffins and Cookies

Cream Bread

||||||||||||||||||||||||||||||||||||||||||||||||||||||||||||||||||||||||||||||||||||||||||||||||||||||

This recipe makes a good bread to slice and use for sandwiches, or excellent dinner rolls (see variation, below). The cottage cheese adds flavor and increases the protein value of the bread.

• **9- by 5-inch (23 by 13 cm) metal loaf pan, lightly greased**

2 tsp	liquid honey	10 mL
$\frac{1}{2}$ cup	warm water	125 mL
2	packages (each $\frac{1}{4}$ oz/8 g) active dry yeast ($4\frac{1}{2}$ tsp/22 mL)	2
$3\frac{1}{2}$ to 4 cups	all-purpose flour, divided	875 mL to 1 L
2 tsp	salt	10 mL
$\frac{1}{2}$ tsp	anise seeds, caraway seeds or dried dillweed (optional)	2 mL
1	egg	1
1 cup	2% cottage cheese	250 mL
$\frac{1}{4}$ cup	unsweetened orange juice	60 mL

1. Dissolve honey in warm water. Sprinkle yeast over water mixture and let stand for 10 minutes; stir well.

2. In a large bowl, combine $2\frac{1}{2}$ cups (625 mL) of the flour, salt and anise seeds (if using). Set aside.

3. In a small saucepan, whisk together egg, cottage cheese and orange juice until well blended. Heat over low heat, whisking constantly, just until warm. Stir in yeast mixture.

4. Add egg mixture to flour mixture and beat with a wooden spoon until well blended. Stir in enough of the remaining flour to make a soft dough that leaves the sides of the bowl.

Nutrients per Serving

Calories	83
Carbohydrate	15 g
Fiber	1 g
Protein	4 g
Total fat	1 g
Saturated fat	0 g
Cholesterol	9 mg
Sodium	237 mg

America's Exchanges	
1	Starch

Canada's Choices	
1	Carbohydrate

Variation

Cream Rolls: After punching down the dough in step 6, divide it into 24 equal portions and form into rolls. Place 2 inches (5 cm) apart on lightly greased baking sheets, cover loosely with plastic wrap and let rise in a warm, draft-free place for 45 to 60 minutes or until doubled in bulk. Bake in upper and lower thirds of a 375°F (190°C) oven, switching pans on racks halfway through, for 20 to 25 minutes or until golden brown. Transfer to wire racks to cool.

5. Transfer dough to a floured work surface and knead for 5 to 10 minutes or until dough is smooth, elastic and no longer sticky. Place dough in a lightly greased bowl, turning to grease all sides. Cover loosely with plastic wrap and let rise in a warm, draft-free place for 1 to $1\frac{1}{2}$ hours or until doubled in bulk.

6. Punch dough down, form into a loaf and place in prepared loaf pan. Cover loosely with plastic wrap and let rise in a warm, draft-free place for 45 to 60 minutes or until doubled in bulk. Meanwhile, preheat oven to 375°F (190°C).

7. Bake for 40 to 45 minutes or until bread is nicely browned and sounds hollow when tapped. Remove from pan and transfer to a wire rack to cool.

Cottage Casserole Bread

|||||||||||||||||||||||||||||||||||||||||||||||||||||||||||||||||||||||||||||||||||||||||||||||||||||||||||||||||||||||||||||||

No kneading is required for this easy bread, which adds a special touch to both everyday meals and meals for guests.

• **6-cup (1.5 L) round casserole dish, lightly greased**

4 tsp	granulated sugar, divided	20 mL
1/4 cup	warm water	60 mL
1	package (1/4 oz/8 g) active dry yeast (2 1/4 tsp/11 mL)	1
1	egg	1
1 1/4 cups	2% cottage cheese	300 mL
2 to 2 1/2 cups	all-purpose flour, divided	500 to 625 mL
1 tbsp	poppy seeds	15 mL
1/2 tsp	salt	2 mL
1/2 tsp	baking soda	2 mL

1. Dissolve 1 tsp (5 mL) of the sugar in warm water. Sprinkle yeast over water mixture and let stand for 10 minutes; stir well.

2. In a small saucepan, whisk together egg and cottage cheese until well blended. Heat over low heat, whisking constantly, just until warm. Stir in yeast mixture.

3. In a large bowl, combine 1 cup (250 mL) of the flour, the remaining sugar, poppy seeds, salt and baking soda. Stir in warmed cottage cheese mixture. Beat with a wooden spoon for about 3 minutes or until mixture becomes elastic. Stir in the remaining flour to form a stiff dough. Cover loosely with plastic wrap and let rise in a warm, draft-free place for about 1 hour or until doubled in bulk.

Nutrients per Serving	
Calories	115
Carbohydrate	19 g
Fiber	1 g
Protein	6 g
Total fat	1 g
Saturated fat	0 g
Cholesterol	17 mg
Sodium	251 mg

America's Exchanges	
1	Other Carbohydrate
1	Lean Meat

Canada's Choices	
1	Carbohydrate
1/2	Meat & Alternatives

Nutrition Tip

Cottage cheese has traditionally contained a lot of salt, with about 400 mg (17% DV) in $1/2$ cup (125 mL). Some brands now contain less. Be sure to check the Nutrition Facts table when shopping and choose the one that's lowest in sodium.

4. Stir down dough and turn out into prepared casserole dish. Cover loosely with plastic wrap and let rise in a warm, draft-free place for 30 to 45 minutes or slightly risen. Meanwhile, preheat oven to 350°F (180°C).

5. Bake for 30 to 35 minutes or until golden brown. Remove from dish and transfer to a wire rack to cool. Cut into 12 wedges.

German Rye Bread

|||||||||||||||||||||||||||||||||||||||||||||||||||||||||||||||||||||||||||||||||||||||||||||||||||||||||||||||||||||||||||||||

Makes 20 slices
Serving size: 1 slice

The caraway seeds are optional, but they do enhance the flavor of this easy-to-make rye bread.

- **Baking sheet or 9- by 5-inch (23 by 13 cm) metal loaf pan, greased**

1 tsp	granulated sugar	5 mL
$\frac{1}{2}$ cup	warm water	125 mL
1	package ($\frac{1}{4}$ oz/8 g) active dry yeast ($2\frac{1}{4}$ tsp/11 mL)	1
$2\frac{1}{2}$ to 3 cups	all-purpose flour, divided	625 to 750 mL
1 cup	rye flour	250 mL
1 tbsp	caraway seeds (optional)	15 mL
2 tsp	salt	10 mL
1 tbsp	butter, melted	15 mL
1 tsp	liquid honey	5 mL

1. Dissolve sugar in warm water. Sprinkle yeast over water mixture and let stand for 10 minutes; stir well.

2. In a bowl, combine 1 cup (250 mL) of the all-purpose flour, rye flour, caraway seeds (if using) and salt. Stir in $\frac{3}{4}$ cup (175 mL) water, butter and honey. Beat with a wooden spoon for 2 to 3 minutes or until smooth. Stir in enough of the remaining all-purpose flour to make a soft dough that leaves the sides of the bowl.

3. Transfer dough to a floured work surface and knead for 5 to 8 minutes or until dough is smooth, elastic and no longer sticky. Place dough in a lightly greased bowl, turning to grease all sides. Cover loosely with plastic wrap and let rise in a warm, draft-free place for about 45 minutes or until doubled in bulk.

Nutrients per Serving

Calories	83
Carbohydrate	17 g
Fiber	1 g
Protein	2 g
Total fat	1 g
Saturated fat	0 g
Cholesterol	2 mg
Sodium	239 mg

America's Exchanges	
1	Starch

Canada's Choices	
1	Carbohydrate

Nutrition Tip

Honey and molasses provide about the same number of calories as an equal amount of granulated sugar.

4. Punch dough down and form into a loaf about 9 inches (23 cm) long. Place on prepared baking sheet, cover loosely with plastic wrap and let rise in a warm, draft-free place for about 45 minutes or until doubled in bulk. Meanwhile, preheat oven to 375°F (190°C).

5. Bake for 30 to 35 minutes or until loaf is lightly browned and sounds hollow when tapped. Remove from pan and transfer to a wire rack to cool.

Harvest Rolls

||||||||||||||||||||||||||||||||||||||||||||||||||||||||||||||||||||||||||||||||||||||||||||||||||||||||||||||||||||||||||

Whole wheat rolls are popular for the extra flavor they give to sandwiches. They also make a nice accompaniment to an autumn supper.

Kitchen Tip

To activate yeast, always use sugar or honey, according to package directions. Artificial sweetener does not work.

- **Baking sheets, lightly greased**

1 tsp	granulated sugar	5 mL
1/2 cup	warm water	125 mL
1	package (1/4 oz/8 g) active dry yeast (2 1/4 tsp/11 mL)	1
1 cup	skim milk	250 mL
1 tsp	light (fancy) molasses	5 mL
1/2 tsp	salt	2 mL
3 cups	whole wheat flour	750 mL
1/2 to 3/4 cup	all-purpose flour, divided	125 to 175 mL

1. Dissolve sugar in warm water. Sprinkle yeast over water mixture and let stand for 10 minutes; stir well.

2. In a large bowl, combine milk, molasses and salt. Stir in yeast mixture. Stir in whole wheat flour until well blended.

3. Spread 1/4 cup (60 mL) of the all-purpose flour on a work surface. Transfer dough to floured surface and knead for 5 to 8 minutes, adding more all-purpose flour as necessary, until dough is smooth, elastic and no longer sticky. Place dough in a lightly greased bowl, turning to grease all sides. Cover loosely with plastic wrap and let rise in a warm, draft-free place for 1 to 1 1/2 hours or until doubled in bulk.

4. Punch dough down, divide into 24 equal portions and form into rolls. Place 2 inches (5 cm) apart on prepared baking sheets. Cover loosely with plastic wrap and let rise in a warm, draft-free place for 1 hour or until doubled in bulk. Meanwhile, preheat oven to 400°F (200°C).

5. Bake in upper and lower thirds of oven, switching pans on racks halfway through, for 12 to 15 minutes or until browned. Remove from pan and transfer to wire racks to cool.

Nutrients per Serving	
Calories	66
Carbohydrate	14 g
Fiber	2 g
Protein	3 g
Total fat	0 g
Saturated fat	0 g
Cholesterol	0 mg
Sodium	55 mg

America's Exchanges	
1	Starch

Canada's Choices	
1	Carbohydrate

Whole Wheat Biscuits

|||||||||||||||||||||||||||||||||||||||||||||||||||||||||||||||||||||||||||||||||||||||||||||||||||||||||

Biscuits really should be served warm to accentuate their delicate texture.

Nutrition Tip

These biscuits each have 4 g less fat than a comparable commercial variety. Because they contain whole wheat flour, they also have four times as much fiber. To boost fiber, you can generally replace up to half the all-purpose flour in a recipe without affecting the results.

Variation

Herb Biscuits: Add 1 tsp (5 mL) dried parsley, ¼ tsp (1 mL) dried basil and ¼ tsp (1 mL) dried thyme to the flour mixture. (This dough also makes great dumplings when spooned over simmering stew or soup.)

- **Preheat oven to 425°F (220°C)**
- **Baking sheet, lightly greased**
- **2-inch (5 cm) round cookie cutter (optional)**

1½ cups	whole wheat flour	375 mL
½ cup	all-purpose flour	125 mL
1 tbsp	baking powder	15 mL
½ tsp	salt	2 mL
2 tbsp	cold margarine or butter	30 mL
1 cup	skim milk	250 mL

1. In a large bowl, combine whole wheat flour, all purpose flour, baking powder and salt. Using a pastry blender or two knives, cut in margarine until mixture resembles coarse crumbs. Using a fork, quickly stir in milk.

2. Transfer dough to a floured work surface and knead for 6 to 8 strokes or just until dough holds together. Roll out to ¾ inch (2 cm) thick. Using cookie cutter, cut into 12 circles (or use a knife to cut into 12 wedges or squares), rerolling scraps, as necessary. Place at least 1 inch (2.5 cm) apart on prepared baking sheet.

3. Bake in preheated oven for 12 to 15 minutes or until lightly browned. Transfer to a wire rack and let cool slightly. Serve warm.

Nutrients per Serving	
Calories	95
Carbohydrate	16 g
Fiber	2 g
Protein	3 g
Total fat	2 g
Saturated fat	0 g
Cholesterol	0 mg
Sodium	201 mg

America's Exchanges	
1	Starch
½	Fat

Canada's Choices	
1	Carbohydrate
½	Fat

Scotch Scones

||||||||||||||||||||||||||||||||||||||||||||||||||||||||||||||||||||||||||||||||||||||||

Scotch scones are so rich and tasty you won't want to add butter. They go well with soups and, when served with a little fruit spread, make a delicious afternoon snack.

Nutrition Tip

When choosing a margarine, look for a non-hydrogenated soft margarine. These are low in saturated fat and do not contain trans fat. Avoid hard margarines, which contain high amounts of saturated and trans fat.

- **Preheat oven to 425°F (220°C)**
- **Large baking sheet, lightly greased**

1¾ cups	quick-cooking rolled oats	425 mL
1½ cups	all-purpose flour	375 mL
¼ cup	granulated sugar	60 mL
1 tbsp	baking powder	15 mL
½ tsp	salt	2 mL
1	egg	1
½ cup	margarine or butter, melted	125 mL
⅓ cup	skim, 1% or 2% milk	75 mL

1. In a large bowl, combine oats, flour, sugar, baking powder and salt.

2. In a small bowl, whisk together egg, margarine and milk. Using a fork, stir into flour mixture until just blended.

3. Transfer dough to a lightly floured surface and pat or roll out into a 12- by 9-inch (30 by 23 cm) rectangle. Cut into 9 rectangles, then cut each diagonally to form 18 triangles. Place at least 1 inch (2.5 cm) apart on prepared baking sheet.

4. Bake in preheated oven for 12 to 14 minutes or until golden brown. Transfer to a wire rack and let cool slightly. Serve warm.

Nutrients per Serving

Calories	135
Carbohydrate	17 g
Fiber	1 g
Protein	3 g
Total fat	6 g
Saturated fat	1 g
Cholesterol	10 mg
Sodium	166 mg

America's Exchanges	
1	Starch
1	Fat

Canada's Choices	
1	Carbohydrate
1	Fat

Popovers

Serve these traditional popovers as a quick bread at mealtime, or use them as shells for savory meat mixtures or as cups for salad.

Kitchen Tips

For drier popovers, at the end of the baking time, turn off the heat and let them dry in the oven for 15 minutes with the door ajar.

Popovers can be frozen in an airtight container, layered with parchment paper or waxed paper, for up to 2 months. Reheat from frozen on a baking sheet in a 375°F (190°C) oven for about 10 minutes or until hot.

- **12-cup muffin pan, sprayed with vegetable cooking spray**

2	eggs	2
1 cup	skim milk	250 mL
¾ cup	all-purpose flour	175 mL
¼ tsp	salt	1 mL

1. In a bowl, using an electric mixer, beat together eggs and milk. Sprinkle with flour and salt; beat until batter is smooth and free of lumps.

2. Divide batter evenly among prepared muffin cups, filling cups no more than half full. Place in a cold oven and set oven to 400°F (200°C). Bake for 30 to 35 minutes or until firm and browned. Pierce popovers to let steam escape. Loosen popovers carefully with a knife. Serve hot.

Nutrients per Serving	
Calories	48
Carbohydrate	7 g
Fiber	0 g
Protein	3 g
Total fat	1 g
Saturated fat	0 g
Cholesterol	31 mg
Sodium	70 mg

America's Exchanges	
½	Starch

Canada's Choices	
½	Carbohydrate

Banana Breakfast Loaf

After you make this loaf, let it cool, wrap it and let it stand overnight to allow the flavors to develop. If you keep the loaf longer than 2 days, store it in the refrigerator.

Kitchen Tip

Do not overmix the batter in step 2. It should be rough or lumpy and stiff.

Nutrition Tip

You will find unsweetened coconut in health food stores and some grocery stores. It is high in saturated fat, so is best used in small quantities.

- **Preheat oven to 350°F (180°C)**
- **8- by 4-inch (20 by 10 cm) metal loaf pan, lightly greased**

1½ cups	whole wheat flour	375 mL
½ cup	unsweetened shredded coconut	125 mL
2 tsp	baking powder	10 mL
½ tsp	baking soda	2 mL
½ tsp	salt	2 mL
1 cup	mashed ripe bananas	250 mL
3 tbsp	vegetable oil	45 mL
2 tbsp	liquid honey	30 mL

1. In a large bowl, combine flour, coconut, baking powder, baking soda and salt.

2. In a small bowl, combine banana, oil and honey until well blended. Stir into flour mixture quickly but gently until just blended.

3. Spread batter evenly in prepared loaf pan. Bake in preheated oven for 45 to 50 minutes or until a tester inserted in the center comes out clean. Let cool in pan on a wire rack for 10 minutes, then transfer to the rack to cool completely. Wrap in waxed paper and let stand overnight before slicing.

Nutrients per Serving	
Calories	115
Carbohydrate	16 g
Fiber	2 g
Protein	2 g
Total fat	5 g
Saturated fat	2 g
Cholesterol	0 mg
Sodium	174 mg

America's Exchanges	
1	Starch
1	Fat

Canada's Choices	
1	Carbohydrate
1	Fat

Orange Nut Bread

||||||||||||||||||||||||||||||||||||||||||||||||||||||||||||||||||||||||||||||||||||||||||||||||||||||||

Try a slice of this bread as a delightful afternoon or evening snack. It's as attractive as it is flavorful.

Kitchen Tip

To grate the orange zest, use the fine side of a box cheese grater or a Microplane-style grater. If you use a five-hole zester, chop the zest into smaller pieces with a knife.

Nutrition Tip

Nuts contain protein and fat. While the fat is the healthy unsaturated type, it still contributes calories, so nuts should generally be used in small quantities.

- **Preheat oven to 350°F (180°C)**
- **8- by 4-inch (20 by 10 cm) metal loaf pan, greased**

1 1/2 cups	all-purpose flour	375 mL
1/4 cup	granulated sugar	60 mL
2 tsp	baking powder	10 mL
1/2 tsp	salt	2 mL
1/3 cup	chopped almonds or walnuts	75 mL
1/4 cup	raisins, chopped	60 mL
2 tbsp	grated orange zest	30 mL
1	egg	1
1/2 cup	unsweetened orange juice	125 mL
2 tsp	vegetable oil	10 mL

1. In a large bowl, combine flour, sugar, baking powder and salt. Stir in almonds, raisins and orange zest.

2. In a small bowl, whisk together egg, orange juice and oil until well blended. Stir into flour mixture just until flour is dampened and fruits and nuts are well distributed.

3. Spread batter evenly in prepared loaf pan. Bake in preheated oven for 40 minutes or until a tester inserted in the center comes out clean. Let cool in pan on a wire rack for 10 minutes, then transfer to the rack to cool completely. Wrap in waxed paper and let stand overnight before slicing.

Nutrients per Serving	
Calories	97
Carbohydrate	17 g
Fiber	1 g
Protein	2 g
Total fat	2 g
Saturated fat	0 g
Cholesterol	12 mg
Sodium	124 mg

America's Exchanges	
1	Starch
1/2	Fat

Canada's Choices	
1	Carbohydrate
1/2	Fat

Best Bran Muffins

Bran muffins are great for breakfast. The night before, combine the dry ingredients and prepare the muffin cups. In the morning, you can mix the muffins in about 5 minutes, then let them bake while you get ready for the day.

Variations

Nutty Bran Muffins: Add ¼ cup (60 mL) chopped walnuts to the flour mixture. This will add 2 g of fat (½ Fat Exchange or ½ Fat Choice) per muffin.

Fruit and Nut Bran Muffins: Add 2 tbsp (30 mL) chopped raisins and 2 tbsp (30 mL) chopped nuts to the flour mixture. Count these additions as a Free Food or Extra.

- Preheat oven to 400°F (200°C)
- 12-cup muffin pan, lightly greased or lined with paper cups

1 cup	all-purpose flour	250 mL
1 cup	natural bran	250 mL
2½ tsp	baking powder	12 mL
1 tsp	ground cinnamon	5 mL
½ tsp	salt	2 mL
⅓ cup	lightly packed brown sugar	75 mL
1	egg	1
1 cup	2% milk	250 mL
¼ cup	vegetable oil	60 mL

1. In a large bowl, combine flour, bran, baking powder, cinnamon and salt.

2. In a medium bowl, whisk together brown sugar, egg, milk and oil until well blended. Stir into flour mixture until just blended.

3. Divide batter evenly among prepared muffin cups. Bake in preheated oven for 20 to 22 minutes or until light golden brown. Let cool in pan on a wire rack for 5 minutes, then transfer to the rack. Serve warm or let cool completely.

Nutrients per Serving	
Calories	125
Carbohydrate	17 g
Fiber	2 g
Protein	3 g
Total fat	6 g
Saturated fat	1 g
Cholesterol	17 mg
Sodium	177 mg

America's Exchanges	
1	Starch
1	Fat

Canada's Choices	
1	Carbohydrate
1	Fat

Apple Honey Spice Muffins

||||||||||||||||||||||||||||||||||||||||||||||||||||||||||||||||||||||||||||||||||||||||||||||||||||||

The honey and shredded apples keep these muffins nice and moist, and the warm spices make them taste reminiscent of apple pie.

Kitchen Tips
Choose a tart, flavorful apple for this recipe. Northern Spy, Empire, Crispin (Mutsu) or Granny Smith are good choices. You'll need about 2 for this recipe.

Use the coarse side of a box grater to shred the apples, or cut them into quarters, cut out the cores and use a food processor with a shredding blade. There's no need to peel them: the skin adds fiber.

- Preheat oven to 375°F (190°C)
- 12-cup muffin pan, lightly greased or lined with paper cups

¾ cup	all-purpose flour	175 mL
¾ cup	whole wheat flour	175 mL
1 tsp	baking powder	5 mL
1 tsp	ground cinnamon	5 mL
½ tsp	ground ginger	2 mL
½ tsp	salt	2 mL
¼ tsp	baking soda	1 mL
Pinch	ground allspice or cloves	Pinch
1	egg	1
¼ cup	vegetable oil	60 mL
¼ cup	liquid honey	60 mL
1½ cups	packed shredded cooking apples (see tip, at left)	375 mL

1. In a large bowl, combine all-purpose flour, whole wheat flour, baking powder, cinnamon, ginger, salt, baking soda and allspice.

2. In a medium bowl, whisk together egg, oil and honey until well blended. Stir in apples. Stir into flour mixture until just blended (the batter will be thick).

3. Divide batter evenly among prepared muffin cups. Bake in preheated oven for 18 to 20 minutes or until tops spring back when lightly touched. Let cool in pan on a wire rack for 5 minutes, then transfer to the rack to cool.

Nutrients per Serving	
Calories	135
Carbohydrate	21 g
Fiber	2 g
Protein	2 g
Total fat	5 g
Saturated fat	1 g
Cholesterol	16 mg
Sodium	155 mg

America's Exchanges	
½	Starch
1	Other Carbohydrate
1	Fat

Canada's Choices	
1	Carbohydrate
1	Fat

Blueberry Oat Muffins

Ever-popular blueberry muffins get a nutritious makeover with added oats and yogurt.

Kitchen Tips

It's worth it to seek out wild blueberries for these muffins. The smaller size and intense blueberry flavor ensure that you get a burst of blueberry in every bite.

Don't thaw frozen berries before adding them to the batter, as thawed berries are more likely to bleed their color into the batter. The baking time with frozen berries will be at the higher end of the range.

- Preheat oven to 400°F (200°C)
- 12-cup muffin pan, lightly greased or lined with paper cups

1 cup	all-purpose flour	250 mL
¾ cup	quick-cooking rolled oats	175 mL
2 tsp	baking powder	10 mL
1 tsp	ground cinnamon	5 mL
½ tsp	baking soda	2 mL
½ tsp	salt	2 mL
¼ cup	packed brown sugar	60 mL
1	egg	1
⅔ cup	1% milk	150 mL
½ cup	1% plain yogurt	125 mL
¼ cup	vegetable oil	60 mL
1 cup	fresh or frozen blueberries, preferably wild	250 mL

1. In a large bowl, combine flour, oats, baking powder, cinnamon, baking soda and salt.

2. In a medium bowl, whisk together brown sugar, egg, milk, yogurt and oil until well blended. Stir into flour mixture until just blended. Gently fold in blueberries.

3. Divide batter evenly among prepared muffin cups. Bake in preheated oven for 20 to 25 minutes or until tops spring back when lightly touched. Let cool in pan on a wire rack for 5 minutes, then transfer to the rack to cool.

Nutrients per Serving

Calories	144
Carbohydrate	20 g
Fiber	1 g
Protein	4 g
Total fat	6 g
Saturated fat	1 g
Cholesterol	17 mg
Sodium	222 mg

America's Exchanges	
1	Starch
1	Fat

Canada's Choices	
1	Carbohydrate
1	Fat

Lemon Poppy Seed Muffins

||||||||||||||||||||||||||||||||||||||||||||||||||||||||||||||||||||||||||||||||||||||||||||||||||||||||||||||||||||||||||||||||

Makes 12 muffins
Serving size: 1 muffin

This version of a classic is just slightly sweet, fragrant with lemon and studded with poppy seeds. It's just perfect for teatime.

Kitchen Tip
Grated lemon zest adds a deep lemon flavor and is essential to these muffins. Use a fine, Microplane-style grater or the fine side of a box grater. If you only have a five-hole zester, chop the strips of zest finely to avoid an unpleasant texture.

- **Preheat oven to 375°F (190°C)**
- **12-cup muffin pan, lightly greased or lined with paper cups**

1 cup	all-purpose flour	250 mL
½ cup	whole wheat flour	125 mL
2 tbsp	poppy seeds	30 mL
1 tsp	baking powder	5 mL
½ tsp	baking soda	2 mL
½ tsp	salt	2 mL
¼ cup	granulated sugar	60 mL
1	egg	1
¾ cup	1% milk	175 mL
¼ cup	vegetable oil	60 mL
	Grated zest of 1 large lemon	
2 tbsp	freshly squeezed lemon juice	30 mL

1. In a large bowl, combine all-purpose flour, whole wheat flour, poppy seeds, baking powder, baking soda and salt.

2. In a medium bowl, whisk together sugar, egg, milk, oil, lemon zest and lemon juice until well blended. Stir into flour mixture until just blended.

3. Divide batter evenly among prepared muffin cups. Bake in preheated oven for 20 to 22 minutes or until tops spring back when lightly touched. Let cool in pan on a wire rack for 5 minutes, then transfer to the rack to cool.

Nutrients per Serving

Calories	133
Carbohydrate	17 g
Fiber	1 g
Protein	3 g
Total fat	6 g
Saturated fat	1 g
Cholesterol	16 mg
Sodium	188 mg

America's Exchanges	
1	Starch
1	Fat

Canada's Choices	
1	Carbohydrate
1	Fat

Raspberry Yogurt Muffins

IIIIIIIIIIIIIIIIIIIIIIIIIIIIIIIIIIIIIIIIIIIIIIIIIIIIIIIIIIIIIIIIIIIIIIIIIIIIIIIIIIIIIIIIIIIIIIIIIIIIIIIIIIIIIIIIIIIIIIIIIIIIII

Makes 12 muffins
Serving size: 1 muffin

The tangy-sweet flavor of raspberries and yogurt are sure to make these muffins one of your new favorites. Be sure to make them when fresh raspberries are in season and throughout the year with frozen berries.

Kitchen Tip
Don't thaw frozen berries before adding them to the batter, as thawed berries are more likely to bleed their color into the batter. The baking time with frozen berries will be at the higher end of the range.

- Preheat oven to 375°F (190°C)
- 12-cup muffin pan, lightly greased or lined with paper cups

1 cup	all-purpose flour	250 mL
½ cup	whole wheat flour	125 mL
1 tsp	baking powder	5 mL
½ tsp	salt	2 mL
¼ tsp	baking soda	1 mL
⅓ cup	packed brown sugar	75 mL
1	egg	1
½ cup	1% plain yogurt	125 mL
½ cup	1% milk	125 mL
3 tbsp	vegetable oil	45 mL
1 cup	fresh or frozen raspberries	250 mL

1. In a large bowl, combine all-purpose flour, whole wheat flour, baking powder, salt and baking soda.

2. In a medium bowl, whisk together brown sugar, egg, yogurt, milk and oil until well blended. Stir into flour mixture until just blended. Gently fold in raspberries.

3. Divide batter evenly among prepared muffin cups. Bake in preheated oven for 20 to 25 minutes or until tops spring back when lightly touched. Let cool in pan on a wire rack for 5 minutes, then transfer to the rack to cool.

Nutrients per Serving

Calories	128
Carbohydrate	20 g
Fiber	1 g
Protein	3 g
Total fat	4 g
Saturated fat	1 g
Cholesterol	16 mg
Sodium	167 mg

America's Exchanges	
1	Starch
1	Fat

Canada's Choices	
1	Carbohydrate
1	Fat

Cornmeal Muffins

Makes 12 muffins
Serving size: 1 muffin

Serve these savory muffins hot for breakfast or as an accompaniment to bean or chili dinners.

Kitchen Tip

The secret to a good muffin is in the mixing. Overmixing creates a tough texture and tunnels. Stir the wet and dry ingredients together until the dryness of the flour *just* disappears. The batter will be lumpy, as it should be.

- **Preheat oven to 400°F (200°C)**
- **12-cup muffin pan, lightly greased or lined with paper cups**

1 cup	cornmeal	250 mL
1 cup	skim milk	250 mL
1¼ cups	all-purpose flour	300 mL
4 tsp	baking powder	20 mL
1 tsp	salt	5 mL
¼ cup	lightly packed brown sugar	60 mL
2	eggs, beaten	2
3 tbsp	vegetable oil	45 mL

1. In a medium bowl, combine cornmeal and milk; let stand for 10 minutes.

2. In a large bowl, combine flour, baking powder and salt.

3. Whisk brown sugar, eggs and oil into cornmeal mixture until well blended. Stir into flour mixture until just blended.

4. Divide batter evenly among prepared muffin cups. Bake in preheated oven for 18 to 20 minutes or until golden brown. Let cool in pan on a wire rack for 5 minutes, then transfer to the rack. Serve warm.

Nutrients per Serving	
Calories	162
Carbohydrate	26 g
Fiber	1 g
Protein	4 g
Total fat	5 g
Saturated fat	1 g
Cholesterol	31 mg
Sodium	319 mg

America's Exchanges	
1½	Starches
1	Fat

Canada's Choices	
1½	Carbohydrates
1	Fat

Crispy Oatmeal Cookies

Do not undercook these cookies if you want them to be flavorful and crisp. They freeze well in an airtight container, so it's a good idea to make a double batch while you are at it.

Kitchen Tips

Store cooled cookies in a cookie tin at room temperature for up to 5 days.

To freeze cookies, layer cooled cookies between parchment paper or waxed paper in an airtight container and freeze for up to 2 months.

- Preheat oven to 350°F (180°C)
- Baking sheets, lightly greased
- 2½-inch (6 cm) round cookie cutter

1 cup	all-purpose flour	250 mL
1 cup	quick-cooking rolled oats	250 mL
1 tsp	ground cinnamon	5 mL
½ tsp	baking soda	2 mL
⅓ cup	lightly packed brown sugar	75 mL
⅓ cup	butter, softened	75 mL
¼ cup	warm water	60 mL

1. In a medium bowl, combine flour, oats, cinnamon and baking soda.

2. In a large bowl, using an electric mixer, cream brown sugar and butter until light and fluffy. Beat in water. Stir in flour mixture until well blended.

3. Transfer dough to a lightly floured work surface and roll out to ⅛-inch (3 mm) thickness. Using cookie cutter, cut out 36 circles, rerolling scraps as necessary. Place 2 inches (5 cm) apart on prepared baking sheets.

4. Bake one sheet at a time in preheated oven for 10 to 12 minutes or until golden brown around edges. Transfer to wire racks and let cool completely.

Nutrients per Serving	
Calories	133
Carbohydrate	18 g
Fiber	1 g
Protein	2 g
Total fat	6 g
Saturated fat	3 g
Cholesterol	14 mg
Sodium	92 mg

America's Exchanges	
1	Starch
1	Fat

Canada's Choices	
1	Carbohydrate
1	Fat

Vegetable Frittata (page 211)

Bean-Stuffed Cabbage Rolls (page 215)

Blueberry Oat Muffins (page 236)

Peanut Butter Cookies (page 242)

Sponge Cake (page 255)

Cranberry Pear Kuchen (page 268)

Pineapple Dream (page 277)

Spicy Pear Spread (page 291) and Spicy Apple Chutney (page 294)

Chocolate Chip Cookies

‖‖‖

Makes 4 dozen cookies
Serving size: 3 cookies

Although the sugar and chocolate have been reduced in this recipe, it will still be a favorite with cookie lovers of all ages.

Kitchen Tips

Store cooled cookies in a cookie tin at room temperature for up to 5 days.

To freeze cookies, layer cooled cookies between parchment paper or waxed paper in an airtight container and freeze for up to 2 months.

● **Preheat oven to 375°F (190°C)**

1 cup	all-purpose flour	250 mL
½ tsp	baking soda	2 mL
½ tsp	salt	2 mL
½ cup	lightly packed brown sugar	125 mL
½ cup	butter, softened	125 mL
1	egg	1
2 tsp	vanilla extract	10 mL
½ cup	quick-cooking rolled oats	125 mL
½ cup	semisweet chocolate chips	125 mL

1. In a medium bowl, combine flour, baking soda and salt.

2. In a large bowl, using an electric mixer, cream brown sugar and butter until light and fluffy. Beat in egg and vanilla. Stir in flour mixture until well blended. Fold in oats and chocolate chips.

3. For each cookie, drop 2 tsp (10 mL) dough onto baking sheets, placing cookies 2 inches (5 cm) apart. Flatten with a fork.

4. Bake one sheet at a time in preheated oven for 10 minutes or until starting to brown around the edges. Transfer to wire racks and let cool completely.

Nutrients per Serving

Calories	143
Carbohydrate	17 g
Fiber	1 g
Protein	2 g
Total fat	8 g
Saturated fat	5 g
Cholesterol	27 mg
Sodium	160 mg

America's Exchanges	
1	Other Carbohydrate
1½	Fats

Canada's Choices	
1	Carbohydrate
1½	Fats

Peanut Butter Cookies

This dough is very easy to handle, and the peanut flavor stands out because of the low sugar content. Use crunchy peanut butter for added texture.

Kitchen Tips

Store cooled cookies in a cookie tin at room temperature for up to 5 days.

To freeze cookies, layer cooled cookies between parchment paper or waxed paper in an airtight container and freeze for up to 2 months.

- **Preheat oven to 350°F (180°C)**
- **Baking sheets, lightly greased**

1 1/2 cups	all-purpose flour	375 mL
1 tsp	baking powder	5 mL
1 tsp	baking soda	5 mL
1/2 tsp	salt	2 mL
2/3 cup	lightly packed brown sugar	150 mL
1/2 cup	shortening	125 mL
2	eggs	2
1 cup	smooth or crunchy peanut butter	250 mL
1 tsp	vanilla extract	5 mL

1. In a medium bowl, combine flour, baking powder, baking soda and salt.

2. In a large bowl, cream brown sugar and shortening until light and fluffy. Beat in eggs, one at a time. Beat in peanut butter and vanilla. Stir in flour mixture until well blended.

3. For each cookie, roll about 2 tsp (10 mL) dough into a ball. Place 2 inches (5 cm) apart on prepared baking sheets. Flatten with a wet fork, forming a crisscross design.

4. Bake one sheet at a time in preheated oven for 8 to 10 minutes or until very light golden brown. Transfer to wire racks and let cool completely.

Nutrients per Serving

Calories	79
Carbohydrate	7 g
Fiber	0 g
Protein	2 g
Total fat	5 g
Saturated fat	1 g
Cholesterol	8 mg
Sodium	85 mg

America's Exchanges	
1/2	Other Carbohydrate
1	Fat

Canada's Choices	
1/2	Carbohydrate
1	Fat

Soft Molasses Spice Cookies

||||||||||||||||||||||||||||||||||||||||||||||||||||||||||||||||||||||||||||||||||||||||||||||

Makes 32 cookies
Serving size: 2 cookies

Aromatic with spices and not too sweet, these soft cookies are perfect with a cup of tea.

Kitchen Tip
These soft cookies are best eaten within a day or two of baking. Store them at room temperature in an airtight container, layered between parchment paper or waxed paper. For longer storage, freeze them for up to 2 months.

- Preheat oven to 375°F (190°C)
- 2 large baking sheets, lined with parchment paper

1¼ cups	all-purpose flour	300 mL
½ cup	whole wheat flour	125 mL
1½ tsp	ground cinnamon	7 mL
½ tsp	baking powder	2 mL
½ tsp	salt	2 mL
½ tsp	ground ginger	2 mL
¼ tsp	baking soda	1 mL
¼ tsp	ground allspice or cloves	1 mL
⅓ cup	packed brown sugar	75 mL
¼ cup	butter, softened	60 mL
1	egg	1
⅔ cup	unsweetened applesauce	150 mL
¼ cup	light (fancy) molasses	60 mL

1. In a medium bowl, combine all-purpose flour, whole wheat flour, cinnamon, baking powder, salt, ginger, baking soda and allspice.

2. In a large bowl, using an electric mixer, cream brown sugar and butter until fluffy. Beat in egg until blended. Beat in applesauce and molasses. Stir in flour mixture until blended.

3. For each cookie, drop 1 level tbsp (15 mL) dough on prepared baking sheets, placing cookies 2 inches (5 cm) apart.

4. Bake in upper and lower thirds of preheated oven for about 15 minutes, switching pans on racks halfway through, until just starting to turn golden around the edges and tops spring back when lightly touched. Let cool on pans on wire racks for 1 minute. Transfer to racks and serve warm or let cool completely.

Nutrients per Serving

Calories	126
Carbohydrate	23 g
Fiber	1 g
Protein	2 g
Total fat	3 g
Saturated fat	2 g
Cholesterol	19 mg
Sodium	132 mg

America's Exchanges	
1½	Other Carbohydrates
½	Fat

Canada's Choices	
1½	Carbohydrates
½	Fat

Shortbread

Makes 5 dozen cookies
Serving size: 2 cookies

Do not undercook shortbread — for the best flavor, it should have a light golden color. It's great at teatime and in packed lunches.

Kitchen Tips
Store cooled cookies in a cookie tin at room temperature for up to 1 week.

To freeze cookies, layer cooled cookies between parchment paper or waxed paper in an airtight container and freeze for up to 2 months.

- Preheat oven to 325°F (160°C)
- 1½-inch (4 cm) round cookie cutter

1¾ cups	all-purpose flour	425 mL
½ cup	white rice flour	125 mL
½ cup	granulated sugar	125 mL
1 cup	butter, at room temperature	250 mL

1. In a medium bowl, combine all-purpose flour and rice flour.

2. In a large bowl, using an electric mixer, cream sugar and butter until light and fluffy. Stir in flour mixture until well blended.

3. Transfer dough to a lightly floured work surface and roll out to ¼-inch (0.5 cm) thickness. Using cookie cutter, cut out 60 circles, rerolling scraps as necessary. Place 1 inch (2.5 cm) apart on baking sheets. Prick with a fork to form a design.

4. Bake in upper and lower thirds of preheated oven, switching pans on racks halfway through, for 22 to 25 minutes or until light golden. Let cool on pans on a wire rack for 2 minutes, then transfer to racks to cool completely.

Nutrients per Serving

Calories	103
Carbohydrate	11 g
Fiber	0 g
Protein	1 g
Total fat	6 g
Saturated fat	4 g
Cholesterol	16 mg
Sodium	44 mg

America's Exchanges	
1	Other Carbohydrate
1	Fat

Canada's Choices	
½	Carbohydrate
1	Fat

Peanut Butter Nuggets

|||||||||||||||||||||||||||||||||||||||||||||||||||||||||||||||||||||||||||||||||||||||||||||||||||||||||||||||||||||||||||||||||||||||||||||||

These crispy nuggets are a tasty addition to a cookie tray for parties.

Kitchen Tip
Store cookies in an airtight container in the refrigerator for up to 1 week.

$\frac{2}{3}$ cup	crushed corn flakes cereal, divided	150 mL
$\frac{1}{2}$ cup	unsweetened shredded coconut	125 mL
$\frac{1}{2}$ cup	smooth or crunchy peanut butter	125 mL
2 tbsp	liquid honey or corn syrup	30 mL

1. In a bowl, combine $\frac{1}{2}$ cup (125 mL) of the corn flakes, coconut, peanut butter and honey; mix thoroughly.

2. For each cookie, roll about 2 tsp (10 mL) into a ball. Roll balls in the remaining corn flakes. Place on a plate and refrigerate until firm.

Nutrients per Serving	
Calories	139
Carbohydrate	9 g
Fiber	2 g
Protein	4 g
Total fat	10 g
Saturated fat	4 g
Cholesterol	0 mg
Sodium	81 mg

America's Exchanges	
$\frac{1}{2}$	Starch
2	Fats

Canada's Choices	
$\frac{1}{2}$	Carbohydrate
2	Fats

Vanilla Crisps

||||||||||||||||||||||||||||||||||||||||||||||||||||||||||||||||||||||||||||||||||||||||||||||||||||||||||||||||||

These vanilla crisps are a lighter version of commercial vanilla wafers, and can be used in place of vanilla wafers in most recipes.

Kitchen Tip

If the baked cookies are not crisp enough for your liking after they've cooled for 10 minutes, return them to the oven, with the heat turned off, for 5 to 10 minutes to crisp.

Variations

Orange Crisps: Replace the vanilla with 2 tsp (10 mL) grated orange zest and 1 tsp (5 mL) freshly squeezed orange juice.

Lemon Crisps: Replace the vanilla with 2 tsp (10 mL) grated lemon zest and 1 tsp (5 mL) freshly squeezed lemon juice.

- Preheat oven to 375°F (190°C)
- Baking sheets, lined with parchment paper

2	eggs, separated, at room temperature	2
1/8 tsp	salt	0.5 mL
1/2 tsp	baking powder	2 mL
1/4 cup	granulated sugar	60 mL
2 tsp	vanilla extract	10 mL
1/3 cup	all-purpose flour	75 mL

1. In a large bowl, using an electric mixer, beat egg whites and salt until frothy. Beat in baking powder until soft peaks form. Beat in sugar until stiff peaks form.

2. In a small bowl, whisk together egg yolks and vanilla. Fold into egg white mixture until just combined. Sift flour over egg mixture and fold in until batter is smooth and very light.

3. For each cookie, drop 2 tsp (10 mL) dough onto prepared baking sheets, placing cookies 2 inches (5 cm) apart.

4. Bake in upper and lower thirds of preheated oven, switching pans on racks halfway through, for 15 to 18 minutes or until golden brown. Let cool on pans on a wire rack for 10 minutes, then transfer to the racks to cool completely.

Nutrients per Serving	
Calories	58
Carbohydrate	9 g
Fiber	0 g
Protein	2 g
Total fat	1 g
Saturated fat	0 g
Cholesterol	41 mg
Sodium	63 mg

America's Exchanges	
1/2	Starch

Canada's Choices	
1/2	Carbohydrate

Almond Crisps

**Makes about
3 dozen cookies**

Serving size: 4 cookies

These crisp, fragrant
cookies are nice as a
treat and work well
in recipes that call for
cookie crumbs.

Kitchen Tips

Store cooled cookies
in a cookie tin at room
temperature for up to 5 days.

To freeze cookies, layer
cooled cookies between
parchment paper or
waxed paper in an airtight
container and freeze for up
to 2 months.

- Preheat oven to 375°F (190°C)
- Baking sheets, lined with parchment paper

2	eggs, separated, at room temperature	2
1/8 tsp	salt	0.5 mL
1/2 tsp	baking powder	2 mL
1/4 cup	granulated sugar	60 mL
2 tsp	almond extract	10 mL
1/3 cup	all-purpose flour	75 mL
1 tbsp	ground almonds	15 mL

1. In a large bowl, using an electric mixer, beat egg whites and salt until frothy. Beat in baking powder until soft peaks form. Beat in sugar until stiff peaks form.

2. In a small bowl, whisk together egg yolks and almond extract. Fold into egg white mixture until just combined. Sift flour over egg mixture, add ground almonds and fold in until batter is smooth and very light.

3. For each cookie, drop 2 tsp (10 mL) dough onto prepared baking sheets, placing cookies 2 inches (5 cm) apart.

4. Bake in upper and lower thirds of preheated oven, switching pans on racks halfway through, for 15 to 18 minutes or until golden brown. Let cool on pans on a wire rack for 10 minutes, then transfer to the racks to cool completely.

Nutrients per Serving	
Calories	61
Carbohydrate	9 g
Fiber	0 g
Protein	2 g
Total fat	2 g
Saturated fat	0 g
Cholesterol	41 mg
Sodium	63 mg

America's Exchanges	
1/2	Other Carbohydrate
1/2	Fat

Canada's Choices	
1/2	Carbohydrate
1/2	Fat

Piña Colada Squares

||||||||||||||||||||||||||||||||||||||||||||||||||||||||||||||||||||||||||||||||||||||||||||||||||||||||||||||||||||||||

Makes 16 squares
Serving size: 1 square

These scrumptious squares are perfect for teatime or dessert. Three layers — light pastry, fruity pineapple and flaky coconut — bake together to make a refreshing concoction that's moist, chewy and crunchy.

Kitchen Tip
For the best texture in the crust, measure the margarine or butter, place it in the freezer for about 15 minutes to harden, then cut it into $1/2$-inch (1 cm) pieces.

- **Preheat oven to 350°F (180°C)**
- **9-inch (23 cm) square metal cake pan, lightly greased**

1 cup	all-purpose flour	250 mL
1 tsp	baking powder	5 mL
$1/4$ tsp	salt	1 mL
$1/4$ cup	margarine or butter, cut into small pieces (see tip, at left)	60 mL
1	egg, separated	1
$1/4$ cup	2% milk	60 mL
1	can (14 oz/398 mL) unsweetened crushed pineapple, with juice	1
2 tbsp	cornstarch	30 mL
2 tsp	rum extract	10 mL
1 tsp	vanilla extract	5 mL
$1/4$ tsp	cream of tartar	1 mL
1 tbsp	granulated sugar	15 mL
1 cup	unsweetened shredded coconut	250 mL

1. In a large bowl, combine flour, baking powder and salt. Using a pastry blender or two knives, cut in margarine until mixture resembles coarse crumbs.

2. In a small bowl, whisk together egg yolk and milk. Stir into flour mixture. Press evenly into bottom of prepared cake pan. Set aside.

3. In a small saucepan, combine pineapple with juice and cornstarch. Bring to a boil over medium heat, stirring; boil, stirring, until thickened. Stir in rum extract and vanilla. Pour over first layer.

Nutrients per Serving	
Calories	123
Carbohydrate	14 g
Fiber	1 g
Protein	2 g
Total fat	7 g
Saturated fat	4 g
Cholesterol	12 mg
Sodium	89 mg

America's Exchanges	
1	Other Carbohydrate
$1\frac{1}{2}$	Fats

Canada's Choices	
1	Carbohydrate
$1\frac{1}{2}$	Fats

Kitchen Tips

Store squares in an airtight container in the refrigerator for up to 3 days.

To freeze, layer cooled squares between parchment paper or waxed paper in an airtight container and freeze for up to 2 months.

4. In a clean bowl, using an electric mixer, beat egg white and cream of tartar until frothy. Beat in sugar until soft peaks form. Fold in coconut. Spread evenly and carefully over pineapple layer. Press down lightly with a fork.

5. Bake in preheated oven for 30 minutes or until top is golden brown. Let cool completely in pan on a wire rack before cutting into squares.

Lemon Fingers

||||||||||||||||||||||||||||||||||||||||||||||||||||||||||||||||||||||||||||||||||||||||||||||||||||||||

Makes 5 dozen cookies

Serving size: 3 cookies

These lemon-flavored sponge bars are similar to lady fingers. Their crispness provides a nice contrast to the smoothness of custards and puddings.

Kitchen Tip

Layer cooled fingers between parchment paper or waxed paper in an airtight container and store at room temperature (or freeze for up to 2 months).

Variations

Orange Fingers: Substitute 1 tbsp (15 mL) grated orange zest and 1 tsp (5 mL) freshly squeezed orange juice for the lemon zest and juice.

Anise Fingers: Substitute 1½ tsp (7 mL) anise seeds and 1 tsp (5 mL) vanilla extract for the lemon zest and juice.

Nutrients per Serving	
Calories	30
Carbohydrate	5 g
Fiber	0 g
Protein	1 g
Total fat	1 g
Saturated fat	0 g
Cholesterol	19 mg
Sodium	31 mg

- **Preheat oven to 375°F (190°C)**
- **9-inch (23 cm) square metal cake pan, lined with parchment paper**

3	egg whites, at room temperature	3
⅛ tsp	salt	0.5 mL
½ tsp	baking powder	2 mL
¼ cup	granulated sugar	60 mL
2	egg yolks, at room temperature	2
1 tbsp	grated lemon zest	15 mL
1 tsp	freshly squeezed lemon juice	5 mL
½ cup	all-purpose flour	125 mL

1. In a large bowl, using an electric mixer, beat egg whites and salt until frothy. Beat in baking powder until soft peaks form. Beat in sugar until stiff peaks form. Beat in egg yolks, lemon zest and lemon juice until well combined. Fold in flour.

2. Spread dough in prepared pan, smoothing top with a knife dipped in water. Bake in preheated oven for 20 minutes or until light brown. Remove from oven, leaving oven on. Immediately loosen edges with a knife, turn out onto a cutting board and remove paper.

3. Cut baked dough into 60 strips, each 2 by ¾ inches (5 by 2 cm). Set strips on their sides on a baking sheet. Bake for 5 minutes. Turn off heat and let dry in oven for 15 minutes. Let cool completely in pan on a wire rack.

America's Exchanges	
1	Free Food

Canada's Choices	
1	Extra

Fudgy Brownies

Sometimes you just need that chocolate fix. Now you can have a fudgy chocolate brownie that's lower in fat.

Kitchen Tip

Store cooled brownies wrapped in plastic wrap or in an airtight container at room temperature for up to 2 days. For longer storage, wrap individually in plastic wrap, then place in a freezer bag or airtight container and freeze for up to 2 months.

- **Blender or immersion blender**
- **8-inch (20 cm) square metal baking pan, lined with foil, leaving a 2-inch (5 cm) overhang, foil greased**

½ cup	packed prunes	125 mL
¼ cup	butter or margarine, cut into cubes	60 mL
¾ cup	boiling water	175 mL
⅔ cup	all-purpose flour	150 mL
½ tsp	baking powder	2 mL
¼ tsp	salt	1 mL
½ cup	unsweetened cocoa powder	125 mL
⅓ cup	granulated sugar	75 mL
1	egg	1
2 tsp	vanilla extract	10 mL

1. In blender or in a heatproof measuring cup, combine prunes, butter and boiling water; let stand for about 30 minutes or until prunes are very soft and mixture is cooled to room temperature. Meanwhile, preheat oven to 350°F (180°C).

2. In a large bowl, combine flour, baking powder and salt. Set aside.

3. Using blender, or immersion blender in measuring cup, purée prune mixture until fairly smooth. Add cocoa, sugar, egg and vanilla; blend until incorporated. Pour over flour mixture and stir until just blended.

4. Spread batter in prepared pan, smoothing top. Bake for 20 minutes or until top is puffed and a tester inserted in the center comes out clean with a few moist crumbs clinging to it. Let cool completely in pan on a wire rack. Using foil overhang as handles, transfer brownies to a cutting board and cut into squares.

Nutrients per Serving	
Calories	55
Carbohydrate	8 g
Fiber	1 g
Protein	1 g
Total fat	2 g
Saturated fat	1 g
Cholesterol	12 mg
Sodium	46 mg

America's Exchanges	
½	Other Carbohydrate
½	Fat

Canada's Choices	
½	Carbohydrate
½	Fat

Homemade Crunchy Granola Bars

||||||||||||||||||||||||||||||||||||||||||||||||||||||||||||||||||||||||||||||||||||||||||||||||||||||||||||

Makes 12 bars
Serving size: 1 bar

It's very easy to make your own granola bars with simple ingredients you're likely to have on hand.

Kitchen Tips

To toast nuts, spread pecan or walnut halves or whole almonds on a baking sheet and bake in 350°F (180°C) oven for about 8 minutes, stirring once, until toasted and fragrant. Immediately transfer to a bowl and let cool. Chop, then measure the nuts.

Store granola bars in a cookie tin at room temperature for up to 1 week.

- **Preheat oven to 350°F (180°C)**
- **8-inch (20 cm) square metal baking pan, lined with foil or parchment paper, leaving a 2-inch (5 cm) overhang**

1½ cups	quick-cooking rolled oats	375 mL
¼ cup	chopped toasted pecans, walnuts or almonds (see tip, at left)	60 mL
¼ cup	ground flax seeds (flaxseed meal)	60 mL
½ tsp	ground cinnamon	2 mL
⅓ cup	liquid honey	75 mL
¼ cup	vegetable oil	60 mL
½ tsp	vanilla extract	2 mL

1. In a large bowl, combine oats, pecans, flax seeds and cinnamon.

2. In a small bowl, whisk together honey, oil and vanilla. Pour over dry ingredients and stir until evenly coated. Using slightly moistened hands or a spatula, firmly press oat mixture into prepared pan.

3. Bake in preheated oven for 15 to 20 minutes or until golden brown and firm. Let cool in pan on a wire rack for 5 minutes. Using foil overhang as handles, transfer granola to a cutting board. Cut into bars and let cool on board until set and firm.

Nutrients per Serving

Calories	144
Carbohydrate	17 g
Fiber	2 g
Protein	2 g
Total fat	8 g
Saturated fat	1 g
Cholesterol	0 mg
Sodium	2 mg

America's Exchanges	
1	Other Carbohydrate
1½	Fats

Canada's Choices	
1	Carbohydrate
1½	Fats

Desserts

Blueberry Cupcakes

Makes 12 cupcakes
Serving size: 1 cupcake

Blueberry cupcakes make a delectable dessert, especially when served with Lemon Pudding Sauce (page 282).

Kitchen Tip

To sour fresh milk for this recipe, pour 2 tsp (10 mL) white vinegar into a measuring cup, then fill with 2% milk to $2/3$ cup (150 mL).

- **Preheat oven to 375°F (190°C)**
- **12-cup muffin pan, lightly greased or lined with paper cups**

1½ cups	all-purpose flour	375 mL
1 tsp	baking powder	5 mL
½ tsp	baking soda	2 mL
½ tsp	salt	2 mL
¼ tsp	ground cinnamon	1 mL
¼ tsp	ground nutmeg	1 mL
6 tbsp	lightly packed brown sugar	90 mL
⅓ cup	butter or margarine	75 mL
1	egg	1
⅔ cup	sour milk (see tip, at left) or buttermilk	150 mL
1 cup	fresh or frozen blueberries	250 mL

1. In a small bowl, combine flour, baking powder, baking soda, salt, cinnamon and nutmeg.

2. In a large bowl, cream brown sugar and butter until light and fluffy. Beat in egg. Stir in flour mixture alternately with sour milk, making three additions of flour and two of milk, until just blended. Fold in blueberries.

3. Divide batter evenly among prepared muffin cups. Bake in preheated oven for 20 minutes or until golden. Let cool in pan on a wire rack for 5 minutes, then transfer to the rack to cool slightly. Serve warm.

Nutrients per Serving	
Calories	144
Carbohydrate	20 g
Fiber	1 g
Protein	3 g
Total fat	6 g
Saturated fat	3 g
Cholesterol	29 mg
Sodium	225 mg

America's Exchanges	
1½	Other Carbohydrates
1	Fat

Canada's Choices	
1	Carbohydrate
1	Fat

Sponge Cake

||||||||||||||||||||||||||||||||||||||||||||||||||||||||||||||||||||||||||||||||||||||||||||||||||||||||||||||||||||||||||||||||||||||

Makes 12 servings

When fresh strawberries, blueberries, peaches or apricots are in season, use this cake as the perfect base for shortcake.

Variation

Sponge Roll: Bake in a 13- by 9-inch (33 by 23 cm) jelly roll pan lined with parchment paper. Let cool, then fill with Cream Topping and Filling (page 280) and roll up as you would a jelly roll. Makes 8 servings.

- **Preheat oven to 400°F (200°C)**
- **8-inch (20 cm) square metal cake pan, lined with parchment paper**

4	egg whites, at room temperature	4
1/4 tsp	cream of tartar	1 mL
1/4 tsp	salt	1 mL
1/3 cup	granulated sugar	75 mL
2	egg yolks	2
2 tsp	almond extract	10 mL
1/2 cup	all-purpose flour	125 mL

1. In a large bowl, using an electric mixer, beat egg whites, cream of tartar and salt until foamy. Beat in sugar, 1 tbsp (15 mL) at a time, until stiff peaks form. Beat in egg yolks and almond extract. Gently fold in flour.

2. Spread batter in prepared pan. Bake in preheated oven for 15 minutes or until cake springs back when lightly touched. Loosen edges with a sharp knife and turn out onto a cake rack lined with paper towels to cool.

Nutrients per Serving

Calories	57
Carbohydrate	10 g
Fiber	0 g
Protein	2 g
Total fat	1 g
Saturated fat	0 g
Cholesterol	32 mg
Sodium	68 mg

America's Exchanges	
1	Other Carbohydrate

Canada's Choices	
1/2	Carbohydrate

Chocolate Sponge Cake

||||||||||||||||||||||||||||||||||||||||||||||||||||||||||||||||||||||||||||||||||||||||||||||||||||||||||||||||

Makes 12 servings

If you love chocolate, you'll love this version of sponge cake.

Kitchen Tip

You get much better volume from egg whites at room temperature than from those that are cold. To speed up the warming, place egg whites in a bowl and set the bowl in a larger bowl with a small amount of lukewarm water in it. Periodically refresh it with more lukewarm water as necessary until the whites are warmed.

- **Preheat oven to 400°F (200°C)**
- **8-inch (20 cm) square or round metal cake pan, lined with parchment paper**

4	egg whites, at room temperature	4
1/4 tsp	cream of tartar	1 mL
1/4 tsp	salt	1 mL
1/3 cup	granulated sugar	75 mL
2	egg yolks	2
1 tsp	vanilla extract	5 mL
1/4 cup	all-purpose flour	60 mL
1/4 cup	unsweetened cocoa powder	60 mL

1. In a large bowl, using an electric mixer, beat egg whites, cream of tartar and salt until foamy. Beat in sugar, 1 tbsp (15 mL) at a time, until stiff peaks form. Beat in egg yolks and vanilla.

2. In a small bowl, combine flour and cocoa. Gently fold into egg mixture.

3. Spread batter in prepared pan. Bake in preheated oven for 15 minutes or until cake springs back when lightly touched. Loosen sides with a sharp knife and turn out onto a cake rack lined with paper towels to cool.

Nutrients per Serving	
Calories	51
Carbohydrate	9 g
Fiber	1 g
Protein	2 g
Total fat	1 g
Saturated fat	0 g
Cholesterol	32 mg
Sodium	68 mg

America's Exchanges	
1/2	Other Carbohydrate

Canada's Choices	
1/2	Carbohydrate

Double Chocolate Roll

Makes 8 servings	

In this delicate sponge roll, chocolate appears twice: in the cake and in the filling. It's a lovely choice for a party and is surprisingly low in fat.

Variation

Peppermint Chocolate Roll: Use peppermint-flavored Cream Topping and Filling (page 280), tinted pink or green, if desired, to fill the roll.

- **Preheat oven to 400°F (200°C)**
- **13- by 9-inch (33 by 23 cm) jelly roll pan or cake pan, lined with parchment paper**

1	batch Chocolate Sponge Cake batter (see recipe, page 256)	1
1	recipe Chocolate Cream Topping and Filling (see variation, page 280)	1

1. Spread cake batter in prepared pan. Bake in preheated oven for 10 minutes or until cake springs back when lightly touched.

2. Immediately loosen edges with a sharp knife and turn out onto a clean cloth. Cut off edges if too crisp. Starting with a short end, roll cake up in cloth. (This prevents the roll from cracking.) Set aside, seam side down, to cool.

3. Unroll and remove cloth. Spread filling evenly over cake. Reroll and place seam side down on serving platter. Cut into 8 slices.

Nutrients per Serving

Calories	144
Carbohydrate	24 g
Fiber	1 g
Protein	7 g
Total fat	3 g
Saturated fat	1 g
Cholesterol	49 mg
Sodium	142 mg

America's Exchanges	
1½ Other Carbohydrates	
½	Fat

Canada's Choices	
1½	Carbohydrates
½	Fat

Ribbon Cream Torte

||||||||||||||||||||||||||||||||||||||||||||||||||||||||||||||||||||||||||||||||||||||||||||||||||||||

Ribbon Cream Torte is our choice for a birthday cake. You can vary the flavor and color of the filling to suit your taste.

| 1 | baked Sponge Cake (see recipe, page 255) | 1 |
| 1 | recipe Cream Topping and Filling (see recipe, page 280) | 1 |

1. Cut cake in half. Split each half horizontally to make 4 thin layers.

2. Spread 3 layers with about 1 cup (250 mL) of the filling. Stack on a plate and top with the remaining layer. Frost top and sides of cake with the remaining filling.

3. Cover loosely and refrigerate until serving time. Cut into 8 slices to serve.

Nutrients per Serving

Calories	158
Carbohydrate	26 g
Fiber	0 g
Protein	7 g
Total fat	3 g
Saturated fat	1 g
Cholesterol	49 mg
Sodium	146 mg

America's Exchanges	
2	Other Carbohydrates
1	Lean Meat

Canada's Choices	
1½	Carbohydrates
½	Fat

Nova Scotia Gingerbread

||||||||||||||||||||||||||||||||||||||||||||||||||||||||||||||||||||||||||||||||||||||||||||||||||||||||||||||||||||||||||||||||

Makes 12 servings

Molasses and a small amount of brown sugar sweeten this old-fashioned cake. It is mellow and soft when warm, with a lightly spiced, heavenly taste.

Kitchen Tip

Wrap cooled cake tightly with plastic wrap and store at room temperature for up to 2 days. For longer storage, place wrapped cake in a freezer bag and freeze for up to 2 months.

- Preheat oven to 350°F (180°C)
- 8- by 4-inch (20 by 10 cm) metal loaf pan, lightly greased

1½ cups	all-purpose flour	375 mL
1 tsp	salt	5 mL
1 tsp	baking soda	5 mL
1 tsp	ground cinnamon	5 mL
1 tsp	ground ginger	5 mL
¼ tsp	ground cloves	1 mL
¼ cup	lightly packed brown sugar	60 mL
¼ cup	shortening	60 mL
1	egg	1
⅓ cup	light (fancy) molasses	75 mL
¾ cup	boiling water	175 mL

1. In a small bowl, combine flour, salt, baking soda, cinnamon, ginger and cloves.

2. In a large bowl, cream brown sugar and shortening until light and fluffy. Beat in egg and molasses. Stir in flour mixture alternately with boiling water, making three additions of flour and two of water, until just blended.

3. Spread batter in prepared pan. Bake in preheated oven for 40 to 45 minutes or until a tester inserted in the center comes out clean. Let cool in pan on a wire rack for 10 minutes, then transfer to the rack to cool completely.

Nutrients per Serving	
Calories	146
Carbohydrate	23 g
Fiber	1 g
Protein	2 g
Total fat	5 g
Saturated fat	1 g
Cholesterol	16 mg
Sodium	311 mg

America's Exchanges	
1½	Other Carbohydrates
1	Fat

Canada's Choices	
1½	Carbohydrates
1	Fat

Light and Lemony Cheesecake

|||||||||||||||||||||||||||||||||||||||||||||||||||||||||||||||||||||||||||||||||||||||||||||||||||||||||||||||||

Makes 8 servings

Dessert lovers delight in the creamy smoothness and tangy taste of this "refrigerator-baked" cheesecake. Serve each slice with 2 tbsp (30 mL) Berry Sauce (page 283), if desired.

Kitchen Tip

To grate the lemon zest, use the fine side of a box cheese grater or a Microplane-style grater. If you use a five-hole zester, chop the zest into smaller pieces with a knife.

Nutrition Tip

Tofu is a low-fat substitute for cream cheese in this recipe, and since it takes on the flavor of the other ingredients, no one will notice that you used tofu instead of cheese.

Variation

For a change, press the crust into a 9-inch (23 cm) pie plate, then fill it. You will end up with a heavenly cheese pie.

Nutrients per Serving	
Calories	162
Carbohydrate	13 g
Fiber	0 g
Protein	9 g
Total fat	8 g
Saturated fat	4 g
Cholesterol	87 mg
Sodium	262 mg

- **Food processor (optional)**
- **Double boiler**

1 1/2 cups	2% cottage cheese or drained soft tofu	375 mL
2 tsp	grated lemon zest	10 mL
1	envelope (1/4 oz/7 g) unflavored gelatin powder	1
1/4 cup	freshly squeezed lemon juice	60 mL
8 tsp	granulated sugar	40 mL
3	egg yolks	3
1/2 cup	2% milk	125 mL
1 tsp	vanilla extract	5 mL
1	Graham Cracker Crust in a 9-inch (23 cm) springform pan (see recipe, page 262)	1

1. In food processor, process cottage cheese until very smooth (or press through a sieve). Stir in lemon zest.

2. Sprinkle gelatin over lemon juice and let stand for 5 minutes to soften.

3. In the top of a double boiler, over simmering water, combine sugar, egg yolks and milk. Cook, stirring, until mixture thickens slightly and coats a metal spoon. Remove from heat and stir in gelatin mixture until all granules dissolve.

4. Transfer to a large bowl and stir in cottage cheese and vanilla. Cover and refrigerate, stirring occasionally, for about 1 hour or until mixture mounds when dropped from a spoon.

5. Spread filling in crust. Cover and refrigerate for about 4 hours or until firm.

America's Exchanges	
1	Other Carbohydrate
1	Lean Meat
1	Fat

Canada's Choices	
1	Carbohydrate
1	Meat & Alternatives
1	Fat

Oatmeal Pie Crust

|||||||||||||||||||||||||||||||||||||||||||||||||||||||||||||||||||||||||||||||||||||||||||||||||||||||||||||||||||||||||||||

Makes 6 servings

Oatmeal contributes to the flaky texture and provides the nutty flavor for this deliciously different pie crust.

Kitchen Tip

If your recipe calls for a baked pastry shell, prick pastry with a fork in several places. Bake in a 400°F (200°C) oven for 10 minutes or until light golden brown.

- **9-inch (23 cm) pie plate**

¾ cup	all-purpose flour	175 mL
½ cup	quick-cooking rolled oats	125 mL
½ tsp	salt	2 mL
4 tbsp	vegetable oil	60 mL
3 to 4 tbsp	ice water	45 to 60 mL

1. In a bowl, combine flour, oats and salt. Slowly drizzle in oil, mixing with a fork. Continue lightly mixing with fork, cutting through mixture, until all dry ingredients are moistened and mixture resembles fine crumbs. Add ice water, a few drops at a time, until mixture begins to form a ball.

2. Pat crumb mixture into pie plate. (Or roll between two sheets of waxed paper. Remove top sheet and turn pastry into pie plate; remove second piece of waxed paper.) Form a rim and flute edges. Fill and bake according to pie recipe.

Nutrients per Serving

Calories	167
Carbohydrate	17 g
Fiber	1 g
Protein	3 g
Total fat	10 g
Saturated fat	1 g
Cholesterol	0 mg
Sodium	196 mg

America's Exchanges	
1	Starch
2	Fats

Canada's Choices	
1	Carbohydrate
2	Fats

Graham Cracker Crust

||||||||||||||||||||||||||||||||||||||||||||||||||||||||||||||||||||||||||||||||||||||||||||||||||||||||||||||||||||||||||||||||||

A touch of cinnamon and nutmeg makes this popular pie crust tasty, and there is no need to add sweetener.

Kitchen Tip

This crust can be used for pies, squares or cakes. Check the recipe you plan to use it for to decide what type of pan is best.

- **9-inch (23 cm) pie plate, 8-inch (20 cm) square cake pan or 9-inch (23 cm) springform pan**

¾ cup	graham cracker crumbs	175 mL
¼ tsp	ground cinnamon	1 mL
¼ tsp	ground nutmeg	1 mL
3 tbsp	melted butter or margarine	45 mL

1. In a bowl, combine graham cracker crumbs, cinnamon, nutmeg and butter.

2. Press into pie plate. Cover and refrigerate for 2 hours before filling.

Nutrients per Serving	
Calories	72
Carbohydrate	6 g
Fiber	0 g
Protein	1 g
Total fat	5 g
Saturated fat	3 g
Cholesterol	11 mg
Sodium	79 mg

America's Exchanges	
½	Other Carbohydrate
1	Fat

Canada's Choices	
½	Carbohydrate
1	Fat

Chocolate Dream Pie

||||||||||||||||||||||||||||||||||||||||||||||||||||||||||||||||||||||||||||||||||||||||||||||||||||||||||||||||||

Makes 8 servings

In this delectable dessert, a crisp, crunchy crust holds a velvety smooth chocolate filling.

Nutrition Tip

By replacing the granulated sugar with an equivalent amount of artificial sweetener, you can reduce the carbohydrate in this recipe by 8 g per serving. In this case, count a serving as 1/2 Other Carbohydrate Exchange or 1/2 Carbohydrate Choice.

Variation

Chocolate Mousse: Prepare filling through step 3. Rinse 6 individual molds or a 4-cup (1 L) jelly mold with cold water. Spoon gelatin mixture into mold(s). Refrigerate for about 4 hours or until set. Makes 6 servings.

1	envelope (1/4 oz/7 g) unflavored gelatin powder	1
1 1/2 cups	skim milk, divided	375 mL
1/4 cup	unsweetened cocoa powder	60 mL
1/3 cup	granulated sugar	75 mL
1 tbsp	cornstarch	15 mL
1	egg yolk	1
1 tsp	vanilla extract	5 mL
1	baked Oatmeal Pie Crust (see recipe, page 261)	1

1. In a small bowl, sprinkle gelatin over 1/4 cup (60 mL) milk and let stand for 5 minutes to soften.

2. In a heavy saucepan, whisk together cocoa and 1 cup (250 mL) milk until well blended. Bring to a boil over medium heat. Reduce heat and simmer for 5 minutes.

3. In a bowl, whisk together sugar, cornstarch, egg yolk and the remaining milk. Stir into cocoa mixture and simmer, stirring, for about 5 minutes or until thickened. Remove from heat and stir in gelatin mixture and vanilla until all granules dissolve. Pour into a bowl and let cool. Refrigerate for about 45 minutes or until partially set.

4. Spoon gelatin mixture into pie crust. Refrigerate for about 4 hours or until set.

Nutrients per Serving	
Calories	195
Carbohydrate	26 g
Fiber	2 g
Protein	5 g
Total fat	8 g
Saturated fat	1 g
Cholesterol	25 mg
Sodium	174 mg

America's Exchanges	
1	Starch
1	Other Carbohydrate
1 1/2	Fats

Canada's Choices	
1 1/2	Carbohydrates
1 1/2	Fats

Strawberry Angel Pie

||||||||||||||||||||||||||||||||||||||||||||||||||||||||||||||||||||||||||||||||||||||||||||||||||||

Makes 6 servings

Fresh or frozen strawberries work equally well in this colorful, light-tasting pie.

Variation

Strawberry Angel Mousse: Prepare filling through step 3. Rinse 6 individual molds or a 4-cup (1 L) jelly mold with cold water. Spoon gelatin mixture into mold(s). Refrigerate for about 4 hours or until set. Makes 6 servings.

3 cups	sliced fresh or frozen unsweetened strawberries	750 mL
1	envelope ($\frac{1}{4}$ oz/7 g) unflavored gelatin powder	1
$\frac{1}{4}$ cup	granulated sugar	60 mL
1 tbsp	cornstarch	15 mL
1	egg yolk	1
1 tsp	vanilla extract	5 mL
$\frac{1}{2}$ tsp	almond extract	2 mL
1	Graham Cracker Crust in a 9-inch (23 cm) pie plate (see recipe, page 262)	1

1. Pour 1 cup (250 mL) water over strawberries and let stand at room temperature for 1 hour.

2. Drain water from strawberries into a saucepan; reserve strawberries. Transfer 2 tbsp (30 mL) liquid to a small bowl, sprinkle gelatin over top and let stand for 5 minutes to soften.

3. Whisk sugar, cornstarch and egg yolk into water in saucepan. Bring to a boil over medium heat, stirring constantly; boil, stirring, for about 3 minutes or until slightly thickened. Remove from heat and stir in gelatin mixture, vanilla and almond extract until all granules dissolve. Pour into a bowl, stir in strawberries and let cool. Refrigerate for about 30 minutes or until partially set.

4. Spoon gelatin mixture into crust. Refrigerate for about 4 hours or until set.

Nutrients per Serving	
Calories	176
Carbohydrate	25 g
Fiber	2 g
Protein	3 g
Total fat	8 g
Saturated fat	4 g
Cholesterol	47 mg
Sodium	112 mg

America's Exchanges	
$1\frac{1}{2}$	Other Carbohydrates
$1\frac{1}{2}$	Fats

Canada's Choices	
$1\frac{1}{2}$	Carbohydrates
$1\frac{1}{2}$	Fats

Mandarin Pie

||||||||||||||||||||||||||||||||||||||||||||||||||||||||||||||||||||||||||||||||||||||||||||||||||||

Serve this cool, refreshing pie with a sprightly garnish of mint or a twist of lemon.

Kitchen Tip

If fresh mandarin oranges are in season, by all means substitute 1 cup (250 mL) orange sections for the canned oranges.

1	envelope (¼ oz/7 g) unflavored gelatin powder	1
2 tbsp	cold water	30 mL
¼ cup	granulated sugar	60 mL
½ cup	boiling water	125 mL
1 tsp	grated orange zest	5 mL
¼ cup	unsweetened orange juice	60 mL
1 cup	low-fat plain yogurt	250 mL
1	can (10 oz/284 mL) unsweetened mandarin oranges, drained	1
1	Graham Cracker Crust in a 9-inch (23 cm) pie plate (see recipe, page 262) Ground cinnamon	1

1. In a medium bowl, sprinkle gelatin over cold water and let stand for 5 minutes to soften.

2. Add sugar and boiling water to gelatin mixture, stirring until all granules dissolve. Stir in orange zest and orange juice. Beat in yogurt until well blended. Let cool. Refrigerate for about 45 minutes or until partially set.

3. Fold oranges into gelatin mixture. Pour gelatin mixture into crust. Sprinkle lightly with cinnamon. Refrigerate for about 4 hours or until set.

Nutrients per Serving	
Calories	175
Carbohydrate	24 g
Fiber	1 g
Protein	4 g
Total fat	8 g
Saturated fat	4 g
Cholesterol	18 mg
Sodium	139 mg

America's Exchanges	
1½ Other Carbohydrates	
1½	Fats

Canada's Choices	
1½	Carbohydrates
1½	Fats

Peachy Blueberry Pie

• Preheat oven to 425°F (220°C)

Makes 8 servings

The two-fruit filling baked in a nutty-tasting pie crust makes an extra-special pie that is bound to become a family favorite.

Nutrition Tip

Fresh fruits and unsweetened fruit juices are sources of sugar. A large apple, for example, contains about 2 tbsp (30 mL) natural sugar.

8 tsp	granulated sugar	40 mL
2 tbsp	cornstarch	30 mL
1/4 tsp	ground nutmeg	1 mL
Pinch	salt	Pinch
1 tbsp	freshly squeezed lemon juice	15 mL
2 cups	sliced fresh or thawed frozen peaches	500 mL
1/2 cup	fresh or partially thawed frozen blueberries	125 mL
1	Oatmeal Pie Crust (see recipe, page 261)	1
1/2 cup	Crunchy Topping (see recipe, page 279)	125 mL

1. In a saucepan, combine sugar, cornstarch, nutmeg, salt, 1/2 cup (125 mL) water and lemon juice; stir until well blended. Bring to a boil over high heat. Cook, stirring, for about 2 minutes or until clear and thickened. Remove from heat and fold in peaches, then blueberries.

2. Immediately spoon filling into pie crust. Sprinkle with topping. Cover loosely with tented foil to prevent overbrowning.

3. Bake in preheated oven for 30 minutes. Remove foil and bake for 10 minutes or until fruit is tender.

Nutrients per Serving

Calories	211
Carbohydrate	29 g
Fiber	2 g
Protein	3 g
Total fat	10 g
Saturated fat	2 g
Cholesterol	4 mg
Sodium	196 mg

America's Exchanges

1	Starch
1	Other Carbohydrate
2	Fats

Canada's Choices

2	Carbohydrates
2	Fats

Baked Rice Pudding

IIIIIIIIIIIIIIIIIIIIIIIIIIIIIIIIIIIIIIIIIIIIIIIIIIIIIIIIIIIIIIIIIIIIIIIIIIIIIIIIIIIIIIIIIIIIIIIIII

Makes 4 servings

This rice pudding is wonderfully smooth and lightly spiced. The secret to its creamy perfection is the twice-cooked rice.

Nutrition Tip

Vanilla extract and other flavorings enhance sweet treats, baked goods and desserts. They perform wonders when sugar is eliminated or used in small amounts. Some of the quantities used in recipes in this book may seem large, but the resultant dishes taste best with these amounts.

- Preheat oven to 350°F (180°C)
- 4-cup (1 L) casserole dish, lightly greased
- Roasting pan

¼ tsp	salt	1 mL
¼ cup	long-grain white rice	60 mL
4 tsp	lightly packed brown sugar	20 mL
¼ tsp	ground cinnamon	1 mL
¼ tsp	ground nutmeg	1 mL
1	egg	1
1¼ cups	2% milk	300 mL
½ tsp	vanilla extract	2 mL
2 tbsp	raisins	30 mL

1. In a small saucepan, bring ½ cup (125 mL) water and salt to a boil over high heat. Add rice, reduce heat to low, cover and simmer for 15 minutes or until rice is tender and liquid is absorbed.

2. In a large bowl, whisk together brown sugar, cinnamon, nutmeg, egg, milk and vanilla. Stir in rice and raisins. Spoon into prepared casserole dish.

3. Place casserole dish in roasting pan, and place roasting pan in preheated oven. Pour boiling water into the roasting pan until it reaches halfway up the sides of the casserole dish. Bake for 30 minutes. Remove from oven and stir. Bake for 30 minutes or until lightly browned.

Nutrients per Serving

Calories	126
Carbohydrate	21 g
Fiber	0 g
Protein	5 g
Total fat	2 g
Saturated fat	1 g
Cholesterol	50 mg
Sodium	199 mg

America's Exchanges	
½	Starch
1	Other Carbohydrate

Canada's Choices	
1½	Carbohydrates
½	Fat

Cranberry Pear Kuchen

||||||||||||||||||||||||||||||||||||||||||||||||||||||||||||||||||||||||||||||||||||||||||||||||||||||

This old-fashioned baked dessert combines two fruits not often seen together — but the combination is perfectly pleasing.

- **Preheat oven to 350°F (180°C)**
- **9-inch (23 cm) round or square glass baking dish, greased**

Fruit Layer

2 cups	cranberries, chopped	500 mL
8 tsp	granulated sugar	40 mL
Pinch	ground cinnamon	Pinch
1 tbsp	cornstarch	15 mL
1/4 cup	cold water	60 mL
1/2	pear or apple, peeled and coarsely chopped	1/2

Kuchen Layer

1 cup	all-purpose flour	250 mL
1 1/2 tsp	baking powder	7 mL
1/2 tsp	salt	2 mL
1/4 tsp	ground cinnamon	1 mL
3 tbsp	granulated sugar	45 mL
1	egg	1
2 tsp	vegetable oil	10 mL
1/2 tsp	vanilla extract	2 mL
1/2 cup	Crunchy Topping (see recipe, page 279)	125 mL

1. *Fruit Layer:* In a saucepan, combine cranberries, sugar, cinnamon and 1 cup (250 mL) water. Bring to a boil over high heat. Reduce heat and boil gently, stirring, for 5 minutes.

2. In a small bowl, whisk together cornstarch and cold water. Stir into cranberry mixture and simmer, stirring, until thickened. Remove from heat and stir in pear. Set aside.

Nutrients per Serving	
Calories	116
Carbohydrate	21 g
Fiber	2 g
Protein	2 g
Total fat	3 g
Saturated fat	1 g
Cholesterol	18 mg
Sodium	149 mg

America's Exchanges	
1 1/2 Other Carbohydrates	
1/2	Fat

Canada's Choices	
1	Carbohydrate
1/2	Fat

Variation

Blueberry Peach Kuchen:
Replace the cranberries with whole blueberries and use 1 peach in place of the pear.

3. *Kuchen Layer:* In a bowl, combine flour, baking powder, salt and cinnamon.

4. In another bowl, whisk together sugar, egg, $\frac{1}{3}$ cup (75 mL) water, oil and vanilla until frothy. Stir into flour mixture until just blended.

5. Spread kuchen layer in prepared baking dish. Pour fruit layer over kuchen layer. Sprinkle with topping.

6. Bake in preheated oven for 45 minutes. Serve warm.

Crêpes Élégantes

Tender crêpes with a brilliant ruby glaze are the perfect dessert for a busy party-giver to serve. Both crêpes and sauce can be made ahead, and the final combination can be done over a burner at the table for an elegant finale to a meal.

Kitchen Tip

The sauce can be made ahead through step 3. Transfer to an airtight container and let cool, then store in the refrigerator for up to 2 days. Reheat in the skillet over medium heat, stirring often, until bubbling before adding the brandy.

● **Blender or food processor**

2 cups	cranberries	500 mL
2 tsp	grated orange zest	10 mL
2 tsp	cornstarch	10 mL
¼ cup	cold water	60 mL
2 tsp	light (fancy) molasses	10 mL
¼ cup	granulated sugar	60 mL
2 tbsp	brandy	30 mL
8	Crêpes (see recipe, page 70)	8
1½ cups	strawberries, sliced	375 mL

1. In a saucepan, combine cranberries, orange zest and 1¾ cups (425 mL) water. Bring to a boil over high heat. Reduce heat and simmer for 5 minutes. Pour into blender.

2. In a small bowl, whisk together cornstarch, cold water and molasses. Add to cranberry mixture and purée for 1 to 2 minutes or until smooth.

3. Return purée to saucepan. Cook, stirring, over medium heat for about 4 minutes or until mixture boils and thickens. Remove from heat and add sugar, stirring until it dissolves.

Nutrients per Serving

Calories	124
Carbohydrate	21 g
Fiber	2 g
Protein	3 g
Total fat	3 g
Saturated fat	1 g
Cholesterol	48 mg
Sodium	27 mg

America's Exchanges	
½	Starch
1	Other Carbohydrate
½	Fat

Canada's Choices	
1	Carbohydrate
½	Fat

Nutrition Tip

Replacing the sugar with an equivalent amount of artificial sweetener will reduce the carbohydrate by 6 g per serving.

Variation

Substitute ³⁄₄ cup (175 mL) raspberries, 1¹⁄₂ thinly sliced peaches or 1 small thinly sliced peeled apple or pear for the strawberries.

4. Transfer sauce to a large skillet and stir in brandy; bring to a boil. Reduce heat and simmer for 1 minute. One at a time, place crêpes in sauce, coating both sides. Fold crêpe in half, then in half again to form a triangle; move to side of skillet. Repeat with remaining crêpes. Add strawberries to other side of skillet and cook, stirring, for 1 minute or until heated through.

5. Spoon a crêpe, sauce and a few strawberries onto a warm dessert plate for each serving.

Cream Puff Shells

||||||||||||||||||||||||||||||||||||||||||||||||||||||||||||||||||||||||||||||||||||||||||||||||||||||||

Makes 30 shells
Serving size: 2 shells

If you want éclairs instead of puffs, shape the paste into little oblong shapes before baking. Whichever one you pick, this is one of the easiest pastries to make.

- **Preheat oven to 400°F (200°C)**
- **Baking sheets, dampened**

⅓ cup	vegetable oil	75 mL
Pinch	salt	Pinch
1 cup	all-purpose flour	250 mL
4	eggs, at room temperature	4
1 tsp	vanilla extract	5 mL

1. In a saucepan, combine 1 cup (250 mL) water, oil and salt. Bring to a rapid boil over high heat. Add flour all at once, beating vigorously with a wooden spoon. Beat until mixture forms a ball and draws away from the sides of the pan. Remove from heat and let cool for 5 minutes.

2. Using an electric mixer, beat in eggs, one at a time, and vanilla. Beat for 1 to 2 minutes or until dough is very smooth and glossy.

3. For each shell, spoon about 1 tbsp (15 mL) dough onto prepared baking sheets, placing shells about 2 inches (5 cm) apart.

4. Bake in upper and lower thirds of preheated oven for 10 minutes. Switch pans on racks. Increase heat to 450°F (230°C) and bake for 12 to 15 minutes or until puffs are lightly browned, crisp and firm to the touch. Slit each puff with the tip of a sharp knife to release steam. Let cool on pans on wire racks before filling.

Nutrients per Serving

Calories	91
Carbohydrate	6 g
Fiber	0 g
Protein	3 g
Total fat	6 g
Saturated fat	1 g
Cholesterol	50 mg
Sodium	36 mg

America's Exchanges	
½	Starch
1	Fat

Canada's Choices	
½	Carbohydrate
1	Fat

Chocolate Almond Cream Puffs

**Makes
30 cream puffs**
Serving size:
2 cream puffs

Since the airy filling is as
light as the puff shells
themselves, these could
be called "chocolate
pillows."

• **Pastry bag fitted with a small plain tube (optional)**

| 2 cups | Chocolate Almond Filling (see recipe, page 281) | 500 mL |
| 30 | Cream Puff Shells (see recipe, page 272) | 30 |

1. Place filling in pastry bag and fill puffs with 1 tbsp
   (15 mL) filling through slit made in puff shell
   (or cut top off and spoon filling into puffs). Serve
   immediately or refrigerate for up to 4 hours.

Nutrients per Serving

Calories	115
Carbohydrate	9 g
Fiber	0 g
Protein	3 g
Total fat	8 g
Saturated fat	2 g
Cholesterol	50 mg
Sodium	43 mg

America's Exchanges	
1/2	Starch
1 1/2	Fats

Canada's Choices	
1/2	Carbohydrate
1 1/2	Fats

Soft Custard

||||||||||||||||||||||||||||||||||||||||||||||||||||||||||||||||||||||||||||||||||||||||||||

Makes 4 servings

Serve this delightful treat as a dessert on its own or as a velvety sauce over a small slice of angel food cake or a small dish of fruit.

• **Double boiler**

2 tbsp	granulated sugar	30 mL
Pinch	salt	Pinch
2	eggs	2
1½ cups	2% milk	375 mL
½ tsp	vanilla extract	2 mL

1. In top of double boiler, whisk together sugar, salt and eggs; stir in milk. Place over simmering water and cook, stirring, until mixture coats a metal spoon. Pour immediately into a cool bowl or pitcher. Stir in vanilla. Use as a sauce or pour into serving dishes when cool.

Nutrients per Serving

Calories	100
Carbohydrate	11 g
Fiber	0 g
Protein	6 g
Total fat	3 g
Saturated fat	1 g
Cholesterol	98 mg
Sodium	144 mg

America's Exchanges

½	Milk
½	Other Carbohydrate
½	Fat

Canada's Choices

1	Carbohydrate
½	Fat

Baked Cinnamon Custard

||||||||||||||||||||||||||||||||||||||||||||||||||||||||||||||||||||||||||||||||||||||||||||||||||||||||||||||||||

Makes 4 servings

Count on baked custard to star as the finale to an everyday meal or an elegant company dinner. If you feel like being innovative, try the variations.

Variations

Saucy Baked Custard:
Place 1 tsp (5 mL) fruit spread or reduced-sugar jam in each custard cup before pouring in custard (or place 4 tsp/20 mL in casserole dish). Omit the cinnamon. Turn out custards onto dessert dishes. Sauce forms over custard.

Baked Coconut Custard:
Place 1 tsp (5 mL) unsweetened shredded coconut in each custard cup before pouring in custard (or place 4 tsp/20 mL in casserole dish).

- Preheat oven to 350°F (180°C)
- 4 individual custard cups or 4-cup (1 L) casserole dish
- Baking pan

2	eggs	2
1	egg yolk	1
1 tbsp	lightly packed brown sugar	15 mL
Pinch	salt	Pinch
1 tsp	vanilla extract	5 mL
1¼ cups	2% milk	300 mL
	Ground cinnamon	

1. In a bowl, lightly beat eggs and egg yolk. Beat in brown sugar, salt and vanilla. Stir in milk. Pour through a fine-mesh sieve into custard cups. Sprinkle lightly with cinnamon.

2. Place cups in baking pan, and place baking pan in preheated oven. Pour boiling water into the baking pan until it comes nearly to the top of the cups. Bake for 45 minutes or until a tester inserted in the center comes out clean. Serve warm or at room temperature or let cool, cover and refrigerate for at least 4 hours, until thoroughly chilled, or for up to 2 days.

Nutrients per Serving

Calories	99
Carbohydrate	7 g
Fiber	0 g
Protein	6 g
Total fat	4 g
Saturated fat	2 g
Cholesterol	144 mg
Sodium	140 mg

America's Exchanges	
½	Other Carbohydrate
1	Fat

Canada's Choices	
½	Carbohydrate
1	Fat

Orange Custard Cloud

||||||||||||||||||||||||||||||||||||||||||||||||||||||||||||||||||||||||||||||||||||||||||||||||||||||||||||||||||||||||||||||||||||||||||||

Makes 8 servings

The delicate flavor and texture of this light orange fluff complement almost any meal. Serve with Berry Sauce (page 283) for a beautiful color contrast.

Kitchen Tip

This recipe contains raw egg whites. If the food safety of raw eggs is a concern for you, substitute 6 tbsp (90 mL) pasteurized liquid egg whites.

Variations

Substitute Peach Nectar (page 38) for the orange juice.

For a richer dessert, replace the egg whites and cream of tartar with 1/4 cup (60 mL) heavy or whipping (35%) cream. Count a serving as 1/2 Other Carbohydrate plus 1 Fat Exchange, or 1/2 Carbohydrate plus 1 Fat Choice.

● **6-cup (1.5 L) jelly mold**

1	envelope (1/4 oz/7 g) unflavored gelatin powder	1
1 tsp	grated orange zest (optional)	5 mL
2 cups	unsweetened orange juice	500 mL
2	egg yolks	2
8 tsp	granulated sugar	40 mL
3	egg whites	3
1/4 tsp	cream of tartar	1 mL

1. In a small bowl, sprinkle gelatin over 1/2 cup (125 mL) orange juice and let stand for 5 minutes to soften.

2. In a saucepan, whisk together the remaining orange juice, orange zest (if using) and egg yolks. Heat over medium heat, stirring constantly, for about 5 minutes or until thick enough to coat a metal spoon. Remove from heat and stir gelatin mixture and sugar until all granules dissolve. Pour into a bowl and let cool. Refrigerate for about 45 minutes or until partially set.

3. In a bowl, using an electric mixer, beat egg whites with cream of tartar until stiff. Fold into gelatin mixture.

4. Rinse jelly mold with cold water. Spoon gelatin mixture into mold. Refrigerate for about 4 hours or until set.

Nutrients per Serving

Calories	67
Carbohydrate	11 g
Fiber	0 g
Protein	3 g
Total fat	1 g
Saturated fat	0 g
Cholesterol	47 mg
Sodium	24 mg

America's Exchanges	
1	Other Carbohydrate

Canada's Choices	
1/2	Carbohydrate
1/2	Meat & Alternatives

Pineapple Dream

||||||||||||||||||||||||||||||||||||||||||||||||||||||||||||||||||||||||||||||||||||||||||||||||||

Makes 8 servings

Pineapple Dream is, as
the Greeks say, "food
fit for the gods." For
a glorious party pie,
pour it into a Graham
Cracker Crust (page 262)
or Oatmeal Pie Crust
(page 261).

Kitchen Tip

Toast coconut in a small dry
skillet over medium heat,
stirring constantly, for 2 to
3 minutes or until golden
and fragrant. Immediately
transfer to a bowl and let
cool.

Nutrition Tip

Cottage cheese has
traditionally contained
a lot of salt, with about
400 mg (17% DV) in $\frac{1}{2}$ cup
(125 mL). Some brands
now contain less. Be sure
to check the Nutrition Facts
table when shopping and
choose the one that's lowest
in sodium.

Nutrients per Serving

Calories	89
Carbohydrate	9 g
Fiber	0 g
Protein	6 g
Total fat	3 g
Saturated fat	3 g
Cholesterol	3 mg
Sodium	130 mg

- **Blender or food processor**

1	envelope ($\frac{1}{4}$ oz/7 g) unflavored gelatin powder	1
$\frac{1}{2}$ cup	unsweetened pineapple juice	125 mL
1 tsp	coconut or almond extract	5 mL
1 cup	2% cottage cheese	250 mL
$\frac{1}{2}$ cup	drained canned unsweetened pineapple chunks	125 mL
1 tsp	granulated sugar	5 mL
1	packet whipped topping mix (for 2 cups/500 mL whipped topping)	1
$\frac{1}{2}$ cup	2% milk	125 mL
2 tsp	unsweetened shredded coconut, toasted (see tip, at left)	10 mL

1. In a small saucepan, sprinkle gelatin over pineapple juice and let stand for 5 minutes to soften.

2. Add coconut extract to gelatin mixture. Heat over low heat until all granules dissolve. Let cool to room temperature.

3. In blender, combine cottage cheese, pineapple and sugar; purée until smooth. Transfer to a serving bowl or dish and stir in gelatin mixture.

4. In a small, deep bowl, using an electric mixer, beat whipped topping mix and milk until stiff peaks form. Fold into cottage cheese mixture. Sprinkle with coconut. Cover and refrigerate for at least 2 hours, until chilled, or for up to 1 day.

America's Exchanges	
$\frac{1}{2}$	Other Carbohydrate
1	Lean Meat

Canada's Choices	
$\frac{1}{2}$	Carbohydrate
$\frac{1}{2}$	Meat & Alternatives

Orange Blocks

||||||||||||||||||||||||||||||||||||||||||||||||||||||||||||||||||||||||||||||||||||||||||||||||||||||||||||||

Makes 32 blocks
Serving size: 1 block

Orange blocks are a cool, colorful confection greatly enjoyed by young people.

Variation

Grape Blocks: Substitute 1 cup (250 mL) unsweetened grape juice and 1 cup (250 mL) water for the orange juice.

- **8-inch (20 cm) square cake pan**

4	envelopes (each ¼ oz/7 g) unflavored gelatin powder	4
2 cups	unsweetened orange juice, divided	500 mL
2 tsp	vanilla extract	10 mL

1. In a large bowl, sprinkle gelatin over 1 cup (250 mL) of the orange juice and let stand for 5 minutes to soften.

2. In a small saucepan, bring the remaining orange juice to a boil over high heat. Stir into gelatin mixture until all granules dissolve. Stir in vanilla.

3. Rinse cake pan with cold water. Pour gelatin mixture into pan. Refrigerate for about 4 hours or until set. Cut into 32 blocks.

Nutrients per Serving

Calories	11
Carbohydrate	2 g
Fiber	0 g
Protein	1 g
Total fat	0 g
Saturated fat	0 g
Cholesterol	0 mg
Sodium	2 mg

America's Exchanges	
1	Free Food

Canada's Choices	
1	Extra

Crunchy Topping

||||||||||||||||||||||||||||||||||||||||||||||||||||||||||||||||||||||||||||||||||||||||||||||||||||||||||

**Makes about
2 cups (500 mL)**
Serving size: 1 tbsp
(15 mL)

A sprinkling of this toasted topping enhances simple puddings, baked custards and fruit cups.

Nutrition Tip
Nuts contain protein and fat. While the fat is the healthy unsaturated type, it still contributes calories, so nuts should generally be used in small quantities.

1/4 cup	butter or margarine	60 mL
1 1/2 cups	quick-cooking rolled oats	375 mL
1/4 cup	lightly packed brown sugar	60 mL
1/4 cup	chopped nuts	60 mL
1/2 tsp	ground cinnamon	2 mL

1. In a skillet, melt butter over medium heat. Stir in oats, brown sugar, nuts and cinnamon; cook, stirring, for about 3 minutes or until golden brown. Remove from heat and spread out on a large plate or baking sheet to cool. Store in an airtight container in the refrigerator for up to 2 months.

Nutrients per Serving	
Calories	41
Carbohydrate	5 g
Fiber	1 g
Protein	1 g
Total fat	2 g
Saturated fat	1 g
Cholesterol	4 mg
Sodium	11 mg

America's Exchanges	
1/2	Fat
1	Free Food

Canada's Choices	
1/2	Fat
1	Extra

Cream Topping and Filling

||||||||||||||||||||||||||||||||||||||||||||||||||||||||||||||||||||||||||||||||

Maple-flavored filling
is marvelous in the
Ribbon Cream Torte
(page 258). If you make
peppermint-flavored
filling, try tinting it
with red or green food
coloring and use it to
make the Peppermint
Chocolate Roll (variation,
page 257).

Variation

*Chocolate Cream Topping
and Filling:* In a saucepan,
combine 2 tbsp (30 mL)
unsweetened cocoa powder
and ¹⁄₂ cup (125 mL) water,
stirring until smooth. Stir in
another ¹⁄₂ cup (125 mL)
water and bring to a boil
over high heat. Substitute
for the boiling water in the
recipe.

1	envelope (¹⁄₄ oz/7 g) unflavored gelatin powder	1
¹⁄₄ cup	cold water	60 mL
1 cup	boiling water	250 mL
³⁄₄ cup	instant skim milk powder	175 mL
¹⁄₄ cup	granulated sugar	60 mL
1 tsp	vanilla extract	5 mL
2 tsp	maple or orange extract (or 1 tsp/5 mL peppermint extract)	10 mL
2 tsp	vegetable oil	10 mL

1. In a large bowl, sprinkle gelatin over cold water and let stand for 5 minutes to soften.

2. Add boiling water to gelatin mixture and stir until all granules dissolve. Let cool for 5 minutes.

3. Add milk powder and sugar to gelatin mixture, stirring until dissolved. Let cool completely, then refrigerate for about 30 minutes or until partially set. Meanwhile, chill the beaters for an electric mixer.

4. Using electric mixer with chilled beaters, beat gelatin mixture on high speed until stiff peaks form. Beat in vanilla, maple extract and oil.

Nutrients per Serving	
Calories	57
Carbohydrate	9 g
Fiber	0 g
Protein	3 g
Total fat	1 g
Saturated fat	0 g
Cholesterol	1 mg
Sodium	35 mg

America's Exchanges	
¹⁄₂	Other Carbohydrate

Canada's Choices	
¹⁄₂	Carbohydrate

Chocolate Almond Filling

||||||||||||||||||||||||||||||||||||||||||||||||||||||||||||||||||||||||||||||||||||||||||||||||||||||||||||||||||||

Chocolate Almond Filling
is superb in cream puffs
(see page 273) and
also makes a beautiful
frosting for Sponge Cake
(page 255).

Kitchen Tip

Toast whole almonds in
a small dry skillet, stirring
constantly, for about
5 minutes or until fragrant.
Immediately transfer to a
bowl and let cool, then chop.

Variation

*Mocha Almond Cream
Filling:* Add 1 tsp (5 mL)
instant coffee granules to
the topping mix before
beating.

1	packet whipped topping mix (for 2 cups/500 mL whipped topping)	1
½ cup	cold 2% milk	125 mL
2 tsp	unsweetened cocoa powder	10 mL
1 tsp	almond extract	5 mL
6	almonds, toasted and chopped (see tip, at left)	6

1. In a small, deep bowl, using an electric mixer, beat whipped topping mix, milk, cocoa powder and almond extract until stiff peaks form. Continue to beat for 2 minutes or until fluffy. Fold in almonds. Store in an airtight container in the refrigerator for up to 1 day.

Nutrients per Serving

Calories	23
Carbohydrate	2 g
Fiber	0 g
Protein	1 g
Total fat	1 g
Saturated fat	1 g
Cholesterol	1 mg
Sodium	6 mg

America's Exchanges	
1	Free Food

Canada's Choices	
1	Extra

Lemon Pudding Sauce

||||||||||||||||||||||||||||||||||||||||||||||||||||||||||||||||||||||||||||||||||||||||||

For a fabulous dessert, drizzle this sauce over piping hot Blueberry Cupcakes (page 254) or Nova Scotia Gingerbread (page 259).

Kitchen Tip

To grate the lemon zest, use the fine side of a box cheese grater or a Microplane-style grater. If you use a five-hole zester, chop the zest into smaller pieces with a knife.

Nutrition Tip

When choosing a margarine, look for a non-hydrogenated soft margarine. These are low in saturated fat and do not contain trans fat. Avoid hard margarines, which contain high amounts of saturated and trans fat.

4 tsp	cornstarch	20 mL
	Finely grated zest of 1 lemon	
1 cup	cold water	250 mL
¼ cup	freshly squeezed lemon juice	60 mL
1	egg	1
2 tsp	margarine or butter	10 mL
8 tsp	granulated sugar	40 mL

1. In a small, heavy saucepan, combine cornstarch, lemon zest, cold water and lemon juice. Beat in egg. Cook over medium heat, stirring constantly, until thickened and clear. Stir in margarine and sugar. Serve warm.

Nutrients per Serving	
Calories	33
Carbohydrate	5 g
Fiber	0 g
Protein	1 g
Total fat	1 g
Saturated fat	0 g
Cholesterol	19 mg
Sodium	14 mg

America's Exchanges	
1	Free Food

Canada's Choices	
1	Extra

Berry Sauce

Makes about
3/4 cup (175 mL)
Serving size: 3 tbsp
(45 mL)

This ruby red sauce is delicious served warm or cold on cheesecake, sponge cake or baked custard.

Kitchen Tips

To serve this sauce warm, heat it in a small saucepan over medium-low heat, stirring often, until starting to bubble.

● **Blender or food processor**

1 cup	raspberries or strawberries	250 mL
	Artificial sweetener equivalent to 1/4 cup (60 mL) granulated sugar	
1 tbsp	freshly squeezed lemon juice	15 mL

1. In blender, combine raspberries and sweetener; purée until smooth. Strain through a fine-mesh sieve to remove seeds, pressing with the back of a spoon to push through as much fruit as possible. Stir in lemon juice. Use immediately or store in an airtight container in the refrigerator for up to 3 days.

Nutrients per Serving

Calories	22
Carbohydrate	5 g
Fiber	0 g
Protein	0 g
Total fat	0 g
Saturated fat	0 g
Cholesterol	0 mg
Sodium	0 mg

America's Exchanges	
1	Free Food

Canada's Choices	
1	Extra

Chocolate Sauce

½ cup	unsweetened cocoa powder	125 mL
2 tsp	cornstarch	10 mL
2 cups	cold water	500 mL
	Artificial sweetener equivalent to 8 tsp (40 mL) granulated sugar	
2 tsp	vanilla extract	10 mL

This sauce is so delectable it disappears quickly. Try drizzling it over ice cream, Sponge Cake (page 255) or fresh pears, or use it as the base for Chocolate Milk (page 52) or Hot Chocolate (page 53).

Variation

Mocha Sauce: Substitute 2 cups (500 mL) strong brewed coffee for the water.

1. In a small bowl, whisk together cocoa and cornstarch.

2. Pour cold water into a saucepan. Whisk in cocoa mixture until no dry bits remain. Bring to a boil over medium heat, stirring frequently. Boil, stirring, for 1 minute or until thickened. Remove from heat and stir in sweetener and vanilla. Cover and let cool. Store in an airtight container in the refrigerator for up to 6 weeks.

Nutrients per Serving

Calories	13
Carbohydrate	3 g
Fiber	1 g
Protein	1 g
Total fat	0 g
Saturated fat	0 g
Cholesterol	0 mg
Sodium	2 mg

America's Exchanges	
1	Free Food

Canada's Choices	
1	Extra

Soft Spreads, Chutneys and Pickles

Cinnamon Apple Jelly

||||||||||||||||||||||||||||||||||||||||||||||||||||||||||||||||||||||||||||||||||||||||||||||

This sparkling jelly
for toast or muffins is
tantalizing and has a
subtle spicy scent.

• **Hot sterilized jar with plastic storage lid or cap**

1 tsp	unflavored gelatin powder	5 mL
1²⁄₃ cups	unsweetened apple juice, divided	400 mL
2 tsp	freshly squeezed lemon juice	10 mL
1	1-inch (2.5 cm) cinnamon stick	1
1	drop yellow food coloring (optional)	1
1	drop red food coloring (optional)	1
	Artificial sweetener equivalent to 4 tsp (20 mL) granulated sugar	

1. In a small bowl, sprinkle gelatin over $\frac{1}{4}$ cup (60 mL) of the apple juice and let stand for 5 minutes to soften.

2. In a medium saucepan, combine the remaining apple juice, lemon juice, cinnamon stick and red and yellow food coloring (if using). Bring to a boil over high heat; boil for about 7 minutes or until reduced by one-third. Remove from heat and stir in gelatin mixture and sweetener until all granules dissolve. Discard cinnamon stick.

3. Pour jelly into hot sterilized jar. Wipe jar rim. Seal with lid. Refrigerate for at least 1 day, until chilled and set. Store in the refrigerator for up to 3 weeks.

Nutrients per Serving	
Calories	13
Carbohydrate	3 g
Fiber	0 g
Protein	0 g
Total fat	0 g
Saturated fat	0 g
Cholesterol	0 mg
Sodium	1 mg

America's Exchanges	
1	Free Food

Canada's Choices	
1	Extra

White Grape Jelly

Makes about 1 cup (250 mL)

Serving size: 1 tbsp (15 mL)

This grape jelly can be made any time of the year and requires no special equipment.

● **Hot sterilized jar with plastic storage lid or cap**

1 tsp	unflavored gelatin powder	5 mL
1²⁄₃ cups	unsweetened white grape juice, divided	400 mL
3	whole allspice or cloves	3
2 tsp	freshly squeezed lemon juice	10 mL
	Artificial sweetener equivalent to 2 tsp (10 mL) granulated sugar	

1. In a small bowl, sprinkle gelatin over ¼ cup (60 mL) of the grape juice and let stand for 5 minutes to soften.

2. In a medium saucepan, combine the remaining grape juice, allspice and lemon juice. Bring to a boil over high heat; boil for about 7 minutes or until reduced by one-third. Remove from heat and stir in gelatin mixture and sweetener until all granules dissolve. Discard allspice.

3. Pour jelly into hot sterilized jar. Wipe jar rim. Seal with lid. Refrigerate for at least 1 day, until chilled and set. Store in the refrigerator for up to 3 weeks.

Nutrients per Serving	
Calories	17
Carbohydrate	4 g
Fiber	0 g
Protein	0 g
Total fat	0 g
Saturated fat	0 g
Cholesterol	0 mg
Sodium	1 mg

America's Exchanges	
1	Free Food

Canada's Choices	
1	Extra

Strawberry Spread

||||||||||||||||||||||||||||||||||||||||||||||||||||||||||||||||||||||||||||||||||||||||||||||||||||||||||||||||||||||||||||||||||||||

**Makes about
1³⁄₄ cups (425 mL)**
Serving size: 2 tbsp
(30 mL)

The tastes of early summer are captured in this berry spread, which freezes beautifully. It's succulent as a cake filling or ice cream sauce.

Variation

Raspberry Spread: Replace the strawberries with fresh or frozen unsweetened raspberries.

• **Hot sterilized jars with plastic storage lids or caps**

1½ tsp	unflavored gelatin powder	7 mL
2 cups	sliced fresh or frozen unsweetened strawberries	500 mL
	Artificial sweetener equivalent to 8 to 12 tsp (40 to 60 mL) granulated sugar	
	Red food coloring (optional)	

1. In a small bowl, sprinkle gelatin over ¼ cup (60 mL) water and let stand for 5 minutes to soften.

2. Place berries in a medium saucepan and bring to a boil over medium heat. Reduce heat and boil gently, stirring occasionally, for 5 minutes. Stir in gelatin mixture, sweetener and food coloring (if using); cook, stirring, for 1 minute or until all granules dissolve. Skim off foam.

3. Ladle spread into hot sterilized jars, leaving ½ inch (1 cm) headspace. Wipe jar rims. Seal with lids. Refrigerate for at least 1 day, until chilled and set. Store in the refrigerator for up to 3 weeks or in the freezer for up to 6 months.

Nutrients per Serving	
Calories	10
Carbohydrate	2 g
Fiber	1 g
Protein	0 g
Total fat	0 g
Saturated fat	0 g
Cholesterol	0 mg
Sodium	1 mg

America's Exchanges	
1	Free Food

Canada's Choices	
1	Extra

Grape Spread

||||||||||||||||||||||||||||||||||||||||||||||||||||||||||||||||||||||||||||||||||||||||||||||||||||||

**Makes about
4 cups (1 L)**
Serving size: 1 tbsp
(15 mL)

What a combination! Grapes and apples mingle to make the darkest, richest spread ever.

Kitchen Tip
Look for blue Concord grapes or the seedless variety, Coronation, at farmers' markets and supermarkets in late summer.

• **Hot sterilized jars with plastic storage lids or caps**

6 cups	blue grapes (about 2 lbs/1 kg)	1.5 L
4	firm apples, cut into chunks (not peeled or cored)	4
Pinch	ground cloves	Pinch

1. In a large pot, combine grapes and apples. Bring to a simmer over medium heat, mashing fruit occasionally. Reduce heat and simmer for 30 minutes or until very soft. Push pulp through a sieve to yield 5 cups (1.25 L) purée; discard solids.

2. Return purée to a clean saucepan and stir in cloves; bring to a boil over medium heat. Reduce heat and simmer, stirring often, for 20 minutes or until thick enough to coat a metal spoon.

3. Ladle spread into hot sterilized jars, leaving $\frac{1}{2}$ inch (1 cm) headspace. Wipe jar rims. Seal with lids. Refrigerate for at least 1 day, until chilled and set. Store in the refrigerator for up to 3 weeks or in the freezer for up to 6 months.

Nutrients per Serving	
Calories	10
Carbohydrate	3 g
Fiber	0 g
Protein	0 g
Total fat	0 g
Saturated fat	0 g
Cholesterol	0 mg
Sodium	0 mg

America's Exchanges	
1	Free Food

Canada's Choices	
1	Extra

Peach Spread

||||||||||||||||||||||||||||||||||||||||||||||||||||||||||||||||||||||||||||||||||||||||||||||||||||||||||||||||||||||||

**Makes about
1²/₃ cups (400 mL)**
Serving size: 1 tbsp
(15 mL)

This golden, fruity jam may be sweetened after cooking with aspartame or liquid artificial sweetener, but we liked the taste better without the added sweetener.

Kitchen Tip
To peel peaches, blanch them 2 or 3 at a time in a pot of boiling water for 1 minute. Immediately transfer to a bowl of ice water and let stand until chilled. Drain well and slip off skins.

• **Hot sterilized jars with plastic storage lids or caps**

2 lbs	peaches (about 8)	1 kg
1 tsp	ascorbic acid color keeper	5 mL
7	whole allspice	7

1. Peel and pit peaches. Place peels and pits in a large saucepan. Chop fruit and place in a bowl. Stir in color keeper and set aside.

2. Add allspice and 2 cups (500 mL) water to saucepan; bring to a boil over high heat. Reduce heat and simmer for about 25 minutes or until liquid is reduced by about three-quarters. Discard peels and pits.

3. Stir in peaches, increase heat and bring to a boil. Reduce heat to medium and cook, stirring and mashing occasionally, for 35 minutes or until very thick. Remove from heat and mash well (or purée in a blender or food processor, or using an immersion blender, if desired).

4. Ladle spread into hot sterilized jars, leaving ½ inch (1 cm) headspace. Wipe jar rims. Seal with lids. Refrigerate for at least 1 day, until chilled and set. Store in the refrigerator for up to 3 weeks or in the freezer for up to 6 months.

Nutrients per Serving	
Calories	11
Carbohydrate	3 g
Fiber	1 g
Protein	0 g
Total fat	0 g
Saturated fat	0 g
Cholesterol	0 mg
Sodium	0 mg

America's Exchanges	
1	Free Food

Canada's Choices	
1	Extra

Spicy Pear Spread

|||||||||||||||||||||||||||||||||||||||||||||||||||||||||||||||||||||||||||||||||||||||||||||||||||||||||||||||||||||||||||||

This thick spread goes
well with both meats
and breads and makes
a splendid gift.

Kitchen Tip
Use a potato masher to
crush pears one layer at
a time. Mash them until
they're juicy but still have
some texture.

Variation
Substitute crushed peeled
pitted peaches for the pears.

• **Hot sterilized jars with plastic storage lids or caps**

2 cups	crushed peeled cored pears (about 4)	500 mL
8	whole cloves	8
1	4-inch (10 cm) cinnamon stick	1
1 tsp	ascorbic acid color keeper	5 mL
2 tsp	freshly squeezed lemon juice	10 mL
1 tsp	unflavored gelatin powder	5 mL
	Artificial sweetener	

1. In a medium saucepan, combine pears, cloves, cinnamon stick, color keeper and lemon juice. Bring to a boil over medium heat. Reduce heat and simmer, stirring frequently, for 10 minutes or until slightly thickened.

2. Meanwhile, in a small bowl, sprinkle gelatin over 2 tbsp (30 mL) water and let stand for 5 minutes to soften. Stir into hot pear mixture and cook, stirring, for about 1 minute or until all granules dissolve. Discard cloves and cinnamon stick. Stir in sweetener to taste.

3. Ladle spread into hot sterilized jars, leaving ½ inch (1 cm) headspace. Wipe jar rims. Seal with lids. Refrigerate for at least 1 day, until chilled and set. Store in the refrigerator for up to 3 weeks or in the freezer for up to 6 months.

Nutrients per Serving	
Calories	14
Carbohydrate	4 g
Fiber	1 g
Protein	0 g
Total fat	0 g
Saturated fat	0 g
Cholesterol	0 mg
Sodium	0 mg

America's Exchanges	
1	Free Food

Canada's Choices	
1	Extra

Pear Plum Spread

||||||||||||||||||||||||||||||||||||||||||||||||||||||||||||||||||||||||||||||||||||||||||||||||||||||||||||||||||||||||||||||

**Makes about
3¼ cups (800 mL)**
Serving size: 1 tbsp
(15 mL)

Smooth pears and tart plums combine in a luscious purée that's perfect on warm-from-the-oven muffins or biscuits.

Kitchen Tip
Including the plum pits in the cheesecloth extracts the pectin and helps with the set of this spread.

- Cheesecloth and kitchen string
- Blender or food processor (optional)
- Hot sterilized jars with plastic storage lids or caps

5	red plums	5
1 tsp	whole cloves	5 mL
1	⅛-inch (3 mm) slice gingerroot (optional)	1
4	pears, peeled and coarsely chopped	4
2 tsp	ascorbic acid color keeper	10 mL
1	3-inch (7.5 cm) cinnamon stick	1
	Artificial sweetener equivalent to 3 tbsp (45 mL) granulated sugar	

1. Remove pits from plums and cut each plum into 8 pieces. Wrap plum pits, cloves and ginger (if using) in a square of cheesecloth and tie into a bundle with string.

2. Place pears in a large saucepan and sprinkle with color keeper. Stir in plums, cinnamon stick and ½ cup (125 mL) water. Bury spice bundle in fruit. Cover and bring to a boil over medium heat. Reduce heat to low and simmer, stirring occasionally, for 15 to 20 minutes or until fruit is tender. Discard spice bag and cinnamon stick.

3. Transfer fruit mixture to blender and purée until smooth (or press through a sieve).

4. Return purée to the saucepan and bring to a simmer over medium heat. Reduce heat and simmer, uncovered, stirring occasionally, for 15 to 20 minutes or until thick enough to coat a metal spoon. Remove from heat and stir in sweetener.

5. Ladle spread into hot sterilized jars, leaving ½ inch (1 cm) headspace. Wipe jar rims. Seal with lids. Refrigerate for at least 1 day, until chilled and set. Store in the refrigerator for up to 3 weeks or in the freezer for up to 6 months.

Nutrients per Serving	
Calories	11
Carbohydrate	3 g
Fiber	0 g
Protein	0 g
Total fat	0 g
Saturated fat	0 g
Cholesterol	0 mg
Sodium	0 mg

America's Exchanges	
1	Free Food

Canada's Choices	
1	Extra

Minted Apple Butter

||||||||||||||||||||||||||||||||||||||||||||||||||||||||||||||||||||||||||||||||||||||||||||||||||||||||||

A hint of mint adds a
delightful twist to this
old-time spread. It is
tasty with ham or lamb,
or on gingerbread or
pancakes.

Kitchen Tip

Choose cooking apples
that soften but keep their
flavor when cooked, such as
McIntosh.

• **Hot sterilized jars with plastic storage lids or caps**

4	cooking apples	4
1 tbsp	dried mint (or 3 tbsp/45 mL chopped fresh mint)	15 mL
1 tsp	ascorbic acid color keeper	5 mL

1. Remove stems from apples and coarsely chop, including cores.

2. Place apples in a large saucepan and add $\frac{1}{2}$ cup (125 mL) water, mint and color keeper. Bring to a boil over high heat. Reduce heat and simmer, stirring occasionally, for about 15 minutes or until apples are tender. Mash until fairly smooth. Simmer, stirring often, for about 10 minutes or until thick. Remove from heat. Press through a sieve and discard solids.

3. Ladle butter into hot sterilized jars, leaving $\frac{1}{2}$ inch (1 cm) headspace. Wipe jar rims. Seal jars with lids. Refrigerate for at least 1 day, until chilled and set. Store in the refrigerator for up to 3 weeks or in the freezer for up to 6 months.

Nutrients per Serving	
Calories	11
Carbohydrate	3 g
Fiber	0 g
Protein	0 g
Total fat	0 g
Saturated fat	0 g
Cholesterol	0 mg
Sodium	0 mg

America's Exchanges	
1	Free Food

Canada's Choices	
1	Extra

Spicy Apple Chutney

|||||||||||||||||||||||||||||||||||||||||||||||||||||||||||||||||||||||||||||||||||||||||||||||||||||||||||||||||||||||||||||||||||

Makes about 3⅓ cups (825 mL)
Serving size: 1 tbsp (15 mL)

This chutney is the perfect accompaniment to curries. It is also excellent as a spread and as a tangy condiment for chicken, pork or ham.

Kitchen Tips
Choose tart cooking apples that keep their flavor when cooked. For a softer texture, use McIntosh apples; for a firmer texture, use Granny Smith, Northern Spy or Empire. You can also use a mixture, for a combination of textures.

The chutney can be served immediately, but the flavors do improve after it's refrigerated for at least 3 days.

• **Hot sterilized jars with plastic storage lids or caps**

4	large apples	4
2 tsp	ascorbic acid color keeper	10 mL
⅓ cup	chopped onion	75 mL
½ cup	chopped red bell pepper	125 mL
½ cup	raisins	125 mL
2 tsp	ground ginger	10 mL
	Grated zest and juice of 1 lemon	
2 tbsp	light (fancy) molasses	30 mL

1. Peel and core apples. Place peels and cores in a small saucepan and add 1 cup (250 mL) water. Cover and bring to a boil over medium heat; boil for 10 minutes.

2. Meanwhile, chop apples and place in a medium saucepan. Stir in color keeper.

3. Discard peels and pits; add cooking liquid to apples. Stir in onion, red pepper, raisins, ginger, lemon zest and lemon juice; bring to a boil over medium heat. Reduce heat and simmer for about 35 minutes, stirring often to prevent sticking, until thickened. Remove from heat and stir in molasses.

4. Ladle chutney into hot sterilized jars, leaving ½ inch (1 cm) headspace. Wipe jar rims. Seal jars with lids. Store in the refrigerator for up to 3 weeks or in the freezer for up to 6 months.

Nutrients per Serving

Calories	16
Carbohydrate	4 g
Fiber	0 g
Protein	0 g
Total fat	0 g
Saturated fat	0 g
Cholesterol	0 mg
Sodium	1 mg

America's Exchanges	
1	Free Food

Canada's Choices	
1	Extra

Pear and Melon Chutney

|||||||||||||||||||||||||||||||||||||||||||||||||||||||||||||||||||||||||||||||||||||||||||||||||||||||||||||||||||||||||||||||||||||

**Makes about
4 cups (1 L)**
Serving size: 1 tbsp
(15 mL)

Your home will be filled with a rich, spicy aroma when you prepare this colorful condiment. Small jars make lovely hostess gifts.

Kitchen Tip
The chutney can be served immediately, but the flavors do improve after it's refrigerated for at least 3 days.

Variation
Substitute peaches or nectarines for the pears.

• **Hot sterilized jars with plastic storage lids or caps**

1 cup	cider vinegar	250 mL
1½ tsp	whole cloves	7 mL
1 tsp	ground ginger	5 mL
1 tsp	ground allspice	5 mL
¾ tsp	ground nutmeg	3 mL
3	cloves garlic, finely chopped	3
2½ cups	chopped onions (about 2 large)	625 mL
½ cup	golden raisins	125 mL
½ cup	dried currants	125 mL
2 tbsp	thinly sliced crystallized ginger	30 mL
5	pears, peeled and chopped	5
2 cups	chopped cantaloupe	500 mL
2 tbsp	light (fancy) molasses	30 mL

1. In a medium saucepan, combine vinegar, cloves, ground ginger, allspice and nutmeg. Bring to a boil over high heat. Reduce heat to low, cover and simmer for 30 minutes.

2. Stir in garlic, onions, raisins, currants and crystallized ginger; cover and simmer for 15 minutes.

3. Stir in pears and cantaloupe; simmer, uncovered, for about 30 minutes, stirring often to prevent sticking, until thickened. Remove from heat and stir in molasses.

4. Ladle chutney into hot sterilized jars, leaving ½ inch (1 cm) headspace. Wipe jar rims. Seal jars with lids. Store in the refrigerator for up to 3 weeks or in the freezer for up to 6 months.

Nutrients per Serving	
Calories	21
Carbohydrate	5 g
Fiber	1 g
Protein	0 g
Total fat	0 g
Saturated fat	0 g
Cholesterol	0 mg
Sodium	2 mg

America's Exchanges	
1	Free Food

Canada's Choices	
1	Extra

Cranberry Orange Relish

||||||||||||||||||||||||||||||||||||||||||||||||||||||||||||||||||||||||||||||||||||||||||||||||||||||||||||||||||

**Makes about
1½ cups (375 mL)**
Serving size: 1 tbsp
(15 mL)

Try this rich, ruby relish
with roast lamb or pork.
It's a no-cook version of
a popular combination.

Kitchen Tip
Scrub the orange peel with
a soft brush under running
water before cutting the
orange.

● **Blender or food processor**

1	orange (unpeeled)	1
4 cups	cranberries	1 L
2 tbsp	chopped crystallized ginger	30 mL
½ tsp	ground cinnamon	2 mL
	Artificial sweetener equivalent to ¼ cup (60 mL) granulated sugar	

1. Cut orange into eighths and remove any seeds. In blender, combine orange, cranberries, ginger and cinnamon; pulse for about 2 minutes or until coarsely chopped. Add sweetener and purée for about 30 seconds or to desired consistency.

2. Transfer to an airtight container and refrigerate for at least 1 day to blend the flavors. Store in the refrigerator for up to 5 days.

Nutrients per Serving	
Calories	15
Carbohydrate	4 g
Fiber	1 g
Protein	0 g
Total fat	0 g
Saturated fat	0 g
Cholesterol	0 mg
Sodium	1 mg

America's Exchanges	
1	Free Food

Canada's Choices	
1	Extra

Hamburger Relish

|||||||||||||||||||||||||||||||||||||||||||||||||||||||||||||||||||||||||||||||||||||||||||||||||||||||||||||||||

The prime time for
relish-making is early
September, when
so many vegetables
are plentiful and
inexpensive.

Kitchen Tip
Rely on a food processor to
ease and speed up the chore
of chopping.

• **Hot sterilized jars with plastic storage lids or caps**

2 cups	finely chopped unpeeled cucumbers	500 mL
1½ cups	finely chopped onions	375 mL
1½ cups	finely chopped celery	375 mL
1 cup	finely chopped green bell peppers	250 mL
½ cup	finely chopped red bell pepper	125 mL
2 tbsp	pickling salt	30 mL
⅔ cup	granulated sugar	150 mL
1½ tsp	celery seeds	7 mL
1½ tsp	mustard seeds	7 mL
2 cups	white vinegar	500 mL
4	drops green food coloring (optional)	4

1. In a very large bowl, combine cucumbers, onions, celery, green peppers, red pepper and pickling salt; cover and let stand overnight. Drain well.

2. In a large saucepan, combine sugar, celery seeds, mustard seeds and vinegar. Add drained vegetables and bring to a boil over high heat. Reduce heat and simmer for 10 minutes or until cucumbers and onions are translucent. Remove from heat and stir in food coloring (if using).

3. Ladle relish into hot sterilized jars, leaving ½ inch (1 cm) headspace. Wipe jar rims. Seal jars with lids. Store in the refrigerator for up to 3 weeks.

Nutrients per Serving	
Calories	15
Carbohydrate	3 g
Fiber	0 g
Protein	0 g
Total fat	0 g
Saturated fat	0 g
Cholesterol	0 mg
Sodium	125 mg

America's Exchanges	
1	Free Food

Canada's Choices	
1	Extra

Pickled Onion Rings

||||||||||||||||||||||||||||||||||||||||||||||||||||||||||||||||||||||||||||||||||||||||||||||||||||||||||||

Serve these sweet and tangy onion pickles with burgers or grilled fish, or as part of an appetizer platter.

Kitchen Tip

The onion rings absorb a little sugar as they stand in their pickle juice. Always drain well before serving.

- **2 hot sterilized pint (500 mL) jars with plastic storage lids or caps**

1	large Spanish onion	1
	Boiling water	
1/3 cup	granulated sugar	75 mL
1/2 tsp	salt	2 mL
1 cup	white vinegar	250 mL
4	drops hot pepper sauce	4

1. Cut onion crosswise into thin slices. Separate into rings and pack into hot sterilized jars. Pour in enough boiling water to cover onions. Let cool, then drain.

2. In a medium saucepan, combine sugar, salt, vinegar, 1 cup (250 mL) water and hot pepper sauce. Bring to a boil over high heat. Pour over onion rings.

3. Wipe jar rims. Seal jars with lids. Refrigerate for at least 2 days to blend the flavors. Store in the refrigerator for up to 2 months.

Nutrients per Serving	
Calories	13
Carbohydrate	3 g
Fiber	0 g
Protein	0 g
Total fat	0 g
Saturated fat	0 g
Cholesterol	0 mg
Sodium	23 mg

America's Exchanges	
1	Free Food

Canada's Choices	
1	Extra

Spicy Pickled Beets

||||||||||||||||||||||||||||||||||||||||||||||||||||||||||||||||||||||||||||||||||||||||||||||||||||||||||||||||||||||||||||

**Makes about
2 cups (500 mL)**
Serving size: 3 slices
(about 2$\frac{1}{2}$ tbsp/37 mL)

Start by cooking fresh beets for this pickle pantry classic. If fresh beets are unavailable, well-drained canned beets will work nearly as well.

Kitchen Tip

You'll need about 6 small beets for this recipe. To cook beets, trim off leaves and long taproots and place in a pot. Add enough cold water to cover by 2 inches (5 cm). Bring to a boil over high heat. Reduce heat and boil gently for about 30 minutes or until tender. Drain well and let cool slightly, then peel off skins.

- Hot sterilized pint (500 mL) jar with plastic storage lid or cap

2 cups	sliced cooked small beets	500 mL
1 tbsp	packed brown sugar	15 mL
2 tsp	whole cloves	10 mL
$\frac{1}{2}$ tsp	ground cinnamon	2 mL
$\frac{1}{4}$ tsp	salt	1 mL
$\frac{1}{2}$ cup	white vinegar	125 mL

1. Place beets in hot sterilized jar and set aside.

2. In a small saucepan, combine brown sugar, cloves, cinnamon, salt, vinegar and $\frac{1}{2}$ cup (125 mL) water. Bring to a boil over high heat. Pour over beets.

3. Wipe jar rim. Seal jar with lid. Refrigerate for at least 8 hours or until beets are pickled. Store in the refrigerator for up to 2 months, removing cloves after 3 days.

Nutrients per Serving	
Calories	17
Carbohydrate	4 g
Fiber	1 g
Protein	0 g
Total fat	0 g
Saturated fat	0 g
Cholesterol	0 mg
Sodium	70 mg

America's Exchanges	
1	Free Food

Canada's Choices	
1	Extra

Peppy Dill Wedges

||||||||||||||||||||||||||||||||||||||||||||||||||||||||||||||||||||||||||||||||||||||||||||||||||||||||||||||||||||

**Makes about
4 cups (1 L)**
Serving size: $1/4$ cup
(60 mL)

Try to use garden-fresh, crisp cucumbers for these perky dills. A variety that is not too seedy is best.

• **Hot sterilized jars with plastic storage lids or caps**

1	large cucumber, quartered lengthwise and cut into 1-inch (2.5 cm) pieces (about 4 cups/1 L)	1
2	cloves garlic (optional)	2
2 tbsp	pickling salt	30 mL
2 cups	ice cubes	500 mL
1 tbsp	dill seeds	15 mL
$1/2$ tsp	hot pepper flakes	2 mL
1 cup	cider vinegar	250 mL

1. In a large glass bowl, combine cucumber, garlic (if using) and pickling salt. Cover with ice cubes. Let stand in a cool place for at least 6 hours or overnight. Drain and rinse well. Drain again.

2. In a large pot, combine dill seeds, hot pepper flakes, vinegar and 1 cup (250 mL) water. Bring to a boil over high heat. Add drained cucumbers and return to a boil; cover and boil for 2 minutes. Discard garlic.

3. Spoon into hot sterilized jars. Wipe jar rims. Seal jars with lids. Refrigerate for at least 1 week to blend the flavors. Store in the refrigerator for up to 2 months.

Nutrients per Serving	
Calories	6
Carbohydrate	1 g
Fiber	0 g
Protein	0 g
Total fat	0 g
Saturated fat	0 g
Cholesterol	0 mg
Sodium	122 mg

America's Exchanges	
1	Free Food

Canada's Choices	
1	Extra

Bread and Butter Pickles

||||||||||||||||||||||||||||||||||||||||||||||||||||||||||||||||||||||||||||||||||||||||||||||||||||||||

**Makes about
4 cups (1 L)**
Serving size: 2 tbsp
(30 mL)

Crisp, crunchy bread and butter pickles are good in or with sandwiches, especially those made with deli cuts or cold roast beef or pork.

● **Hot sterilized jars with plastic storage lids or caps**

1	clove garlic	1
4 cups	cucumber slices (1/8 inch/3 mm thick)	1 L
1 cup	thinly sliced onion	250 mL
2 tsp	pickling salt	10 mL
2 cups	ice cubes	500 mL
1/3 cup	granulated sugar	75 mL
1 1/2 tsp	mustard seeds	7 mL
1 tsp	celery seeds	5 mL
1/2 tsp	ground turmeric	2 mL
1 cup	cider vinegar	250 mL

1. In a large glass bowl, combine garlic, cucumber, onion and pickling salt. Cover with ice cubes. Let stand in a cool place for at least 6 hours or overnight. Drain and rinse well. Drain again.

2. In a large pot, combine sugar, mustard seeds, celery seeds, turmeric, vinegar and 1 cup (250 mL) water. Bring to a boil over high heat. Add drained cucumber mixture and return to a boil; boil for 2 minutes. Discard garlic.

3. Spoon into hot sterilized jars. Wipe jar rims. Seal jars with lids. Refrigerate for at least 1 week to blend the flavors. Store in the refrigerator for up to 2 months.

Nutrients per Serving	
Calories	12
Carbohydrate	3 g
Fiber	0 g
Protein	0 g
Total fat	0 g
Saturated fat	0 g
Cholesterol	0 mg
Sodium	43 mg

America's Exchanges	
1	Free Food

Canada's Choices	
1	Extra

Appendix 1
7-Day Meal Plan

The daily menus below provide approximately 1,750 calories per day. An asterisk (*) indicates a recipe in this book. The menus were calculated with skim milk (2 to 3 cups/500 to 750 mL per day). Substituting 1% milk for skim milk will add 5 to 8 grams of fat and 45 to 72 calories per day.

You can vary these menus by substituting equivalent foods. For example, a medium potato (2 Starch Exchanges or 2 Carbohydrate Choices) can be replaced with two selections from the Starch Exchange list (see pages 306–308) or the Carbohydrate Choice lists (see page 318–323). Use the

	Day 1	Day 2	Day 3	
Breakfast	1 Best Bran Muffin* ½ grapefruit 1 serving Strawberry Instant Breakfast*	¾ cup (175 mL) oatmeal ½ cup (125 mL) milk 1 soft-cooked egg 1 slice whole wheat toast 1 tbsp (15 mL) Strawberry Spread* ½ cup (125 mL) orange juice	1 whole wheat English muffin with 1 oz (30 g) reduced-fat Cheddar cheese and sliced tomato 1 shredded wheat biscuit ½ cup (125 mL) milk	
Lunch	1 oz (30 g) sliced turkey ½ oat bran bagel 1 tsp (5 mL) margarine 1 cup (250 mL) Orange and Sprout Salad* 1 small apple 1 Blueberry Oat Muffin*	6 tbsp (90 mL) Tuna Salad* on 2 slices whole wheat bread 1½ cups (375 mL) Wholesome Pasta and Veggie Salad* 1 Apple Honey Spice Muffin*	1 cup (250 mL) Hearty Beef Minestrone* 1 hard-cooked egg ½ cup (125 mL) Potato Salad* Lettuce and cherry tomatoes 1 tbsp (15 mL) All-Purpose Balsamic Vinaigrette* 1 small pear	
Snack	1 Lemon Poppy Seed Muffin* 1 cup (250 mL) milk	1 high-fiber low-fat granola bar 1 cup (250 mL) milk	4 whole wheat crackers 1 tbsp (15 mL) Pear Plum Spread* 1 cup (250 mL) milk	
	continued on page 304	*continued on page 304*	*continued on page 304*	

Exchange and Choice information with each recipe to identify dishes that contain similar nutrients, Exchanges and Choices. For example, Best Bran Muffins (page 234), Blueberry Oat Muffins (page 236), Lemon Poppy Seed Muffins (page 237) and Raspberry Yogurt Muffins (page 238) all contain 1 Starch Exchange and 1 Fat Exchange, or 1 Carbohydrate Choice and 1 Fat Choice, and one can replace another.

Day 4	Day 5	Day 6	Day 7
1 Best Bran Muffin* 1 serving Chocolate Banana Instant Breakfast*	½ whole wheat English muffin with 1 oz (30 g) reduced-fat Swiss cheese 1 small apple 1 shredded wheat biscuit ½ cup (125 mL) milk	1 slice whole wheat toast 1 tbsp (15 mL) peanut butter ⅔ cup (150 mL) toasted oat cereal O's ½ cup (125 mL) milk ½ cup (125 mL) orange juice	1 cup (250 mL) diced melon (e.g., cantaloupe or honeydew) with ⅓ cup (75 mL) low-fat plain yogurt and 2 tbsp (30 mL) low-fat granola 2 slices whole wheat toast 1 tsp (5 mL) margarine
½ cup (125 mL) whole wheat macaroni with ½ cup (125 mL) Spaghetti Sauce* and 4 Meatballs* Lettuce with shredded carrot and ⅙ avocado 1 tbsp (15 mL) All-Purpose Balsamic Vinaigrette* ¾ cup (175 mL) fresh pineapple chunks	1½ cups (375 mL) Chicken Soup* 1 serving Classic Greek Salad* ½ of a 6-inch (15 cm) whole wheat pita 1 small pear	1 cup (250 mL) Fish Chowder* 1 wedge Cottage Casserole Bread* ⅔ cup (150 mL) Marinated Vegetable Medley* Cherry tomatoes 1 Raspberry Yogurt Muffin*	1 serving Vegetable Frittata* ½ cup (125 mL) Confetti Peas* ⅔ cup (150 mL) Sesame Ginger Brown Rice Salad* ½ cup (125 mL) canned juice-packed fruit cocktail
4 crispbread rye crackers 1 tbsp (15 mL) Strawberry Spread* 1 cup (250 mL) milk	4 whole wheat crackers 1 tbsp (15 mL) Spicy Pear Spread 1 cup (250 mL) milk	3 Crispy Oatmeal Cookies* 1 cup (250 mL) milk	1 slice Banana Breakfast Loaf* 1 cup (250 mL) milk
continued on page 305	*continued on page 305*	*continued on page 305*	*continued on page 305*

	Day 1	Day 2	Day 3	
Dinner	¾ cup (175 mL) Beef Burgundy* Cabbage ¼ medium acorn squash, baked 1 medium potato, baked 1 tsp (5 mL) margarine 2 Soft Molasses Spice Cookies* ½ cup (125 mL) fruit cocktail	½ cup (125 mL) Cucumber and Fruit Salad* 1 serving Chicken and Snow Pea Stir-Fry* Broccoli 1 cup (250 mL) soba noodles 1 serving Strawberry Angel Pie*	1 cup (250 mL) Lamb Curry* 1 cup (250 mL) whole wheat couscous Green beans 1 serving Marinated Cucumbers* 1 serving Baked Cinnamon Custard*	
Snack	1 slice whole wheat toast 1 tbsp (15 mL) Strawberry Spread* 1 cup (250 mL) milk	⅔ cup (150 mL) toasted oat cereal O's ½ cup (125 mL) milk ½ small banana	2 oat bran cookies 1 serving Hot Chocolate*	

Day 4	Day 5	Day 6	Day 7
1 serving Crispy Baked Fish* 1 serving Sautéed Broccoli and Red Peppers* 1 medium potato, baked 1 tsp (5 mL) margarine 1 serving Nova Scotia Gingerbread* 2 tbsp (30 mL) unsweetened applesauce	1 cup (250 mL) Chili Con Carne* Carrot, cucumber and celery sticks 2 tbsp (30 mL) Eggplant Dip* 1 slice whole wheat bread 1 tsp (5 mL) margarine 1 serving Mandarin Pie*	1 Stuffing-Topped Pork Chop* with ¼ cup (60 mL) unsweetened applesauce ¾ cup (175 mL) Skinny Scalloped Potatoes* ¾ cup (175 mL) Thyme-Scented Carrots* 1 Crêpe Élégante*	1 skinless chicken breast barbecued with 1 tbsp (15 mL) Speedy Barbecue Sauce* 1 tbsp (15 mL) Cranberry-Orange Relish* 1 serving Scalloped Sweet Potatoes* ¾ cup (175 mL) Green Beans with Water Chestnuts* 1 serving Peachy Blueberry Pie*
⅔ cup (150 mL) toasted oat cereal O's ½ cup (125 mL) blueberries ½ cup (125 mL) milk	½ cup (125 mL) bran flakes ½ small banana ½ cup (125 mL) milk	1 slice whole wheat toast 1 tbsp (15 mL) Strawberry Spread* 1 serving Hot Chocolate*	1 slice Orange Nut Bread* 1 serving Hot Chocolate*

Appendix 2
Exchange Lists for Diabetes

||||||||||||||||||||||||||||||||||||||||||||||||||||||||||||||||||||||||||||||||||||||||||||||||||||||||||||||||||||||||||||||

The information in this appendix will help you plan your meals. It is excerpted with permission from *Choose Your Foods: Exchange Lists for Diabetes*, © American Dietetic Association and American Diabetes Association, 2008. To purchase the complete lists, visit www.eatright.org/shop or www.shopdiabetes.org.

Starch

Cereals, grains, pasta, breads, crackers, snacks, starchy vegetables and cooked beans, peas and lentils are starches. In general, 1 starch is:

- ½ cup of cooked cereal, grain or starchy vegetable
- ⅓ cup of cooked rice or pasta
- 1 oz of a bread product (such as 1 slice of bread)
- ¾ to 1 oz of most snack foods (some snack foods may also have extra fat)

A choice on the Starch list has 15 grams of carbohydrate, 0 to 3 grams of protein, 0 to 1 grams of fat and 80 calories.

Bread		
Food	Serving Size	Notes
Bagel, large (about 4 oz)	¼ (1 oz)	
Bread, reduced-calorie	2 slices (1½ oz)	More than 3 grams of dietary fiber per serving
Bread, white, whole-grain, pumpernickel, rye, unfrosted raisin	1 slice (1 oz)	
Chapati, small, 6 inches across	1	
Hot dog bun or hamburger bun	½ (1 oz)	
Naan, 8 inches by 2 inches	¼	
Pita, 6 inches across	½	
Taco shell, 5 inches across	2	If prepared with added fat, count as 1 Starch + 1 Fat
Tortilla, corn or flour, 6 inches across	1	

Cereals and Grains

Food	Serving Size	Notes
Barley, cooked	1/3 cup	
Cereal, bran	1/4 cup	More than 3 grams of dietary fiber per serving
Cereal, cooked (oats, oatmeal)	1/2 cup	
Cereal, shredded wheat, plain	1/2 cup	
Couscous	1/3 cup	
Grits, cooked	1/2 cup	
Kasha	1/2 cup	
Millet, cooked	1/3 cup	
Pasta, cooked	1/3 cup	
Polenta, cooked	1/3 cup	
Quinoa, cooked	1/3 cup	
Rice, white or brown, cooked	1/3 cup	
Wild rice	1/2 cup	

Whole Grains

Whole grains and grain products contain the entire grain seed of a plant. They are rich in fiber, vitamins, minerals and phytochemicals. Here are some tips for including more whole grains in your diet:

- Choose whole-grain foods more often. Whole-grain foods include whole-wheat flour, whole oats/oatmeal, whole-grain cornmeal, popcorn, buckwheat, buckwheat flour, whole rye, whole-grain barley, brown rice, wild rice, bulgur, millet, quinoa and sorghum.

- Read food labels carefully. If a product label says "100% whole grain," it must contain at least 16 grams of whole grain per serving. A "whole grain" stamp identifies foods that have at least a 1/2 serving of whole grains (3 grams of whole grains).

- Add several tablespoons of cooked grains to stews, soups and vegetable salads.

- Monitor your blood glucose carefully to find out the effect whole grains have on you.

Starchy Vegetables

Food	Serving Size	Notes
Cassava	⅓ cup	
Corn kernels	½ cup	
Parsnips	½ cup	More than 3 grams of dietary fiber per serving
Peas, green	½ cup	More than 3 grams of dietary fiber per serving
Plantain, ripe	⅓ cup	
Potato, baked with skin	¼ large (3 oz)	
Potato, boiled, all kinds	½ cup or ½ medium (3 oz)	
Spaghetti/pasta sauce	½ cup	
Squash, winter (acorn, butternut)	1 cup	More than 3 grams of dietary fiber per serving
Yam, sweet potato, plain	½ cup	More than 3 grams of dietary fiber per serving

Crackers and Snacks

Food	Serving Size	Notes
Crackers, saltine-type	6	
Crackers, whole wheat regular	2–5 (¾ oz)	If serving contains more than 4 g fat, count as 1 Starch + 1 Fat
Crackers, lower-fat or crispbreads	2–5 (¾ oz)	More than 3 grams of dietary fiber per serving
Popcorn, no fat added	3 cups	More than 3 grams of dietary fiber per serving

Beans, Peas and Lentils
(The choices in this list count as 1 Starch + 1 Lean Meat)

Food	Serving Size	Notes
Baked beans	⅓ cup	More than 3 grams of dietary fiber per serving
Beans, cooked (black, garbanzo, kidney, lima, navy, pinto, white)	½ cup	More than 3 grams of dietary fiber per serving
Lentils, cooked (brown, green, yellow)	½ cup	More than 3 grams of dietary fiber per serving
Peas, cooked (black-eyed, split)	½ cup	More than 3 grams of dietary fiber per serving
Refried beans, canned	½ cup	More than 3 grams of dietary fiber per serving; 480 milligrams or more of sodium per serving

Fruits

Fresh, frozen, canned and dried fruits and fruit juices are on this list. In general, 1 fruit choice is:

- ½ cup of canned or fresh fruit or unsweetened fruit juice
- 1 small fresh fruit (4 oz)
- 2 tablespoons of dried fruit

A choice on the Fruits list has 15 grams of carbohydrate, 0 grams of protein, 0 grams of fat and 60 calories.

Fruits
(The weight listed includes skin, core, seeds and rind)

Food	Serving Size	Notes
Apple, unpeeled, small	1 (4 oz)	
Banana, extra-small	1 (4 oz)	
Cantaloupe, small	⅓ melon or 1 cup cubed (11 oz)	
Figs, dried	1½	
Figs, fresh	1½ large or 2 medium (3½ oz)	More than 3 grams of dietary fiber per serving
Fruit cocktail	½ cup	
Grapefruit, large	½ (11 oz)	
Grapes, small	17 (3 oz)	
Mango, small	½ fruit (5½ oz) or ½ cup	
Orange, small	1 (6½ oz)	More than 3 grams of dietary fiber per serving
Peaches, canned	½ cup	
Peaches, fresh, medium	1 (6 oz)	
Strawberries	1¼ cup whole berries	More than 3 grams of dietary fiber per serving

Fruit Juices

Food	Serving Size	Notes
Apple juice/cider	½ cup	
Fruit juice blends, 100% juice	⅓ cup	
Orange juice	½ cup	

Milk

Milks and yogurts are grouped in three categories — fat-free/low-fat, reduced-fat or whole — based on the amount of fat they have.

- For fat-free (skim) and low-fat (1%) milks and yogurts, a choice has 12 grams of carbohydrate, 8 grams of protein, 0 to 3 grams of fat and 100 calories.
- For reduced-fat (2%) milks and yogurts, a choice has 12 grams of carbohydrate, 8 grams of protein, 5 grams of fat and 120 calories.
- For whole milks and yogurts, a choice has 12 grams of carbohydrate, 8 grams of protein, 8 grams of fat and 160 calories.

Nutrition Tips

- Milk and yogurt are good sources of calcium and protein.
- The higher the fat content of milk and yogurt, the more saturated fat and cholesterol it has.
- Children over the age of 2 and adults should choose lower-fat varieties, such as skim, 1% or 2% milks or yogurts.
- If you choose 2% or whole-milk foods, be aware of the extra fat.

Milk and Yogurts

Food	Serving Size	Count As
Evaporated milk, fat-free or low-fat (1%)	½ cup	1 Fat-Free Milk
Evaporated milk, whole	½ cup	1 Whole Milk
Yogurt, plain or flavored with an artificial sweetener, fat-free or low-fat (1%)	⅔ cup (6 oz)	1 Fat-Free Milk
Yogurt, plain, reduced-fat (2%)	⅔ cup (6 oz)	1 Reduced-Fat Milk
Yogurt, plain, whole milk	1 cup (8 oz)	1 Whole Milk

Dairy-Like Foods

Food	Serving Size	Count As
Chocolate milk, fat-free	1 cup	1 Fat-Free Milk + 1 Carbohydrate
Chocolate milk, whole	1 cup	1 Whole Milk + 1 Carbohydrate
Rice drink, flavored, low-fat	1 cup	2 Carbohydrates
Rice drink, plain, fat-free	1 cup	1 Carbohydrate
Soy milk, light	1 cup	1 Carbohydrate + ½ Fat
Soy milk, regular, plain	1 cup	1 Carbohydrate + 1 Fat

Sweets, Desserts and Other Carbohydrates

You can substitute food choices from this list for other carbohydrate-containing foods (such as those found on the Starch, Fruit or Milk lists) in your meal plan, even though these foods have added sugars or fat. One choice has 15 grams of carbohydrate, variable amounts of fat and variable calories.

Nutrition Tips

- The foods on this list do not have as many vitamins and minerals as the choices on the Starch, Fruits or Milk lists. When choosing Sweets, Desserts and Other Carbohydrate foods, you should also eat foods from other lists to balance out your meals.
- Many of these foods don't equal just a single choice. Some will also count as one or more fat choices.

Food	Serving Size	Count As
Brownie, small, unfrosted	1¼-inch square, ⅞-inch high (about 1 oz)	1 Carbohydrate + 1 Fat
Cookies, chocolate chip	2 cookies (2¼ inches across)	1 Carbohydrate + 2 Fats
Pudding, regular (made with reduced-fat milk)	½ cup	2 Carbohydrates
Honey	1 tbsp	1 Carbohydrate
Jam or jelly, regular	1 tbsp	1 Carbohydrate
Sugar	1 tbsp	1 Carbohydrate
Syrup, chocolate	2 tbsp	2 Carbohydrates
Syrup, light (pancake-type)	2 tbsp	1 Carbohydrate
Syrup, regular (pancake-type)	1 tbsp	1 Carbohydrate
Cranberry sauce, jellied	¼ cup	1½ Carbohydrates
Sweet and sour sauce	3 tbsp	1 Carbohydrate
Fruit juice bars, frozen, 100% juice	1 bar (3 oz)	1 Carbohydrate
Ice cream, light	½ cup	1 Carbohydrate + 1 Fat
Yogurt, frozen, fat-free	⅓ cup	1 Carbohydrate
Granola or snack bar, regular or low-fat	1 bar (1 oz)	1½ Carbohydrates

Nonstarchy Vegetables

Vegetable choices include the nonstarchy vegetables in the list below as well as the starchy vegetables found in the Starch list (page 308). Vegetables with small amounts of carbohydrate and calories are nonstarchy vegetables. In general, 1 nonstarchy vegetable choice is:

- $\frac{1}{2}$ cup of cooked vegetables or vegetable juice
- 1 cup of raw vegetables

A choice on this list has 5 grams of carbohydrate, 2 grams of protein, 0 grams of fat and 25 calories.

Asparagus	Mushrooms (all kinds, fresh)
Beans (green, wax, Italian)	Okra
Broccoli	Onions
Cabbage (green, bok choy, Chinese)	Pea pods
Carrots*	Peppers (all varieties)*
Celery	Radishes
Cucumber	Spinach
Green onions	Squash (summer, crookneck, zucchini)
Greens (collard, kale, mustard, turnip)	Swiss chard
Jicama	Tomatoes (fresh or canned)
Mung bean sprouts	

* More than 3 grams of dietary fiber per serving

Meat and Meat Substitutes

Meat and meat substitutes are rich in protein. Foods from this list are divided into four groups: lean meat, medium-fat meat, high-fat meat and plant-based proteins.

- A lean meat choice has 0 grams of carbohydrate, 7 grams of protein, 0 to 3 grams of fat and 100 calories.
- A medium-fat meat choice has 0 grams of carbohydrate, 7 grams of protein, 4 to 7 grams of fat and 130 calories.
- A high-fat meat choice has 0 grams of carbohydrate, 7 grams of protein, 8 or more grams of fat and 150 calories.
- A plant-based protein choice has variable amounts of carbohydrate, 7 grams of protein, variable amounts of fat and variable calories.

Lean Meats and Meat Substitutes

Food	Amount	Count As	Notes
Beef, Select or Choice grades trimmed of fat: ground round, roast (chuck, rib, rump), round, sirloin, steak (cubed, flank, porterhouse, T-bone), tenderloin	1 oz	1 Lean Meat	
Cheeses with 3 grams of fat or less per oz	1 oz	1 Lean Meat	
Cottage cheese	¼ cup	1 Lean Meat	
Egg whites	2	1 Lean Meat	
Fish, fresh or frozen, plain: catfish, cod, flounder, haddock, halibut, orange roughy, salmon, tilapia, trout, tuna	1 oz	1 Lean Meat	
Lamb: chop, leg or roast	1 oz	1 Lean Meat	
Poultry, without skin: Cornish hen, chicken, domestic duck or goose (well-drained of fat), turkey	1 oz	1 Lean Meat	
Processed sandwich meats with 3 grams of fat or less per oz: chipped beef, deli thin-sliced meats, turkey ham, turkey kielbasa, turkey pastrami	1 oz	1 Lean Meat	
Salmon, canned	1 oz	1 Lean Meat	
Tuna, canned in water or oil, drained	1 oz	1 Lean Meat	

Medium-Fat Meats and Meat Substitutes

Food	Amount	Count As	Notes
Beef: corned beef, ground beef, meatloaf, Prime grades trimmed of fat (prime rib), short ribs, tongue	1 oz	1 Medium-Fat Meat	
Cheeses with 4–7 grams of fat per oz: feta, mozzarella, pasteurized processed cheese spreads, reduced-fat cheeses, string	1 oz	1 Medium-Fat Meat	
Egg	1	1 Medium-Fat Meat	High in cholesterol, so limit to 3 per week

High-Fat Meats and Meat Substitutes

These foods are high in saturated fat, cholesterol and calories and may raise blood cholesterol levels if eaten on a regular basis. Try to eat 3 or fewer servings from this group per week.

Food	Amount	Count As	Notes
Bacon, turkey	3 slices (½ oz each before cooking	1 High-Fat Meat	480 milligrams or more of sodium per serving
Cheese, regular, American, blue, Brie, Cheddar, hard goat, Monterey Jack, queso, Swiss	1 oz	1 High-Fat Meat	
Processed sandwich meats with 8 grams of fat or more per oz: bologna, pastrami, hard salami	1 oz	1 High-Fat Meat	
Sausage with 8 grams of fat or more per oz: bratwurst, chorizo, Italian, knockwurst, Polish, smoked, summer	1 oz	1 High-Fat Meat	480 milligrams or more of sodium per serving

Plant-Based Proteins

Because carbohydrate content varies among plant-based proteins, you should read the food label. *For dried legumes, see page 308.*

Food	Amount	Count As	Notes
Meatless burger, soy-based	3 oz	½ Carbohydrate + 2 Lean Meats	More than 3 grams of dietary fiber per serving
Nut spreads: almond butter, cashew butter, peanut butter, soy nut butter	1 tbsp	1 High-Fat Meat	
Tempeh	¼ cup	1 Medium-Fat Meat	
Tofu	4 oz (½ cup)	1 Medium-Fat Meat	
Tofu, light	4 oz (½ cup)	1 Lean Meat	

Portion Sizes

Portion size is an important part of meal planning. The Meat and Meat Substitutes list is based on cooked weight (4 oz of raw meat is equal to 3 oz of cooked meat) after bone and fat have been removed. Try using the following comparisons to help estimate portion sizes:

- 1 oz cooked meat, poultry or fish is about the size of a matchbox.
- 3 oz cooked meat, poultry or fish is about the size of a deck of playing cards.
- 2 tbsp peanut butter is about the size of a golf ball.
- The palm of a woman's hand is about the same size as 3 to 4 oz of cooked, boneless meat. The palm of a man's hand is a larger serving.
- 1 oz cheese is about the size of 4 dice.

Fats

Fats and oils have mixtures of unsaturated (polyunsaturated and monounsaturated) and saturated fats. Foods on the Fats list are grouped together based on the major type of fat they contain. In general, 1 fat choice equals:

- 1 teaspoon of regular margarine, vegetable oil or butter
- 1 tablespoon of regular salad dressing

A choice on the Fats list contains 5 grams of fat and 45 calories.

Monounsaturated Fats

Food	Serving Size
Avocado, medium	2 tbsp (1 oz)
Nuts: almonds, cashews, mixed (50% peanuts)	6 nuts
Nuts: pecans	4 halves
Oil: canola, olive, peanut	1 tsp
Olives, black (ripe)	8 large
Olives, green, stuffed	10 large

Polyunsaturated Fats

Food	Serving Size
Margarine: stick, tub (trans fat–free) or squeeze (trans fat–free)	1 tsp
Mayonnaise and mayonnaise-style salad dressing, reduced-fat	1 tbsp
Nuts: pine nuts	1 tbsp
Nuts: walnuts, English	4 halves
Oil: corn, cottonseed, flaxseed, grape seed, safflower, soybean, sunflower	1 tsp
Seeds: flax (whole), pumpkin, sunflower, sesame	1 tbsp

Portion Tip

Your thumb is about the same size and volume as 1 tbsp of salad dressing, mayonnaise, margarine or oil. It is also equal to 1 oz of cheese. A thumb tip is about 1 teaspoon of margarine, mayonnaise or other fats and oils.

Saturated Fats

Food	Serving Size
Bacon, cooked, regular or turkey	1 slice
Butter, stick	1 tsp
Coconut milk, light	$\frac{1}{3}$ cup
Coconut milk, regular	$1\frac{1}{2}$ tbsp
Cream, half-and-half	2 tbsp
Cream cheese, reduced-fat	$1\frac{1}{2}$ tbsp ($\frac{3}{4}$ oz)
Cream cheese, regular	1 tbsp ($\frac{1}{2}$ oz)
Sour cream, light	3 tbsp
Sour cream, regular	2 tbsp

Free Foods

A "free" food is any food or drink choice that has less than 20 calories and 5 grams or less of carbohydrate per serving.

Selection Tips

- Most foods on this list should be limited to 3 servings (as listed here) per day. Spread out the servings throughout the day. If you eat all 3 servings at once, it could raise your blood glucose level.
- Food choices listed here without a serving size can be eaten whenever you like.
- Drink choices without a serving size listed can be consumed in any moderate amount.

Low-Carbohydrate Foods

Food	Serving Size
Cabbage, raw	$\frac{1}{2}$ cup
Carrots, cauliflower or green beans, cooked	$\frac{1}{4}$ cup
Cucumber, sliced	$\frac{1}{2}$ cup
Gelatin, dessert, sugar-free unflavored	
Jam or jelly, light or no sugar added	2 tsp
Salad greens	
Sugar substitutes (artificial sweeteners)	
Syrup, sugar-free	2 tbsp

Condiments

Food	Serving Size
Barbecue sauce	2 tsp
Ketchup	1 tbsp
Honey mustard	1 tbsp
Lemon juice	
Mustard	
Parmesan cheese, freshly grated	1 tbsp
Pickle relish	1 tbsp
Salsa	¼ cup
Taco sauce	1 tbsp
Vinegar	

Drinks

Food	Serving Size
Bouillon or broth, low-sodium	
Carbonated or mineral water	
Cocoa powder, unsweetened	1 tbsp
Coffee, unsweetened or with sugar substitute	
Diet soft drinks, sugar-free	
Drink mixes, sugar-free	
Tea, unsweetened or with sugar substitute	
Water	

Seasonings

(Be careful with seasonings that contain sodium or are salts, such as garlic salt, celery salt and lemon pepper)

Food	Serving Size
Flavoring extracts (for example, vanilla, almond, peppermint)	
Garlic	
Herbs, fresh or dried	
Nonstick cooking spray	
Pimento	
Spices	
Hot pepper sauce	
Wine, used in cooking	
Worcestershire sauce	

Appendix 3
Canadian Diabetes Association Choice Lists

||||||||||||||||||||||||||||||||||||||||||||||||||||||||||||||||||||||||||||||||||||||||||||||||||||||||||||||||||||||||

The information in this appendix will help you plan your meals. It is excerpted with permission from *Beyond the Basics: Meal Planning for Healthy Eating, Diabetes Prevention and Management*, © Canadian Diabetes Association, 2007. For a longer list of foods, visit www.diabetes.ca/files/Long%20list%20Dec%202005.pdf.

Grains and Starches

This food group includes all types of breads and cereals, as well as rice, corn, pasta and potatoes. Grains are an excellent source of carbohydrate and fiber, and are an important part of every meal. Choosing whole grains more often will help you to meet the higher fiber recommendations for those with diabetes. Whole grains are foods such as whole-grain breads, whole wheat pasta, barley, oatmeal, brown rice and wild rice.

Carbohydrate foods do raise blood glucose levels. People with diabetes should choose food sources of carbohydrate with a low glycemic index rather than a high glycemic index more often to optimize blood glucose control. Foods with a low glycemic index are digested more slowly and cause a more gradual and lower rise in blood glucose.

The foods in this group are an excellent source of fiber, which can be divided into soluble and insoluble fiber. Include both types when you're planning meals. Soluble fiber, found in foods such as dried beans, peas, lentils and oats, can help to control blood glucose and lower cholesterol and triglycerides. Insoluble fiber, found in foods such as whole-grain breads and cereals and brown rice, can help keep bowel movements regular.

Each serving in this group contains about 15 grams of available carbohydrate and 3 grams of protein.

Tips for Meal Planning

- Eat a choice from this food group at every meal. The best choices are those that are lower in fat and higher in fiber.
- Limit the amount of fat added to these foods in preparation. Choose baked or boiled potatoes instead of french fries.
- Whole-grain crackers or mini-size cereals can be part of a healthy snack.
- There are many kinds of grains. Why not try barley or quinoa with dinner instead of potato or rice?
- Read labels to check for whole grains, both in the ingredient list and in the Nutrition Facts table, which lists the fiber in each serving.

Choose More Often

Food Item	Serving Size	Available Carbohydrate (g)	Protein (g)	Fat (g)	Glycemic Index
Whole wheat bread	1 slice (28 g)	11	3	1	medium
Rye bread	1 slice (32 g)	14	3	1	medium
Chapati, roti, prata	1 piece (44 g)	19	3	5	medium
All-bran cereal	½ cup (125 mL)	15	4	1	low
Oatmeal, cooked	¾ cup (175 mL)	16	5	2	medium
Shredded wheat cereal	1 biscuit	16	2	trace	high
Corn on the cob	½ ear (73 g)	16	3	trace	low
Corn kernels	½ cup (125 mL)	14	2	1	medium
Barley, pearled, cooked	½ cup (125 mL)	20	2	trace	low
Quinoa, cooked	⅓ cup (75 mL)	13	3	1	low
Rice, brown and white, long-grain, cooked	⅓ cup (75 mL)	13	2	trace	low
Pasta, whole wheat, cooked	½ cup (125 mL)	14	3	trace	n/a
Potato, boiled or baked	½ medium (84 g)	15	2	trace	medium
Potato, mashed	½ cup (125 mL)	17	2	1	high
Sweet potato, mashed	⅓ cup (75 mL)	16	1	trace	medium
Lentil soup	1 cup (250 mL)	15	8	2	low
Minestrone	1½ cups (375 mL)	15	6	4	low

Choose Less Often

Food Item	Serving Size	Available Carbohydrate (g)	Protein (g)	Fat (g)	Glycemic Index
White bread	1 slice (30 g)	13	3	1	high
Hamburger or hot dog bun	½ bun (22 g)	11	3	1	medium
Bagel	½ bagel (3-inch/ 7.5 cm diameter, 29 g)	14	3	trace	high
Bran or corn flakes cereal	½ cup (125 mL)	13	2	trace	high
Puffed rice cereal	1 cup (250 mL)	12	1	trace	high
French fries	10 strips (50 g)	14	2	4	high
Chicken noodle soup	2 cups (500 mL)	17	8	5	n/a

Fruits

Most people should choose fruit rather than juice more often and eat a variety for good health. Fruits are an important source of carbohydrate, fiber, vitamins and minerals. They are also naturally low in fat and generally have a low glycemic index. Fresh, frozen, canned and dried fruits are healthy choices. If possible, choose fresh fruit in season most often. Enjoy canned fruit in light syrup or juice and use the label to help you choose the appropriate portion size.

Each serving in this group contains about 15 grams of available carbohydrate and 1 gram of protein.

Tips for Meal Planning

- Choose fruit instead of juice for the benefit of about 2 grams of fiber per serving. For the highest amount of fiber, choose whole fruit, wash it well and eat the skin (if it's edible).
- Enjoy fruit at meals and for snacks.
- Try preserving fruit at home when it is in season. That way, you can control the amount of added sugar at a reasonable cost.
- Look for ways to add fruits to recipes. Fruits blend well with cheese, ham, pork, poultry, shellfish and wild game.
- The serving size for most fresh fruits is the size of a fist. For canned fruit or juice, it is $\frac{1}{2}$ cup (125 mL). For dried fruit, it is usually 2 tbsp (30 mL).

Choose More Often					
Food Item	Serving Size	Available Carbohydrate (g)	Protein (g)	Fat (g)	Glycemic Index
Apple	1 small (106 g)	12	trace	trace	low
Banana	1 small (101 g)	20	1	trace	low
Cantaloupe	1 cup (250 mL) cubed	12	1	trace	medium
Cherries	15 medium (102 g)	14	1	trace	low
Grapefruit, all colors	1 small (240 g)	22	1	trace	low
Grapes, red and green	$\frac{1}{2}$ cup (125 mL) or 15 medium (80 g)	14	1	trace	low
Orange	1 medium (131 g)	12	1	trace	low
Strawberries	2 cups (500 mL) whole (288 g)	16	2	1	n/a
Fruit cocktail, canned in light syrup	$\frac{1}{2}$ cup (125 mL)	16	1	trace	medium
Peaches, canned in light syrup	$\frac{1}{2}$ cup (125 mL)	17	1	trace	low

Choose Less Often					
Food Item	Serving Size	Available Carbohydrate (g)	Protein (g)	Fat (g)	Glycemic Index
Apple juice	½ cup (125 mL)	14	trace	trace	low
Orange juice	½ cup (125 mL)	13	1	trace	low
Tomato juice or 100% vegetable juice (such as V8)	1 cup (250 mL)	8	2	0	n/a
Raisins	2 tbsp (30 mL)	14	1	trace	medium

Milk and Alternatives

This group is beneficial for bone health and blood pressure. It includes milk, yogurt and fortified soy beverage products. It is the best source of calcium and vitamin D. Most people should have two to three servings of milk products per day. If you don't like to drink milk, try it in milk-based soups or puddings. This food group provides calcium, protein, carbohydrate and fat.

Each serving in this group contains about 15 grams of available carbohydrate and 8 grams of protein; fat content varies with the type of milk.

Tips for Meal Planning

- Choose lower-fat options (for example, skim or 1% milk).
- If you do not use milk, ensure that milk alternatives are fortified with calcium and vitamin D.
- If you do not drink milk, add powdered milk to soups, puddings, custards and so on to boost the protein and calcium content.
- If you do not consume calcium-rich products on a regular basis, consult with a dietitian about other sources of calcium and vitamin D.

Healthy Choices					
Food Item	Serving Size	Available Carbohydrate (g)	Protein (g)	Fat (g)	Glycemic Index
Milk, canned, evaporated	½ cup (125 mL)	13	9	10	n/a
Milk, whole (3.25%)	1 cup (250 mL)	11	8	8	low
Milk, 2%	1 cup (250 mL)	12	8	5	n/a
Milk, 1%	1 cup (250 mL)	12	8	2	n/a
Milk, skim	1 cup (250 mL)	12	8	trace	low
Milk, chocolate, 1%	½ cup (125 mL)	13	4	1	n/a
Soy beverage, fluid	1 cup (250 mL)	15	9	5	low
Yogurt, flavored, low-fat, artificially sweetened	¾ cup (175 mL)	15	8	trace	low

Other Choices

This group includes a wide variety of foods often thought of as snacks or treats, such as popcorn, prepared puddings, licorice, granola bars and cookies. Treats and snacks can add variety to a meal plan, but they often lack vital nutrients, such as fiber, vitamins and minerals, and are high in calories. Use the Nutrition Facts table on package labels to help you make healthier choices. Because of their higher calorie count, many of the foods in this group should be eaten only occasionally, as eating them more often may make it more difficult to control your weight.

Each serving in this group contains about 15 grams of available carbohydrate; protein and fat content varies.

Tips for Meal Planning

- Foods in this group should be used only to add interest to meals and snacks or as an occasional treat. They should not be the main part of your diet.
- The foods in the "Choose More Often" section are healthier choices, as they are lower in fat.
- The Nutrition Facts table on food labels provides a lot of information that makes it easier to pick out a healthier snack.

Choose More Often

Food Item	Serving Size	Available Carbohydrate (g)	Protein (g)	Fat (g)	Glycemic Index
Milk pudding	½ cup (125 mL)	12	4	trace	low
Popcorn, air-popped, low-fat	3 cups (750 mL)	18	2	1	low

Choose Less Often

Food Item	Serving Size	Available Carbohydrate (g)	Protein (g)	Fat (g)	Glycemic Index
Brownie, unfrosted	2-inch (5 cm) square	12	2	7	low
Cookies, chocolate chip	2 medium	18	1	7	n/a
Cola	⅓ cup (75 mL)	14	trace	trace	n/a
Ice cream	½ cup (125 mL)	17	3	8	low
Popsicle	1 bar (55 g)	16	1	0	n/a
Chocolate bar	½ bar (21 g)	13	3	8	medium
Granola bar, oatmeal type	1 bar (28 g)	18	3	6	medium
Jell-O, regular	½ cup (125 mL)	18	2	0	n/a
Pretzels, low-fat	7 large or 30 sticks	17	2	1	high

Vegetables

Vegetables have many health benefits. You should eat a minimum of four servings of vegetables every day. Choose a wide variety of brightly colored vegetables in season, especially those that are dark green or orange. Vegetables are an excellent source of vitamins, minerals and fiber. They are low in calories and fat, and most are low in carbohydrate. Because of this, vegetables can usually be considered a free food.

Some vegetables, such as acorn squash, butternut squash and peas, are high in carbohydrate. When you eat 1 cup (250 mL) or more of these vegetables, count them as 15 g of carbohydrate, or 1 Carbohydrate Choice.

Tips for Meal Planning

- Fill half your plate with vegetables for a good boost to your nutrition at a low calorie cost.
- Choose a variety of vegetables in season for the peak taste and nutritional value.
- Vegetables lose vitamins when stored, so purchase only the amount you can use within a few days.
- Frozen and canned vegetables without added salt are good alternatives to fresh, but avoid those packed in sauce.
- Add new vegetables to your menus. Try some of the recipes in this book, such as Asparagus Rice Pilaf (page 134) or Lubeck Cabbage (page 138).
- Add flavor and variety by seasoning with herbs and spices instead of adding butter, margarine or oil.

Healthy Choices					
Food Item	**Serving Size**	**Available Carbohydrate (g)**	**Protein (g)**	**Fat (g)**	**Glycemic Index**
Acorn squash*	1 cup (250 mL) mashed	19	2	trace	n/a
Asparagus	4 spears	1	1	trace	n/a
Beans, yellow or green	1 cup (250 mL)	6	6	trace	n/a
Bell peppers, all colors	1 medium	5	1	trace	n/a
Broccoli	1 cup (250 mL) chopped	6	4	trace	n/a
Butternut squash, baked*	1 cup (250 mL) cubed	19	2	trace	n/a
Cabbage, cooked	1 cup (250 mL)	4	2	trace	n/a
Carrots	1 cup (250 mL) chopped	8	1	trace	low
Lettuce	1 cup (250 mL) shredded	1	1	trace	n/a
Peas*	1 cup (250 mL)	14	8	trace	low
Spinach	1 cup (250 mL)	2	5	trace	n/a
Tomatoes, fresh	1 cup (250 mL) chopped	6	2	trace	n/a
* These vegetables are high in carbohydrate and are not considered a free food.					

Meat and Alternatives

Foods in this group are an excellent source of protein and an important source of essential vitamins and minerals, such as B vitamins, iron, calcium and zinc. One of the main functions of protein is to build and repair body tissue. As most of the foods in this group contain little or no carbohydrate, they should have little effect on blood glucose. Choose a portion size that is about the size of a deck of cards.

A serving in this group contains about 7 grams of protein and usually 3 to 5 grams of fat. Count ½ cup (125 mL) of cooked kidney beans, lentils and other legumes as 1 Meat and Alternatives Choice and 1 Carbohydrate Choice.

Choose More Often					
Food Item	Serving Size	Available Carbohydrate (g)	Protein (g)	Fat (g)	Glycemic Index
Beef, lamb, pork, chicken, turkey, game	1 oz (30 g) cooked	0	7	1–5	n/a
Minced or ground meat (lean or extra-lean)	2 tbsp (30 mL)	0	7	3–5	n/a
Low-fat processed luncheon meats or fresh deli meats	1 oz (30 g)	0	7	1–5	n/a
Canned tuna, salmon or shellfish, drained	¼ cup (60 mL)	0	7	1–5	n/a
Fish fillet or steak (mackerel, salmon, trout), fresh or frozen	1 oz (30 g) cooked	0	7	0–2	n/a
Skim milk cheese (<7% MF)	2 by 1 by 1 inch (5 by 2.5 by 2.5 cm) (30 g)	0	7	0–3	n/a
Light cheese (<20% MF)	2 by 1 by 1 inch (5 by 2.5 by 2.5 cm) (30 g)	0	7	0–5	n/a
Cottage cheese (1% to 2% MF)	¼ cup (60 mL)	0	7	1	n/a
Whole egg (regular or with added omega-3s)	1 large	0	6	5	n/a
Chickpeas, kidney beans, lentils, soaked	½ cup (125 mL)	10–15	7	0–2	low
Baked beans	½ cup (125 mL)	18	7	2	medium
Peanut butter	2 tbsp (30 mL)	4–5	7	15	n/a
Tofu, regular	1¾ by ¾ inches (4 by 2 cm) (85 g)	2	7	1–4	n/a

Tips for Meal Planning

- Food from this group should take up about a quarter of the plate.
- Protein foods are often forgotten at breakfast. Quick and easy choices include low-fat cheese, hard-cooked eggs and peanut butter.
- Fatty fish, such as salmon, sardines and mackerel, supply omega-3 fatty acids. Try to eat at least two servings of fish per week.
- Lean red meats (labeled "lean" or "extra-lean") are an excellent source of iron. In moderation, they can be part of a healthy diet.

Choose Less Often

Food Item	Serving Size	Available Carbohydrate (g)	Protein (g)	Fat (g)	Glycemic Index
Ground beef, medium fat	2 tbsp (30 mL)	0	7	5–6	n/a
Regular-fat prepared meat (bologna, wieners)	1 slice or wiener (30 g)	0	5	5–8	n/a
Chicken wings	2 wings (45 g)	0	7	10–12	n/a
Regular cheese (>21% MF)	2 by 1 by 1 inch (5 by 2.5 by 2.5 cm) (30 g)	0	7	5–10	n/a

Fats

This group contains oils, spreads, nuts, margarine and butter. Fats are often added to food in cooking or processing. We need fat in our diet to provide insulation, to protect our vital organs, to store energy and to make hormones. Fats are important, but a little is enough. It's very important to choose the right type and amount of dietary fat, especially for people with diabetes. Fat has twice the calories of carbohydrate or protein, so it is an important factor in weight control. Excess fat can also increase your risk of heart disease. Fats are mainly of three types: saturated, polyunsaturated and monounsaturated. While saturated fats (in such foods as fatty meat) can cause blood cholesterol to rise, monounsaturated and polyunsaturated fats (in vegetable fats such as canola and olive oil) help to lower blood cholesterol and should be chosen more often.

Tips for Meal Planning

- Substitute lower-fat foods, such as yogurt, for higher-fat sour cream in dips, dressings and so on.
- Use broth, water or reduced-sodium vegetable juice instead of fats in cooking.
- Avoid deep-frying.
- Spray oil with a pump spray to control the amount used.

Recommended in Small Amounts Only

Food Item	Serving Size	Available Carbohydrate (g)	Protein (g)	Fat (g)
Margarine, non-hydrogenated, regular	1 tsp (5 mL)	trace	trace	4
Oils (canola, olive)	1 tsp (5 mL)	0	0	5
Olives, black	8 large (35 g)	1	trace	5
Sunflower seeds, dry-roasted	1/3 oz (10 g)	2	2	5
Walnuts, black	1/3 oz (10 g)	1	trace	6

Choose Less Often

Food Item	Serving Size	Available Carbohydrate (g)	Protein (g)	Fat (g)
Bacon	1 slice	trace	3	3
Gravy	2 tbsp (30 mL)	n/a	n/a	5
Mayonnaise, regular	1 tsp (5 mL)	2	trace	5
Sour cream, regular	2 tbsp (30 mL)	1	1	5

Extras

This group includes foods that are low in calories, carbohydrate and other nutrients. These foods, such as coffee, tea, spices and condiments, are used to add flavor and variety to meals and snacks. Some foods in this group, such as sauces, may add calories, carbohydrate and sodium to meals, so it is important to read the labels carefully and use the portion size suggested.

Food Item	Serving Size	Available Carbohydrate (g)	Protein (g)	Fat (g)
Cocoa powder	1 tbsp (15 mL)	3	1	1
Barbecue sauce*	1 tbsp (15 mL)	2	trace	trace
Ketchup*	1 tbsp (15 mL)	4	trace	trace
Salsa	1/4 cup (60 mL)	3	1	trace
* These foods may have a high level of sodium.				

Library and Archives Canada Cataloguing in Publication

Canada's 250 essential diabetes recipes / Sharon Zeiler, editor.

Includes index.
ISBN 978-0-7788-0269-3

   1. Diabetes—Diet therapy—Recipes. I. Zeiler, Sharon II. Title: Canada's two hundred fifty essential diabetes recipes.

RC662.Z45 2011   641.5'6314   C2010-907390-8

250 essential diabetes recipes / Sharon Zeiler, editor.

Includes index.
ISBN 978-0-7788-0270-9

   1. Diabetes—Diet therapy—Recipes. I. Zeiler, Sharon II. Title: Two hundred fifty essential diabetes recipes.

RC662.Z455 2011   641.5'6314   C2010-907393-2

Index

|||||||||||||||||||||||||||||||||||||||||||||||||||||||||||||||||||||||||||||||||||||||||||||||||||||||||||||||||||||||||||||||||||

Note: Recipe titles followed by "(v)" refer to a variation of the recipe on that page.